THE END OF DEMOCRACY? II

THE END OF DEMOCRACY?
II
A Crisis of Legitimacy

Edited by
MITCHELL S. MUNCY

Introduction by
J. BUDZISZEWSKI

SPENCE PUBLISHING COMPANY • DALLAS
1999

Published in the United States by
Spence Publishing Company
501 Elm Street, Suite 450
Dallas, Texas 75202

Library of Congress Cataloging-in-Publication Data

The end of democracy? II : a crisis of legitimacy / edited by
Mitchell S. Muncy.
p. cm.
Sequel to previously published book with same title: The end of
democracy : the celebrated First Things debate, with arguments
pro and con, 1997.
Includes bibliographical references and index.
ISBN 1-890626-10-4 (pbk.)
1. Political questions and judicial power—United States. 2.
Legitimacy of governments—United States. 3. Conservatism—
United States. 4. Christianity and politics—United States. 5.
United States—Social policy—1993- I. Muncy, Mitchell S.
(Mitchell Shannon), 1968-
KF5130.A75 E53 1999
321.8´0973—dc21   98-48483

Printed in the United States of America

CONTENTS

v

PART II
LESSONS FROM THE PAST

PART III
EXTRAORDINARY POLITICS?

Preface

Mitchell S. Muncy

SEQUELS OFTEN SUPPLY only the dregs of the first effort to an audience that it is hoped will not notice—at least not until they have paid their money. But the present volume is far from a mere postscript to its predecessor. Indeed, it would be more accurate to say that the first volume is an introduction to the second.

The opinion pieces of *The End of Democracy? The Judicial Usurpation of Politics* mark the terrain on which the debate will take place. Now, four of the *First Things* symposiasts, joined by six new contributors, fully, patiently, and incisively re-present their arguments and consider our crisis of self-government in its broader historical and cultural context. The problem of judicial usurpation is very old, has only recently roused "conservatives," and, most important, runs much deeper than lamentations about "judicial activism."

Unlike the contributors to the earlier volume, contributors to *The End of Democracy? II* unanimously assent to the

First Things symposiasts' central claims, which George W. Carey (though not one of the original symposiasts) states succinctly in his essay: "The old regime, that which corresponded with the principles, values, and goals of the original Constitution, is dying. It has been mortally wounded by an opportunistic attack at a vital point that totally distorts its allocation of powers and authority. Conversely, the attacking forces have provided none of the rationale and justification for a new regime; they are seemingly content to operate within the shell of the older regime, pretending as if they are its true heirs."

Some may consider, then, that this volume lacks "balance." Yet it should be clear that the task here is quite different from that of the first volume. As Gary Glenn affirms in his essay, if our constitutional order is truly in crisis, then it is incumbent upon those who have diagnosed the crisis to articulate and defend their position in detail according to the constitutional principles which they believe have been violated. They must provide a principled ground for a resolution of our difficulties.

Even favorable reviews of the first volume have tended to portray the controversy as a passing family feud. Perhaps this is understandable: commentators nowadays spend much more time reacting to arguments than responding to them, and reactions pass. Yet the articles listed in the bibliography in the first volume, which contains nearly 250 items, leave no doubt that the controversy is of interest because of the constitutional questions engaged, not simply because it may signal developments (or amusing quarrels) within conservatism. Reviews continue to appear, though not in conservative journals, and each semester politics and law professors purchase the book for their courses.

Perhaps the most telling indication of the broad and enduring relevance of the debate is (at this writing) the most recent—in the *New York Times Magazine.* In the October 11, 1998, issue, Andrew Sullivan devotes a considerable part of his cover story to the influence, which he considers deep and detrimental, of *First Things*, complete with a freeze-frame of Richard John Neuhaus in which he appears to wag a sanctimonious finger at the world. The quotations Sullivan chooses to capture the spirit of the journal come from *The End of Democracy?*. Sullivan's highly tendentious account of conservatism aside, he does reveal that, over two years after its publication, the symposium still has a powerful effect on its genuine opponents. The conservative critics (who certainly hold no brief for the judicial status quo) seem to have moved on, possibly in a tacit admission, as Father Neuhaus suggests, "that they perhaps overreacted." But clearly, those who believe their political and cultural convictions impugned by the symposium still consider it a salient sign of contradiction.

Aristotle calls a "natural slave" one whose affairs are managed by others because he is either unwilling or unable to manage them for himself. The slave may be prosperous, but he not self-governing—and he is not a citizen. Perhaps the reason for the reaction to and the lasting importance of the *End of Democracy?* debate is that in the face of the question, "Do you want to be a free citizen, or are you content with prosperous servitude?," all sense that they cannot avoid answering and that in answering they reveal themselves.

The essays of Richard John Neuhaus, Russell Hittinger, and Robert P. George appeared in the *Loyola Law Review* 44 (1998): 83-133 under the title "Conference on Judicial

Usurpation" and are reprinted with permission. Professors Arkes, Glenn, Holloway, and Vaughan granted permission to print their copyrighted essays. The essay by Scott H. Moore appeared in *Pro Ecclesia* 7:1 (1998): 17-47 under the title "The End of Convenient Stereotypes" and is reprinted with permission. The essay by George W. Carey appeared in *Liberty under Law: American Constitutionalism, Yesterday, Today, and Tomorrow*, Kenneth L. Grasso and Cecilia Rodriguez Castillo, eds. (Lanham, Md.: Rowman & Littlefield, 1997), 71-84, under the same title and is reprinted with permission.

There are many to whom I owe thanks for work on this volume. Dean John Makdisi of the Loyola of New Orleans Law School commissioned the essays in Part 1, sponsored the conference in October 1997 at which they were first presented, and gave his unqualified support to their publication in this volume. He was assisted by Adam Zuckerman, editor of the *Loyola Law Review* for the academic year 1997-98. Professor Stephen Krason of the Society of Catholic Social Scientists organized the conference from which the papers in Part 11 were drawn and assisted in their acquisition for this volume. My special thanks go to Gary Glenn for his invaluable assistance in the preparation of the papers in Part 11 and to Kenneth Grasso for drawing my attention to Professor Carey's essay. Finally, I thank Father Richard John Neuhaus for his generous and continued support for Spence Publishing. Flaws in this volume should, of course, be attributed only to its editor.

INTRODUCTION

J. Budziszewski

I F YOU WANT TO KNOW WHY the United States is in constitutional crisis, a good place to begin thinking about it is the series of outrages perpetrated by the 1992 Supreme Court decision *Planned Parenthood v. Casey,* which upheld the outcome, though not the reasoning, of the infamous abortion decision *Roe v. Wade.*

The first atrocity was that the *Casey* Court reaffirmed what it would seem that no government can affirm without undermining its own authority: a private right to use lethal violence for any reason whatsoever against an unprotected class of persons.

The second was that the Court upheld *Roe* even while admitting that it may have been decided unconstitutionally. "[W]e are satisfied," say the jurists, "that the immediate question is not the soundness of *Roe*'s resolution of the issue, but the precedential force that must be accorded the ruling." In effect this statement sets the Court itself in the place of the Constitution, and it seems that the justices intend no less, for they declare explicitly that "the rule of law" depends on citizens' accepting their decisions.

The third was that the Court unilaterally established a religion, something the Constitution explicitly forbids—the religion of radical selfism. By contrast with the Founders, who pledged themselves to the laws of nature and of nature's God, they announce a "right to define one's own concept of existence, of meaning, of the universe, and of the mystery of human life." Unborn children may be killed, it seems, because each person decides for himself which rules have "meaning" and who counts as "human."

I hope it is obvious that in such a polity no one else can long be safe. Indeed, the wonder of it all is how one thing leads to another. Having declared that the Constitution somehow includes a right to define reality, the judges *must* put themselves in its place: If he wishes to survive, any king who says "Everything is permitted" must add "But I decide for everyone what 'everything' includes." To take a longer view of the matter, in order to justify violating the natural law against killing the Court has at last found it necessary to defy the principle of our own republican government (the balance of powers), the principle of all republican government (that the weak have equal standing with the strong), and the principle of government as such (that rule is ordained to protect, not destroy).

As time has passed, several lower courts have followed the logic of the *Casey* "mystery passage" to conclusions, involving euthanasia and assisted suicide, even more murderous than its authors are yet willing to approve, and in the meantime the Court has shown greater and greater readiness to assert itself against all attempts to clip its wings. It was against this background that in November 1996 a quiet intellectual journal with a reputation for sobriety decided to do something. *First Things*, perhaps the most widely read contemporary magazine of politics and religion, published a symposium entitled (please note the question mark) *The End of Democracy?*

Substantive evils like abortion had been criticized in *First Things* before. So had the procedural evil whereby all of the important decisions about how to live are pre-empted by usurping courts. Various remedies, such as constitutional amendment and Article III legislation, had often been mooted, and the violent fringe had been firmly rejected. So how was the symposium new? For good or for ill, what distinguished it was its willingness to raise the question "whether we have reached or are reaching the point where conscientious citizens can no longer give moral assent to the existing regime" and to consider, without endorsement, the rights and wrongs of responses "ranging from non-compliance to resistance to civil disobedience to morally justified revolution."

In view of the controversy that followed, I think it is important to measure the tone of some of the most widely quoted passages from the introduction by the editors of *First Things*. Indeed, many critics appear to have drawn their swords without reading further.

> Perhaps the United States, for so long the primary bearer of the Democratic idea, has itself betrayed the idea and become something else.
>
> . . . .
>
> [The Founders] had no illusions that the people would always decide rightly. . . . but the principle was

clear: legitimate government is government by the consent of the governed. The Founders called this order an experiment, and it is in the nature of experiments that they can fail. . . . The proposition advanced in the following essays is this: The government of the United States of America no longer governs by the consent of the people.

. . . .

The courts have not, and perhaps cannot, restrain themselves, and it may be that in the present regime no other effective restraints are available. If so, we are witnessing the end of democracy.

. . . .

Among the most elementary principles of Western Civilization is the truth that laws which violate the moral law are null and void and must in conscience be disobeyed.

. . . .

America is not and, please God, will never become Nazi Germany, but it is only blind hubris that denies it can happen here and, in peculiarly American ways, may be happening here.

. . . .

What is happening now is a growing alienation of millions of Americans from a government they do not recognize as theirs; what is happening now is an erosion of moral adherence to this political system.... What is happening now is the displacement of a constitutional order by a regime that does not have, will not obtain, and cannot command the consent of the people.

. . . .

"God and country" is a motto that has in the past come easily, some would say too easily, to almost all

Americans. What are the cultural and political consequences when many more Americans, perhaps even a majority, come to the conclusion that the question is "God *or* country"?

Although the editors anticipated charges of irresponsibility and alarmism—defending themselves with the reminder that "it is the Supreme Court that has raised the question of the legitimacy of its law"—they were clearly unprepared for the hurricane of criticism which followed. Rubbing salt in the wound is that many of the critics had been close allies. While *First Things* had viewed itself as pushing its good friends a little further in the direction to which they were already logically committed by their premises, not all who felt the push thought it so little or so friendly. Two distinguished neoconservatives, Gertrude Himmelfarb and Peter Berger, resigned from the editorial board. Walter Berns, whose connection with the journal had been more rarified, resigned from the editorial advisory board. *Commentary* sponsored a symposium just to respond to the *First Things* symposium. But the readership held firm, the many defenders of the symposium were as spirited as its critics, and the editors took comfort in the fact that what had opened with a quarrel might continue as a conversation.

A previous volume by Spence Publishing chronicled the quarrel. The present volume attempts to advance the conversation. In Part I, the editor of *First Things* and three of the original symposiasts (Richard John Neuhaus, Russell Hittinger, Hadley Arkes, and Robert P. George) consider the arguments of their critics. Part II (with reflections by Gary D. Glenn, Carson Holloway, and Frederick Vaughan) puts the problem of judicial usurpation in historical perspective, and Part III (with essays by Scott H. Moore and George W. Carey) ponders the meaning of the controversy.

THE ORIGINAL OBJECTIONS

Greater attention is due criticisms from those whom the symposiasts had counted among their allies. Most of these reproaches are explicit, but a few must be teased out from between the lines.

First, the symposiasts are said to lack a properly conservative disposition. Their shortsightedness is said to make them ignore the great strides their cause has already made,[1] their radicalism to threaten the political alliances by which these gains have been won,[2] and their absolutism to poison the negotiation and compromise on which their future gains depend.[3] Moreover, critics allege, their pessimism discourages people from seeking political remedies for political problems,[4] their shallowness encourages them to seek political remedies even though the problems are really cultural,[5] and their intemperance eggs on crazies who would emulate the violence of the foe.[6] Besides, some add, the comparisons which the symposiasts offer are not only undiscriminating but offensive: Usurping judges are not like Nazis,[7] and abortion is not like the Holocaust.[8]

Second, critics maintain that although the judicial usurpation of legislative power is both deep and disturbing, there is something inappropriate about the manner in which the symposiasts frame their complaints. To some these complaints seem *overheated*, because usurpations by one branch or another are a pervasive fact of political life.[9] To some they seem *hypocritical*, because the real gripe of the symposiasts is supposed to be not who legalized abortion but the sheer fact that it was legalized.[10] Some even hint that they are *futile* because the American people have passively consented to what their courts have done.[11]

Next are objections to the extraconstitutional forms of resistance which some of the symposiasts consider. The critics do not charge that resistance can *never* be justified, but that constitutional democracy makes it problematic. Some make the point that under constitutional democracy, the laws merely reflect what the people want.[12] Others remark that the democratic opportunities for changing a law are never exhausted.[13] A final rebuke is that the proponents of civil disobedience have somehow overlooked the fact that the laws which they protest are literally impossible to disobey: They do not command evil, but merely permit it.[14]

Finally, some critics are troubled by the religious views by which most of the symposiasts are moved. A few critics maintain that religion and religious morality do not belong in the public square at all; the genius of our constitutional system, they say, is that passions are defused by the relegation of all such things to the private realm.[15] Most critics concede religion a place, but not the place the symposiasts want it to have. Just what place they think that is, or what place they propose themselves, is by no means clear. Perhaps the idea is that religion may be invoked in debate about particular laws, but not in reference to the constitutional framework within which such debate is held. Or perhaps the point is that religion may be invoked generically, but never in "sectarian" terms.[16] Whether or not these views are the precisely the ones the critics have in mind, they are widely held in the culture.

Were the symposiasts really so intemperate and radical? In some instances the critics seem to have misunderstood their language; in others they seem to have understood it perfectly well but rejected it. Some of the misunderstandings appear downright silly. For example, a surprising number of critics complained that America is not a "regime," taking that expression as a snotty 1990s equivalent of the 1960s slam "Amerika." The problem here is merely that the symposiasts were writing in Academic dialect while their critics were reading in Trade Media. Since everyone on both sides of the dispute is bilingual, it is hard to see why there should have been any confusion.

The genuine disagreements are more difficult to deal with, although they become somewhat manageable once disentangled from the agreements. Because neither side thinks that our *present* circumstances justify anything like insurrection, the critics ask "How could you think of bringing it up?" Because both sides can imagine circumstances *becoming* so bad that some kind of resistance would be justified, the symposiasts ask "Why won't you let us worry out loud?" As I read the state of the conversation, a tacit agreement has been reached not to say much about extreme responses which no one thinks are yet upon us. A gap remains about whether civil disobedience is ripe for discussion; we will return to the problem twice more because it arises in several contexts.

Have the symposiasts ignored the strides their cause has already made and endangered the political alliances which achieved them? When Gertrude Himmelfarb says conservatives have begun to think the unthinkable and do the undoable she is speaking of past and future reforms in the realms of welfare, Medicare, and Social Security. Yet even she admits that in the realms the symposiasts care about most deeply, "the situation may be getting worse rather than better." This suggests that the conservative coalition has been better for some kinds of social and cultural activists than for others, and it hardly seems immoderate to ask that its terms be renegotiated. From one point of view, that is all the symposiasts were doing. As to the charges that they discouraged people from seeking political remedies for political problems and encouraged them to seek political remedies to cultural problems, the essays in this volume make it pretty clear that there is no "either-or." Both political activism and cultural persuasion are necessary, and neither endeavor can get far without the other. That seems to be a point on which both sides can agree, so the next stage of the conversation should be how to coordinate the two endeavors.

The charge of absolutism involves a different kind of disagreement. Both the symposiasts and their critics think abortion and euthanasia are wrong; both are willing to oppose them; and both support halfway measures like prohibiting partial-birth or third-trimester abortions. So what's the problem? The problem is that *how* wrong it is to take innocent human life is not just an academic question—it determines strategy. If abortion and euthanasia are bad only in the way that budget deficits are bad, then we should strike a "win some, lose some" pose and be willing to make lots of tradeoffs between saving human lives and our many other goals. But if they are bad in the way that stuffing Jews into gas chambers was bad, then it is morally unthinkable to make our peace with them: Human lives cannot be traded off. Halfway measures may be the only available pathway to complete prohibition, but even so we should be willing to sacrifice almost anything to achieve them. As to those offensive analogies, it all comes down to whether we take our premises seriously: If an abortion is really a murder then thirty-seven million abortions are really a Holocaust. They are not something that could happen here; they are happening here. Who has the better argument? On one point the symposiasts are right: The fact that our local oligarchy privatizes the pogrom does not make it any less a pogrom, and the burden is on their critics to show why ending it is no more important than Social Security reform. But on another point their critics are right: the privatization of the pogrom does make vague talk about "resistance" a little glib, and the burden is on the symposiasts to explain more clearly what they have in mind in the here and now.

The indictment for overheated arguments supposes that judicial usurpation is not much different from the legislative and executive usurpations the republic has suffered in the past. I think this a dubious claim and will take it up again in the conclusion. On the other hand, the indictment for futility is grave and may be true. If the charge were that passive consent makes the complaints of the symposiasts *inappropriate,* then it would be sufficient to note, as several of them have, that the life of a republic depends not on passive but active consent; after all, the passive sort exists even under despotism. But what if the citizens no longer *want* a republic? If the judicial preemption of deliberations about our common life were ended, they might be made to care; but can they be made to care enough to end the preemption? As the symposiasts and even most critics agree, the only way to know their temper is to try them. Ahead is a long unexplored road of education, entreaty and exhortation. We scarcely know what might be required of us: all the more reason for continuing this conversation.

What of the indictment for hypocrisy? Would the symposiasts be so hot for democracy if the culture of death had been promoted not by a renegade judiciary, but by the representatives of the sovereign people? The question seems unanswerable, but it conceals a fallacy. Ancient democracy meant that the most numerous group or class could do as it pleased. Constitutional democracy—which is really more like what Aristotle called "polity," mixed government, but ennobled by the biblical understanding that human beings bear the image of God—means that many groups share power on principles of equal dignity, institutional balance, and natural justice. This is what the Founders meant when they spoke of a *novus ordo seclorum,* a new order for the ages, and a reversion to the failed model of antiquity would represent not the perfection of democracy but its corruption. In the constitutional sense, it would be no more "democratic" for a voting majority to prey on an unprotected class than for judges to tell them they may do so. The clarity with which the symposiasts elucidate this theme is one of the greatest achievements of the present volume. Of course it is one thing to admit that a majority can act undemocratically, and another to say what should be done if it does. Checks and balances are not a complete answer, for a determined and unscrupulous majority can subvert any restraints the mind of man can devise. The Founders counted on checks not to force bad men to act justly, but to slow down imperfect men until they could come to their senses by themselves. But all that is becoming academic. The problem in our era is that usurping judges use the checks entrusted to them not to protect the Constitution but to destroy it, and the majority has so far been too torpid to act.

Constitutional democracy *does* make some forms of resistance problematic, in particular revolution. On this point the symposiasts and their critics agree. I am one of those who doubt whether revolution can ever be justified; however, all sober theories of justified revolution insist, among other things, both that peaceful alternatives to revolution must have been exhausted *and* that the majority, on whose consent the authority of every government depends, must concur.[17] So long as the republic continues, these conditions can never be satisfied. As I understand them, the contributors to the original symposium did not mean to deny the claim; their point is that if the judicial branch continues to entrench its usurpations, a day may come when the republic can *no longer* be said to continue. As I understand the critics, however, the point is true but idle. If that day should come it will have arrived only through the sloth of the usurped majority, and a people that lets their liberties slip through their fingers will hardly stoop to pick them up. In the meantime, talk of revolution can only inflame unstable minds. Both sides make good points; let us call this match a draw.

Civil disobedience is another matter altogether. Whereas revolution responds to a government that has no right to legislate, civil disobedience responds to a law that cannot in good conscience be obeyed. The "regime" does not have to be "illegitimate" for a law to be unconscionable. I hope readers will forgive me for what may seem scholastic hairsplitting, but it seems to me that much of the *End of Democracy?* confusion is based on the failure of both sides to make necessary distinctions of principle. After that should come case-by-case prudential judgment, which has hardly begun even now.

According to the classical analysis, from Thomas Aquinas, a law can be unjust in either of two ways, and the difference makes a difference. Some laws are unjust because they hinder our relationship to God, for example because they violate the commands of the Decalogue: do not murder, do not steal, do not bear false witness, and so on. Others are unjust because they hinder our life in this world, for example because they serve private rather than public interest, impose disproportionate burdens, or exceed the authority of government. Concerning laws unjust in the first way, our duty is simple: we *must* disobey. A law unjust in the second way *may* be disobeyed, but there is a catch. Thomas framed it in negative terms, suggesting that if the harm of the ensuing scandal or disturbance would be even greater than the harm of the law itself, the law should be obeyed. Martin Luther King framed it in positive terms, suggesting that whoever *does* disobey must choose means that do *not* cause avoidable scandal or disturbance—for example by accepting the full legal penalty for breaking the law. John Calvin allowed only subordinate magistrates to resist the second kind of unjust law, because they share in the public authority; others argue that in a republic, citizenship is a public office too.

It is important to remember that civil disobedience is not just a Christian idea. Jewish law firmly maintains the superiority of God's law to man's, and the first known case of civil disobedience to unjust laws is from Torah—the refusal of Hebrew midwives to obey Pharaoh's edict to kill male Hebrew infants, recorded in Exodus 1:15-21.[18] At stake in our own day is the killing not just of infants but of the unborn, disabled, aged, sick, or merely depressed. Several varieties of killing are already legal; several others are on the verge.

The argument that permissive laws cannot be disobeyed is weaker than it looks, because ultimately the culture of death cannot be sustained by permissive laws alone. It requires that certain monies change hands, certain officials do what they are told, certain voices be silenced, and certain information be suppressed. For a small example, in the 1994 case *Madsen v. Women's Health Center, Inc.*, the Supreme Court upheld a provision of Florida law establishing a thirty-six-foot zone around an abortion clinic within which demonstrations were permitted by supporters of abortion—but not by supporters of life. A possible mode of civil disobedience for those who hold no office but their citizenship might have been to pray peacefully and silently within the zone, then accept the legal penalty for demonstration. For their part, judges and magistrates might have cooperated in enforcing preexisting laws against violence and trespass by persons of all persuasions, but refused to recognize ordinances which imposed harsher penalties just for holding the pro-life position. The penalty for them would presumably have been removal from office. A judge might also protest a law in a manner which does *not* involve civil disobedience by entering a judgment of conviction, but suspending the sentence.[19]

My aim is not to recommend mass violations of the thirty-six-foot rule but to show that the option of disobedience cannot be ruled moot just because the government has not (yet) commanded us to abort our own children or euthanize our own grandmothers. The manifold regulations and intricate fiscal arrangements of the modern state present a myriad opportunities to draw the line, and these need to be patiently considered. One crucial point is that even though laws and ordinances like the thirty-six-foot rule form part of the support structure for the culture of death, *in themselves* they are unjust only in the second way, not in the first. They don't directly violate commands of God such as *do not murder;* they merely undermine the temporal common good, in this case by imposing disproportionate punishments and burdening the pro-life view with official opprobrium. In such cases civil disobedience is not an unconditional duty but a matter of discretion—something to be weighed according to whether, in the circumstances, it will do more good or harm. For example, a disadvantage of drawing the line *here* is that hostile journalists do all they can to obscure the difference between praying in the driveway and planting a bomb in the waiting room. Then there is the fact that the knowledge of blood flowing freely only a few feet away is such a terrible goad that the distinction may disappear for some demonstrators too. These are powerful objections. But they are *prudential* objections, so there is no reason why the conversation between the symposiasts and their critics should end.

The greatest obstacle to intelligent discussion about morality and religion in the public square is not a difference in principles, but a muddle in logic. It is literally impossible to eject either morality or religion from deliberation, not because people are stubborn but because decision and neutrality are inconsistent terms. All laws and regulations, from the prohibition of homicide to the list of allowable deductions from the income tax, embody suppositions about what is good and right. If the morality of Moses and Jesus is ejected, its place will merely be filled by another morality—the morality, perhaps, of Peter Singer, the newly appointed Ira W. DeCamp Professor of Bioethics at the University Center for Human Values at Princeton University, who believes that human babies have no greater moral value than snails. Moreover, the *Casey* Court had one thing right—all suppositions about what is good and right rest on larger suppositions about the "meaning of existence." Secularism is not a way of getting on without such suppositions, but a way of getting on without admitting to anyone what they are. It is, in short, a fraud.

If I say that euthanasia should be illegal because murder violates the law of God, then obviously I suppose that there is a God, that he has a law, that this law ought to be obeyed, that it forbids murder, that euthanasia is murder, and that he commands the government to back him up on such a point. If instead I say that euthanasia should *not* be illegal, then obviously I suppose *either* that there is no God, or that even if there is a God he has no law, that even if he has a law it need not be obeyed, or that even if it must be obeyed it does not forbid murder, or that even if it does forbid murder euthanasia is not murder, or that even if euthanasia is murder God does not command the government to back him up on such a point. It is not enough to have no suppositions—at some point there must be a contrary supposition. That contrary supposition may be "secular," but it is still "religion" in that it is still about the meaning of the universe. The relevant distinction is not between a secular public life and a religious public life, but between a public life informed by a secular religiosity and a public life informed by the older religiosity which it opposes. A particular *kind* of morality and religion can be pushed out of the public realm, but morality and religion *as such* cannot be pushed out of the public realm.

What goes for deliberation goes for deliberation about deliberation. It is no use to say that religion may be invoked in debate about particular laws but not in reference to the constitutional framework within which such debate is held. To banish the religions which call themselves religions is merely to free the religions which do not call themselves religions from the burden of competition—whether the utilitarian religion of Expedience, the yuppie religion of Autonomy, or the mammonist religion of Wealth.

What goes for deliberation also goes for passion. Walter Berns suggests that by pushing morality and religion out of the public square, the Founders cooled those specially dangerous passions which wreck republics. This could be true only if the kinds of morality and religion they are supposed to have pushed out of the public square (assuming they pushed out any) are more responsible for reckless passion than the kinds that would have taken their place. Empirical grounds for such a claim would seem to be lacking. Passions have not noticeably cooled among contemporary secularists who demonstrate for the privilege of killing their close relatives. The most famous secularists of the century, leaders of revolutions in China, Russia, and Germany, were even said to be rather warm. It is sometimes held that Western secularism has brought an increase in the number of those who do terrible things in cold blood, but if this is true, one would think it would count against the secular sensibility rather than for it.

Much more difficult to deal with is the idea that "generic" religious considerations may be invoked in the public square but that "sectarian" considerations should be avoided—that one may speak of God, but not quote him. What makes the problem difficult is the vagueness of the idea of generic religion.

One possibility is that generic religion is "neutral" religion: just those ideas about God, good, and evil that all human beings embrace. The problem here is that no such ideas exist. Theravada Buddhists, for example, do not believe in a God at all, and Hindus believe that what they call God is beyond good and evil. Another possibility is that generic religion is "general revelation": not the ideas all humans do embrace, but the ones they all *ought* to embrace because God has "written them on their hearts." Here the problem is different; some traditions maintain strongly the reality of general revelation, while others deny it. Paradoxically, then, even the appeal to the generic presupposes the particular; for insight into what we hold in common, we must fall back on traditions we do not hold in common. The result is that to say "You must not speak of God except generically" is to say "The most important things about God you must not speak."

Another way to put the problem is that what is known to all is not admitted by all. Hebrew and Christian scriptures portray the human race as in denial. This may seem an abstract point. In reality it is very practical. Consider for example the abortionist. We say the duty to protect innocent human life is known to every human being. The abortionist says it cannot be, because it is not known to him. What do we say? "Forgive us, we are mistaken, we thought you knew but you do not"? No, we say "You are lying.[20] Perhaps also to yourself, but you are lying. You say you do not know, but you do. On this point, we know what you know better than you know what you know." It is not from the lowest common denominator that we know this, not from Hallmark Cards, not from the Gallup Poll, but from the Book of Romans, from the magisterium of the Church, from the seven laws given to the sons of Noah and explained by learned rabbis. No wonder the symposiasts quote from the "sectarian" documents of their traditions.

Their critics have a point. Not even Scripture says believers must always be quoting Scripture. When Paul spoke to the Athenians he began not with the law and prophets, but with what they knew already, quoting their poets and commenting on their altar "To An Unknown God." Just so must we begin with modern pagans.

But must we never stop beginning? Must all our anthems be nursery rhymes? Must we always serve porridge, never meat? Richard John Neuhaus denies it: "Short of the Kingdom," he says, "our public or political task in an inescapably pluralistic world is to find common moral ground for establishing and maintaining a humane life together. Christianity is unique in providing conceptual and practical resources for doing precisely that."[21] We return to this question in the conclusion.

THE LESSONS OF HISTORY

Almost everything has been discovered, said Aristotle. In certain moods, one agrees. The *End of Democracy?* symposium took place mostly in the present and future tenses, inasmuch as the symposiasts and their critics focused on what is happening, what may happen, and what we are to do. For people of conservative temper, though, the most important things are the permanent things, and the crucial tense is past: Today and tomorrow take root in the deep soil of yesterday. The contributors to this part of the book seek insight into the nature and course of judicial usurpation by delving into history.

The meaning of judicial usurpation, says Gary D. Glenn, is that judges think and act as though their own decisions, rather than the Constitution of 1789, were the true Constitution or the law of the land. This makes them incapable of self-restraint, for if the Constitution is only what they say it is, then it follows that nothing they do can be unconstitutional.

From the heat of the controversy after the *End of Democracy?* symposium, one might get the impression that the case against usurpation is new. In fact, Glenn explains, it is very old; only its embrace by conservatives is new. We may begin its history with Abraham Lincoln, who conceded that judges may construe ambiguous constitutional language, but denied that they are the Constitution's sole interpreters. Insisting the power of interpretation is shared among the branches, he held that when legislative interpretations of constitutional language are sufficiently venerable, courts should defer to them rather than embarking on fresh ones.

Glenn would prefer that the Lincolnian view of the courts and the Constitution had prevailed. Unfortunately, for most of our own century the argument against judicial usurpation has been carried by statesmen of another cast of mind, statesmen whose strategy for upholding popular sovereignty has been to denigrate the prestige of the Constitution itself. Carefully he marks the steps in its fatal progression. First, Theodore Roosevelt proposed that Supreme Court decisions should be limited by popular referenda—in effect abolishing the distinction between the permanent and the transient will of the people, which is the foundation of the Constitution's authority. Next Woodrow Wilson suggested that between the Founders' time and our own, history turned an invisible corner; tyranny having become impossible, constitutional restraints have become unnecessary. Franklin Roosevelt was impatient with the very idea of restraints; for him the important thing about the Constitution is not that it limits power but that it grants it. According to Robert Jackson, judges who claim to speak for the Constitution are really expressing the dominant opinions and interests of the generation in which they were appointed. Rexford Tugwell made the even more radical claim that the Constitution is whatever the judges say it is; the textual authority to which they appeal is merely a necessary fiction.

Having come this far, the Progressive argument turned a somersault and became its opposite. For if the fiction is necessary, why not regard it as noble? And if really the Constitution has no stable meaning, how can judges be called usurpers? The avatar of this line of thought was William Brennan, who declared that a judge's role is not to find meaning in the Constitution, but to give meaning to the Constitution. What matters is neither the permanent *nor* the transient will of the people, but the will of the judiciary itself, as directed toward individual rights. Once adversaries, the judicial culture and the Progressive culture merge and pursue the same ideal—not the sovereignty of the people, but the sovereignty of self.

If judges cannot be checked, Glenn warns, we may be

forced to choose between the usurpations we can live with and the usurpations we cannot. However, the historical record of attempts to rein in a usurping judiciary have been spotty. During ordinary times, when the people and their government are divided (just as the Founders planned), courts (not as they planned) can do very much as they please. In fact experience has shown that restraints require the alignment of four factors which do not often coincide.

The first is calamity; there must be an emergency so terrible for the nation that although we may prepare for it, no decent person would hope for it. The second is political luck; in the calamity of the Civil War, the element of luck was that the delegates of the seceding states had withdrawn themselves from Congress. The next is sound doctrine; there must be some corner of the national consciousness in which the knowledge of the proper role of courts and Constitution is preserved. Here, incidentally, lies the importance of events like the *End of Democracy?* debate.

The fourth and final factor is leadership equal to the day. Most important, it must be equal to the fact that the sovereign people have already been corrupted—in no small measure through the decisions of the courts themselves. Although ordinary folk are still more decent than Supreme Court justices, they are not less relativistic. Too good to demand that new atrocities be legalized, they are no longer good enough to demand that the old ones be decommissioned.

Alexis de Tocqueville shared our fear that democracy might degenerate into despotism. Carson Holloway holds that he achieved keener insight into the nature and tendencies of democracy because of his deeper appreciation of the aristocratic alternative. According to the symposiasts, the emerging judicial order is undemocratic in at least two ways: that the most important questions about how we shall live together are now made by a small unelected elite, and that this elite holds the moral traditions of the people in contempt so that its answers are at odds with those the people would have given. Tocqueville anticipated both. The reason, thinks Holloway, is that he was willing to press an inquiry the symposiasts avoid: whether the seeds of despotism may lie in democracy itself. In short, Tocqueville would view our problem less in terms of "judicial usurpation" than in terms of "public abdication." Whereas the symposiasts and their critics merely deplore the popular apathy, Tocqueville probed its causes.

The Frenchman's analysis runs as follows. Democracy and aristocracy are not just political but social orders. From this point of view, the chief characteristic of aristocracy is the fixity of social class, while the chief characteristic of democracy is its fluidity. In a society with fixed social classes, each class takes its lot for granted. In a society with fluid social classes, no one does. The rich are preoccupied by the danger of loss, the poor by the prospect of gain. The upshot is that while in aristocracies the universal human longing for comfort is attenuated, in democracies it becomes all-consuming. No one finds time for activities that do not promise gain. Therefore, unless opposite tendencies are somehow set in motion, democratic souls will view the privilege of self-government as a burden and distraction. So long as the economy flourishes they will be only too happy to let it go.

Convinced that Tocqueville's diagnosis fits our culture

precisely, Holloway goes on to consider the great thinker's prescription. In the aristocratic condition of society, where rich and poor alike are sunk in torpor, fixed on the other world but disinterested in this one, the highest expression of aristocratic statesmanship is to encourage the pursuit of prosperity. But democratic souls suffer the opposite condition, and only religion can turn them from private comforts to public duties. Therefore the highest expression of democratic statesmanship is to encourage the blossoming of faith: in particular, belief in the doctrine of immortality, so that they will learn to lift their eyes from the near and mundane to the far and sublime. To encourage such belief, statesmen must act as if they shared it. This means that they must conform strictly to religious morality, not only in their private lives, but in the great affairs of state.

If all this is true, then the anti-religious actions of our judiciary "are not only symptoms of the prime democratic disease, but . . . an attack on the remedy." Unfortunately, explains Holloway, some of the symposium's critics miss this point, regarding "religion as democracy's bane and materialism as its salvation." Their fear is so extreme that they regard even a level playing field as an invitation to theocracy. If Tocqueville is anywhere near the mark this is most unlikely. The danger in democracy is not that the people will yield to bad religious influences but that they will fail to yield to good ones.

Interestingly, though Glenn and Holloway begin from different premises, they converge on some of the same conclusions. Both remark the coincidence of a kind of "decency" and a kind of torpor; as Holloway puts it, although the people may not approve of the judiciary's "moral innovations," neither do they care about them. For both this makes the prospects for remedy discouraging. Where the conclusions of Glenn and Holloway do differ, they are asking different questions, contemplating different kinds of remedy.

Glenn, viewing judicial tyranny as a political problem, reflects on the unusual circumstances which might make short-term political statesmanship effective; Holloway, viewing it as a political symptom of a social problem, reflects on the permanent qualities of human nature which might make long-term spiritual statesmanship effective. Depressing our hopes are the facts that democratic beings tend to lack imagination, belittle the wisdom of their ancestors, and deny what they cannot understand. Resurrecting them is the fact that human beings have inclinations deeper than those given them by democracy. As a greater authority than Tocqueville put it, man does not live by bread alone.

Frederick Vaughan dissects a reason for judicial usurpation which the symposiasts have not so far considered: the perversion of equity. Law is a clumsy instrument for achieving justice, in large part because no system of general rules, however just, can perfectly accommodate the infinite variety of circumstances to which they must be applied. Equity, therefore, is "the correction of that wherein the law, by reason of its universality, is deficient." In Vaughan's words, it is the necessary power of judges to "do the right thing" in cases where going by the books would produce injustice, to set aside the letter of the law for the sake of its spirit or intention. As with other judicial powers, so with equity: The problem is not that judges should not have it, but that they distort it. Vaughan argues that this distortion is rooted in the faulty but influential theories of John Austin, and that the pre-Austinian understanding of equity must be restored.

In Aristotle's thought, equity merely fulfills what the legislator himself would have done had he foreseen what it were impossible to foresee. Though so different from Aristotle in most ways, Thomas Hobbes labors to make this point his own, explaining that judges act not as the sovereign, but for it: the power of equity in no wise authorizes them to use their "private reason." This is his reason for rejecting Sir Edward Coke's definition of equity as an "artificial perfection" of reason which judges have but which lawmakers lack. Lord Francis Bacon concurs, calling judges "lions, but yet lions under the throne." Baron Montesquieu, commenting on English institutions from France, seems to refuse judges any equity power at all, insisting that their judgements be "ever conformable to the letter of the law." Although rejecting this extreme position and returning to the Aristotelian understanding of equity, William Blackstone agrees that "law without equity" is a lesser evil than "equity without law," for the latter would "make every judge a legislator, and introduce most infinite confusion." But then we come to Austin, who cannot imagine what judges are if not legislators, or how any danger could lie in allowing them a power he thought they could not help but use. By erasing the line between judgment and legislation, he destroyed the distinction between the use and abuse of equity. Indeed, as Austin sees it, the problem with judges is not that they legislate but that they do it timidly, narrowly, and piecemeal rather than boldly, broadly, and all at once.

Following Gary McDowell, Vaughan shows that for America, the Austinian moment arrived in *Brown v. Board of Education* (1955), when the Supreme Court shifted its attention from the actual injuries of particular individuals as shown in the facts of the case, to the hypothetical injuries of entire social classes as suggested by sociological theory. His deeper interest, however, is in the underlying reasons for the Austinian triumph, of which he proposes two: a change in legal instruction, which emphasized the reasoning of judges and encouraged the incorporation of the social sciences into the study of law, and a rise of interest in judicial protection of human rights, which developed in the wake of World War II. He closes his essay with an illustration of how, once the Austinian virus had found a suitable host in the American idea of judicial review, it made its way around the world.

Though each of the contributors to this section would like to end judicial usurpation, each draws attention on a different kind of remedy. Glenn, viewing it as a political problem, focuses on political remedy; Holloway, viewing it as a political symptom of a social problem, focuses on spiritual remedy; and Vaughan, viewing it as a problem of judicial doctrine, focuses on educational and procedural remedy. The obstacle, he fears, is that the schools will resist the old and wise understanding of equity's inherent problems and that the courts will resist the old and strict distinction between equity and law. What are the prospects that the resistance can be broken? This question he leaves in an intriguing dangle. An optimist might urge that sheer institutional inertia has been overcome before, and so might be overcome again. A pessimist might reply that institutional inertia is never sheer; there is a difference between prodding people to give in to the temptations of power, and prodding them to give it up.

Glenn seems to take for granted the judicial will to power. I think he is right to do so, but cannot help noticing that no one in the discussion has commented how this undermines the theory of the judiciary propounded by the Framers. The Federalists assumed that the judiciary would be the *least* dangerous branch because it held neither the purse nor the sword; in resting in this assumption they seem to have forgotten their own warning that for checks and balances to work, the branches must be given not only the means of self-defense but the motive to use them. Congress surely has checks, but its motive is *not* to use them because the courts provide its members cover for their reluctance to make hard decisions for which voters might punish them at the polls.

On this point, we might do well to broaden our focus so that it takes in not only the Framers but the opponents of the Constitution. Several of the Anti-Federalists were especially deft at lancing judicial pretensions. The Federalists, they charged, had extrapolated too freely from the services of English courts in resisting royal absolutism, forgetting that judicial independence would have an entirely different meaning in a country without a king.[22] They had also extrapolated too freely from the moderating influence that judges had exerted on the turbulent legislatures of the states, forgetting that in the natural course of political development, legislatures become less arbitrary and courts become more.[23] They had assumed that checks and balances would be a zero-sum game, forgetting the permanent advantages of collusion.[24] They had failed to anticipate that the legislature would look to the judiciary in order to understand its powers.[25] And they had failed to anticipate the sophisms and fictions by which the judiciary would expand its own.[26] The point is not that the Constitution is rubbish but that it may require what James Madison called "auxilliary precautions."

As we have seen, both Glenn and Holloway are confident that ordinary people are better than Supreme Court justices. They may be slothful, they may be low-minded, they may be relativistic, yet they retain a shred of decency. Comparatively, this is no doubt true, yet I wonder if they are too sanguine. Have the contributors to the discussion underestimated the malignancy of vice—its tendency, once rooted in a single moral faculty, to metastasize and overrun the others? Take lust, for example. From the annals of this controversy one might almost think it were an elitist innovation rather than the thoroughly democratic vice that it is. Isn't the motive which sexual incontinence provides for committing abortion at least as powerful as the motives which judicial ideology provides for allowing it? Once having outraged their own consciences by these acts against defenseless life, don't ordinary people have to twist a dozen other sensibilities to rationalize it? Once twisted, don't these sensibilities engender further crimes? From prurience to euthanasia, the road would seem to be fairly straight. Few thinkers would have believed this thirty years ago; fewer and fewer can deny it today.

The fine balance of Vaughan's essay provides a signal service to our discussion, for he sheds equal light on the necessity and on the danger of the equity power. Worth mentioning is the unexpected fact that from Vaughan's point of view Hobbes winds up as the symposiasts' ally; to others he has seemed their enemy, and the "Hobbesian streak" of some of the symposiasts' critics has been much discussed. Something can be said on both sides.[27] Vaughan is right that a Hobbesian judge would never usurp a Hobbesian sovereign. On the other hand, from a Hobbesian sovereign there is no appeal to the natural law. It isn't that Hobbes repudiates the natural law, but that he regards the sovereign as its only voice. In fact he thinks that apart from its expression in positive laws, natural law isn't even "law" but merely private prudence. The reason that only the sovereign can say what it means is that only the sovereign can bring it to legal life.

Our Supreme Court justices pretend to a similar role, but vis-à-vis the Constitution rather than the natural law. As they say in *Casey,* "If the Court's legitimacy should be undermined, then so would the country be in its very ability to see itself through its constitutional ideals." That is to say, "You speak of the Constitution, but you have no eyes to read it but ours. We are not just its only actual, but its only possible interpreters." If this were true, of course, then the Court were indeed the sovereign and democracy had indeed met its end.

EXTRAORDINARY POLITICS?

A paradox of history is that although the past is the source of the future, the future is not just the past "more so." One does not have to deny development to see that an oak is not much like an acorn. Have we come to one of those moments (much more than a moment to mortals) when even the way things change is changing? A name is needed. Borrowing from the history of war we could call them "revolutions," but a term with such warlike connotations would just get the symposiasts in trouble with their critics again. Borrowing instead from the history of science, where a distinction is made between the "normal" science which takes place within paradigms and the "extraordinary" science which takes place between them, Scott H. Moore suggests "extraordinary politics." That will do.

Debate about the proper relation of religion and politics is one of the perennial occupations of American politics. Moore's claim is that the terms of this debate are changing in such a radical way as to call its continuation into question. Terms like "liberal" and "conservative," which have always been misleading, now tell us nothing whatsoever about who can make alliance. Moore offers two epitomes of our disarray: on what used to be called the right, the quarrel over the *End of Democracy?* symposium, and on what used to be called the left, the quarrel over the appointment of an activist priest named Michael Baxter to the theology faculty of Notre Dame. Yet the individuals and issues involved in these two quarrels are intricately intertwined in ways that "right" and "left" cannot describe.

Moore focuses especially on the bitterness of those who describe both Baxter and the *First Things* symposiasts as "sectarian." According to theologian Richard McBrien, what "sectarians" believe is that the Church is the only place God acts and that an "otherworldly salvation" is the Church's only mission. No such belief is asserted by any of the parties charged. What some of them do embrace is a view on which we touched previously—that "there are no religiously generic resources," that "one must employ confessionally particular resources" even to speak of common concerns, that "the scandal of particularity cannot be removed without compromising authentically Christian convictions." This opinion is anathema to many of *First*

Things' critics—and no wonder, thinks Moore. For centuries, the terms of engagement between religion and politics have been shaped by the Enlightenment delusion that the scandal of particularity could be expunged. Now, in Moore's view, some are saying that the emperor has no clothes, and the ministers of his eminence are wroth; the one thing the modern polity cannot tolerate is an unassimilable confession.

In developing these ideas Moore has much to say about theologian Stanley Hauerwas, a renowned promoter of the particularist view, who not only directed Baxter's dissertation but serves on the editorial board of *First Things.* The editor, Richard John Neuhaus, interests Moore for a different reason: Moore uses him to illustrate the dilemma of Christian thinkers "tortured" by the tension between the "confessionally particular" and the "religiously generic."[28] In one of the most provocative sections of the essay he contrasts Neuhaus with Gertrude Himmelfarb, taking as his point of departure a Baylor University symposium at which both spoke about the idea of a Christian university. While Himmelfarb embraced neutrality, Neuhaus rejected it; while Himmelfarb spoke of the role of faith in the larger picture, Neuhaus spoke of the role of other things within the larger picture framed by faith.

The political meaning of Himmelfarb's vision is that legitimacy depends on pure procedural criteria and is unaffected by any actual evils to which the requisite procedures may lead. Moore's answer is that in the end, such a system merely affirms the resultant evils over all procedural challenges. Neutrality is merely another substantive commitment in disguise, and abortion has blown its cover. We are in for extraordinary politics.

Moore is hopeful. Formerly, labels like "liberal" and "conservative" burdened reflection on the political meaning of Christianity by encouraging Christians to "co-opt and be co-opted by" groups who did not share their faith. Abortion changed all that too, because if conservatism meant limiting the government then conservatives should have supported it, while if liberalism meant protecting the weak then liberals should have opposed it. Agreement among Christians may be as hard to reach without the labels as with them, but "perhaps there will be more integrity."

George Carey, too, thinks the terms of American debate are changing beyond recognition, but he focuses more tightly on jurisprudence. After all, the quarrel over judicial usurpation is a quarrel over the proper limits to the power of one of the branches. Many such disputes have erupted during our history, and in the past they could usually be put to rest by consulting the Constitution. The present dispute is different, because it concerns the nature of the Constitution itself. Is the design of the Founders compatible with a judicial power to set aside their actual words and intentions, in the name of "values" of which they were ignorant but which our judges deem "inherent" or "implicit" in their text? Carey sometimes calls this "looking beyond the text to its spirit," but we must take care. As we saw in Vaughan, the "spirit" of the law was traditionally viewed as its intention—what the legislators would have said if they had foreseen the particular case. By contrast, what activists call its "spirit" has nothing to do with the intention, and may even contradict it. No one really supposes that the delegates to the Philadelphia convention wanted to legalize abortion, euthanasia, or homosexual union, to abolish most of the law of obscenity, libel, and slander, or to drive religion from the public square. Yet all these "values" are supposed to be "inherent" in the document they produced.

What Carey asks, then, is whether the Constitution is a dead letter—whether "our system operates as if we lack basic agreement as a people about the character of the Constitution," exactly the kind of agreement that writing it down was supposed to guarantee. He argues that the very gap between traditionalists and activists suggests that the answer is "Yes." We have entered a "kritarchy," a reign of judges, a "constitutional cosmos" completely different from the one in which the Framers dwelt. He quotes Russell Hittinger from the original symposium: "[W]e live today under an altered constitutional regime, where the rules are no longer supplied by a written document but by federal courts defining the powers of government *ad hoc,* through their own case law."

Is the new regime legitimate? How could it be? Carey points out that not only have its defenders offered virtually nothing to justify it, but they could not. The shape of the thing they defend is far too vague. In the strict sense it is not a "regime" at all, but a "movement" which has been just successful enough to inflict fatal damage on the old regime. Hence the answer to the title question, "The Philadelphia Constitution: Dead or Alive?" is "Not dead yet, but dying."

Can the old regime be resuscitated? One obstacle is the inherited reverence Americans hold for the judiciary. Carey thinks this awe would be dissipated if only the people were better educated about the Framers' intentions, but here we come to the second obstacle: Because activists love not just power but particular results, opposing them, even by education, seems partisan. For now, these obstacles are too great to overcome, but as the constitutional system enters into deeper and deeper crisis, the public may at last demand an accounting.

Moore is certainly right that religious neutrality is a fraud and that its unmasking would be something extraordinary in American politics. I wonder, though, whether "confessional particularists" have fully grasped what it means to blow its cover. Oftentimes, they escape from the Modernist trap only to fall into the Postmodernist trap. The former works like this:

1. Neutrality and objectivity are the same.

2. Objectivity is possible, therefore neutrality is also possible.

3. Christians do not believe in neutrality, therefore they must not believe in objectivity either.

4. Therefore, Christians should shut up.

But the latter works like this:

1. Neutrality and objectivity are the same.

2. Neutrality is impossible, therefore objectivity is also impossible.

3. Christians believe in objectivity, therefore they must believe in neutrality too.

4. Therefore, Christians should shut up.

The fact is that neutrality and objectivity are *not* the same. To be neutral, if that were possible, would be to have no presuppositions whatsoever. To be objective, by contrast, is to presuppose the truths of that "general" revelation which God has made available even to those who reject the more particular revelations of scripture. In order to escape from the Modernist frying pan without falling into the Postmodernist fire, believers must unmask neutrality but embrace objectivity. This is a tricky distinction, and not all who write about the end of the Enlightenment have troubled to make it.

These points are not merely academic. Consider for example the Free Exercise provision of the First Amendment religion clause. Its genius, says Richard John Neuhaus, is to guarantee "that a self-governing people would be able to name the transcendent authority by which they, the people, would themselves be governed." That is well put, but see how quickly we get into trouble if we do not keep our presuppositions straight. Not just any transcendent authority may be named; even today no court in the land would be insane enough to allow the free exercise of a religion which involved the release of nerve gas in the public subways. To count as a "religion" within the Founders' frame of reference, a sect must at least acknowledge the truths of general revelation. Neuhaus gets it exactly right when he writes a few lines later, "The Founders knew and said that this constitutional order is not a machine that can run of itself, that it must constantly be justified—that is to say, legitimized—by appeal to moral truth and, ultimately, to "the laws of nature and of nature's God.'"[29] How provident it was that in the Founding generation, the dominant confession of faith (Christian) and the dominant current of religious skepticism (Deist) agreed about these laws; they concurred in general revelation even while disagreeing about special revelation. Precisely this concurrence made the American experiment possible. Precisely its disintegration calls the experiment into question today.

I am a little ashamed to say anything more about Carey's essay, because its crystalline perspicuity makes such a fitting end to the volume. Though not, I hope, to the conversation. What I most admire about it is the voice of the teacher, and if Carey is right, that is the voice in which many more of us will have to speak if our questionable experiment in democracy is to have any future at all. More people must be brought into the conversation. It is in the nature of a republic that it cannot be sustained just by a chat among intellectual elites, even if they are dissident elites who still believe in it.

In order to open the conversation, we need to talk more about the problem Carey mentions in his conclusion—that our efforts to teach what the Framers intended will inevitably seem partisan. In a sense they are. We do have different commitments than the usurpers do, not only as to procedure, but also as to substance. We are no more neutral than they are; we are only more objective. A fair examination of the Founding documents does not support their claim to fulfill the intention of these texts, so they must ultimately take refuge in hocus-pocus like "non-interpre-tivist" interpretation. A fair presentation of their goals does not support their claim to fulfill the moral law, so they must ultimately take refuge in jabberwocky like a "different" moral law that lets everyone do as he likes. For a while people can be overawed by such incantations, but eventually they say "I don't get it—it seems like double-talk." At that point we can say "It is" and show them the mirrors, if only they are willing to look.

It may seem a terrible waste of time that so much of our teaching must be un-teaching, that almost all our effort must be expended just to prepare for Lesson One. I think we do very well to reach Lesson One—if we do reach it. Certainly the Founders reached no further. Lesson One is the highwater mark of all previous generations; speaking strictly of human wisdom, there is no Lesson Two.

PART I

A Crisis of Legitimacy

Rebuilding the
Civil Public Square

Richard John Neuhaus

I N NOVEMBER 1996, the journal *First Things* published
a symposium entitled "The End of Democracy? The
Judicial Usurpation of Politics."[1] I must note that
in the storm that swirled and continues to swirl around
the symposium, the question mark in the title has been
generally ignored. In fact, numerous articles critical of
the symposium claimed that its editors and participants
were flatly asserting the death of democracy.[2] I do not
want to make too much of this, lest it be thought we were
only posing a question. We did much more than that:
Our assertion was that ominous developments in our political order now force that question upon us, and force
it urgently.

The urgency of our national situation is reflected in
the conclusion of the editorial introduction to the original symposium:

What is happening now is the displacement of a constitutional order by a regime that does not have, will not obtain, and cannot command the consent of the people. If enough people do not care or do not know, that can be construed as a kind of negative consent, but it is not what the American people were taught to call government by the consent of the governed. We hope that more people know and more people care than is commonly supposed and that it is not too late for effective recourse to whatever remedies may be available. It is in the service of that hope that we publish this symposium.[3]

Many of the hundreds of published commentaries on the symposium missed that note of hope. Indeed a common criticism, often made by those who did not engage in the substance of the argument, was that the "tone" or "mood" of the discussion was alarmist, even apocalyptic. Lest there be any misunderstanding, I should note that the response to the symposium has been overwhelmingly positive.

But some reactions were, to put it gently, less than approving.[4] Resignations from the *First Things* editorial board and cries of outrage greeted publication of the symposium. But without these powerfully negative reactions, the argument might not have received the attention it has. I am glad to say that personal friendships have survived, and some who reacted most negatively have, at least privately, come to think that they perhaps overreacted. This does not mean that we should now lightly put these disagreements behind us. It is important to understand the alarm that met what we said.

First, much was made of our use of the term *regime*. Americans, for understandable reasons, do not think of their government as a regime. Regimes are what we call authoritarian and totalitarian governments. *Regime*, of course, is a term more familiar to certain streams of political philosophy, where it does not bear the odium associated with its popular usage. This is more than a quibble over words. We must nurture a popular understanding that all forms of government are human contrivances for the order and rule of things public, and that a time-honored term for that order and rule is *regime*.

The American Founders were keenly aware that they were contriving a new thing—what they, with a touch of hubris, termed a *novus ordo seculorum,* a new order for the ages. They frequently spoke of their work as an "experiment." As in other spheres of human activity, so also in politics: Experiments can succeed, and experiments can fail. What we were and are suggesting is that the American experiment may be failing. That observation may be alarming, but I do not think it is alarmist.

I was bemused by the critics who suggested that we should permanently retire the language of experiment altogether. After two hundred years, they said, this constitutional order is no longer an experiment. It has, they said, been definitively vindicated and is an unquestionable success. Certainly nobody should doubt the astonishing achievements and demonstrated resilience of the American experiment. But this seems to me a very dangerous way of thinking. When Americans no longer understand our political system as an experiment, it will be a troubling sign that the experiment has ended. To entertain the possibility that this is happening is a form of patriotic adherence to the founding vision.

The judgment that the American experiment has

ended, or is irreversibly on the way to termination, is premature. It is irresponsibly premature. But precisely in the hope that the American experiment not end, we must ask hard questions. And so we asked in the opening editorial

> What are the consequences when many millions of children are told and come to believe that the government that rules them is morally illegitimate?. . . "God and country" is a motto that has in the past come easily, some would say too easily, to almost all Americans. What are the cultural and political consequences when many more Americans, perhaps even a majority, come to the conclusion that the question is "God *or* country?" What happens not in "normal" times, when maybe America can muddle along, but in a time of great economic crisis, or in a time of war when the youth of another generation are asked to risk their lives for their country? We do not know what would happen then, and we hope never to rind out.[5]

Note that these are cautionary questions in the future tense. Yet some critics recast them as descriptive questions in the present tense, thereby presenting the entire discussion as recklessly alarmist.[6] In sobering fact, millions of Americans—by no means limited to weekend militias and the black helicopter crowd—are questioning the legitimacy of the government by which they are ruled. Conventional wisdom holds that these citizens are either apolitical or alienated by the sleaziness of politics today. No doubt there is truth in both views. But the judicial usurpation of politics has contributed powerfully to a widespread suspicion that our political system has lost the first mark of democratic legitimacy—namely, the doctrine in the Declaration of Independence that just government is derived from the consent of the governed.

That is the argument advanced in the remarkable statement, *We Hold These Truths*—signed by three Roman Catholic cardinals, twelve bishops and archbishops, and a wide range of Protestant and Orthodox leaders—which appeared in the October 1997 issue of *First Things*.[7] Historians have noted that such a statement is without precedent in American history. The document has even more support than indicated by the signatories, and through such organizations as James Dobson's Focus on the Family, Gary Bauer's Family Research Council, and the National Association of Evangelicals, the argument about judicial usurpation and the legitimacy of the regime is being disseminated to and engaged in by millions of Americans. Those who think this is a marginal phenomenon have, I would suggest, a very tenuous hold on the moral, cultural, and political dynamics of American public life today.

While we should guard against alarmism or crisis-mongering, this is a time for sober deliberation about the future of an experiment that is still, in Lincoln's phrase, "the last, best hope of earth"—at least among temporal forms of government. So I am surprised at the number of distinguished intellectuals who seem to believe that any comparison between what may be happening in this country and the great tyrannies of history is somehow beyond the pale. This seems to me a profoundly misguided reaction. It suggests that authoritarian and totalitarian governments are irrelevant aberrations, and that constitutional democracy is the historical norm. A better case can be made for the opposite. The marvelously insouciant assumption that "it cannot happen here" seems to me quite without warrant.

It is certainly true that complaints about "judicial activism" are old hat. Many on both the Right and Left cynically observe that the phrase *judicial activism* means court decisions one does not like. Behind that observation, however, is the abandonment of any effort to determine the appropriate role of the courts in our constitutional order, as though there were, in fact, no Constitution at all. The so-called realism that asserts that "the law is the law is the law" should be named for what it is: the abdication of the rule of law. Those who think the law requires no legitimation from sources other than itself ridicule the idea of a crisis of legitimacy. But those Americans, including conservative thinkers, whose business it is to reflect upon such matters, are properly concerned.

While the present argument engages judicial activism, the problem of judicial usurpation is qualitatively different. Judicial activism is an abuse of power; judicial usurpation involves a redefinition of the constitutional order. The judicial usurpation of politics is a direct challenge to the constituting premises of our political order; namely, that just government is derived from the consent of the governed; that the consent of the governed is to be understood in the strong sense of self-government; and that in a self-governing republic, political sovereignty belongs to the people and is exercised through their elected representatives who are accountable to those whom they represent. Of course many today view such civics textbook definitions of our political system as quaint and naïve. Intellectuals, which is to say professional complexifiers, remind us that things are a great deal more complicated than the civics textbooks would have it, and they are of course right.

Cutting through our sophisticated complexifications, however, the argument about the judicial usurpation of politics advances a number of simple propositions that are disturbingly true. Politics, in this connection, is understood in its Aristotelian sense of free people deliberating how we ought to order our life together. That is another way of describing what the Founders meant by self-government. The "ought" in Aristotle's definition indicates that politics is, in its nature if not typically in its practice, a moral enterprise.

When it comes to the big questions of the right ordering of our life together, the courts, led by the Supreme Court, have again and again said, in effect, that the American people are not capable of self-government. The *Planned Parenthood v. Casey*[8] decision most egregiously expresses this idea in its declaration of what might be called the Führer principle, saying that "the people will be tested" by whether they follow the lead of the Court and acquiesce in *Roe v. Wade*'s [9] putative settlement of the abortion question.[10]

The Court's effective declaration that the American people are not capable of self-government through the representative institutions of this republic is not simply motivated by judicial ambition to rule. Legislators bear a heavy burden of responsibility for our present circumstances. As the religious leaders declared in *We Hold These Truths*, "Too often, legislators prefer to leave difficult and controverted questions to the courts. This must be called what it is, an abdication of their duty in our representative form of democratic government. Too often, too,

Christian legislators separate their convictions from their public actions, thus depriving our politics of their informed moral judgment. The other side of judicial usurpation is legislative dereliction."[11]

The timidity of the legislature and the consequent creation of a vacuum that the courts are all too ready to fill are closely related to long-standing confusions about the place of moral judgment—and especially religiously-grounded moral judgment—in our constitutional order. For fifty years now, perhaps best dated from the *Everson v. Board of Education* decision of 1947,[12] the separation of church and state has been construed to mean the separation of religion from public life. The result is what I have elsewhere called "the naked public square."[13] The naked public square is one in which it is impossible to deliberate how we ought to order our life together because the deepest convictions of the deliberators are ruled out of order. For the great majority of Americans, moral judgment is inexplicably, however confusedly, connected with religion. In a long series of decisions, the Supreme Court and the other courts following in its judicial wake have manifested a deep-seated suspicion of, if not clear hostility to, religion and its attendant moral judgments. They frequently suggest that religion is a "sectarian" threat to the public order that must be grudgingly tolerated because of the regrettable but inescapable first freedom protected by the First Amendment.[14]

Going further in *Lee v. Weisman*,[15] the Court seemed to suggest that "an ethic and a morality which transcend human invention" is in fact religion, and therefore forbidden ground for law.[16] *Romer v. Evans* cavalierly dismissed thousands of years of moral teaching regarding the right ordering of human sexuality as an "irrational animus."[17] And then, of course, there is the notorious mystery passage from *Casey*: "At the heart of liberty is the right to define one's own concept of existence, of meaning, of the universe, and of the mystery of human life."[18] This last statement flies in the face of all that the Founders meant by "ordered liberty," liberty ordered to the truth, and not least to the truths of what the Declaration of Independence calls the "Laws of Nature and of Nature's God."[19]

Some respected students of constitutional law tell us that we need not worry about such statements: they are merely reckless dicta, rhetorical flourishes of justices who let their inner poet or inner philosopher out to play from time to time. Perhaps. But dicta have a way of insinuating themselves into later jurisprudence. Witness the great mischief done by Jefferson's dictum in a private letter about "a wall of separation" between church and state. I believe such dicta deserve the closest attention, for they reveal the underlying assumptions of the Court—or at least of some on the Court—about the relationship between law and moral judgment. If even one justice of the Supreme Court were to advance ideas about the Court's authority as radical as those advanced by *Casey*, there should be cause for concern. When these ideas are advanced by three justices and stand on the record as the Court's understanding of its place in our political order, there is cause for alarm.

While frequently paying lip-service to "moral neutrality," the courts just as frequently present themselves as the guardians of the nation's conscience. As Justice Antonin Scalia has noted, the pretense of neutrality is a thin disguise for the judicial imposition of an alternative morality that reflects the legal and cultural milieu from which judges typically come. The courts have thus become, more and more, belligerents in our much-discussed culture wars—and belligerents, with remarkable consistency, on one side of the great questions regarding how we ought to order our life together.

The procedural liberalism that pretends to be morally neutral, all the while imposing its own morality under the guise of protecting the law from the religiously-tainted morality of the people, is well described by Pope John Paul II in his 1991 encyclical on the free and just society, *Centesimus Annus*: "Authentic democracy is possible only in a State ruled by law, and on the basis of a correct conception of the human person. It requires that the necessary conditions be present for the advancement both of the individual through education and formation in true ideals, and of the 'subjectivity' of society through the creation of structures of participation and shared responsibility."[20]

That, it seems to me, is not a bad definition of what the Founders meant by self-government. The pope then states in that crucial passage:

> Nowadays there is a tendency to claim that agnosticism and skeptical relativism are the philosophy and the basic attitude which correspond to democratic forms of political life. Those who are convinced that they know the truth and firmly adhere to it are considered unreliable from a democratic point of view, since they do not accept that truth is determined by the majority, or that it is subject to variation according to different political trends. It must be observed

in this regard that if there is no ultimate truth to guide and direct political activity, then ideas and convictions can easily be manipulated for reasons of power. As history demonstrates, a democracy without values easily turns into open or thinly disguised totalitarianism.[21]

"Open or thinly disguised totalitarianism"[22] is strong language, but I think it is fully warranted. "Those who are convinced that they know the truth and firmly adhere to it are considered unreliable from a democratic point of view. . . ."[23] Many in the legal academy and on the bench consider the American people unreliable from a democratic point of view. Indeed, from a skeptical and relativistic democratic point of view, the Founders themselves are unreliable. The overwhelming majority of Americans, like the Founders, may not be convinced that they know all the truth, and they may not always adhere to the truth they know, but they do believe there is truth, including moral truth.

Nonetheless, there are those who contend that the system contrived by the Founders was deliberately built on the nonfoundation of agnosticism and skeptical relativism. Generations of Americans have now been mis-educated by this bowdlerized and radically secularized account of the founding. This version takes Thomas Jefferson as the lodestar of the founding vision and largely ignores all those who were involved (as Jefferson was not) in the writing and ratification of the Constitution. Our Founders understood themselves to be orthodox Christians, generally of a Protestant and Calvinist kind. It is inconceivable that they would have approved a constitutional order hostile to their deepest convictions, as the courts have in recent decades interpreted the Constitution to be. And even Jefferson, while he was surely a theological skeptic, was hardly a moral skeptic or proponent of moral relativism. While he may have been as confused in his moral reasoning as he was in his theology, his entire life and voluminous writings bear witness to his conviction that the American order is premised upon moral truths to which it must be held accountable.

So we find ourselves in circumstances quite new and quite recent. That the Constitution is an instrument to protect the government against the American people has been proposed by the courts only in the last fifty years. What an irony that the great problem in America today is not the tyranny of the majority, as Toqueville feared, but the tyranny of a minority, one that has largely captured the judiciary to advance its own purposes. Perhaps the majority will acquiesce in such tyranny. Many, perhaps most, Americans seem to have accepted the courts' view that they—unruly, bigoted, racist, and potentially despotic—must be protected from themselves and that the purpose of the Constitution is to protect the rights of minorities against such a tyrannous majority as they might be. Certainly the Constitution, and particularly the Bill of Rights, is designed to protect minorities, but it is first of all an instrument to assure self-government to a people deemed capable of self-government. And a Constitution that is increasingly pitted against the majority will, in time, become an ineffectual instrument in protecting minorities.

Our present difficulties proceed in part from the profound influence of the famous 1954 Supreme Court school desegregation decision, *Brown v. Board of Education*.[24] Whether or not one agrees with its reasoning, the American people have effectively ratified its conclusion. This, more than any other one event in our recent history, has cloaked the Court in an aura of moral superiority. The standard telling of the story is that because the constitutionally defined political process could not resolve the question of racial segregation, the Court had to break the deadlock. Whatever the truth in that telling, and I think it considerable, the Court set forth on a course that could not and should not be sustained. With strong support from the makers of public opinion, the Court thought itself on a moral roll, so to speak. That roll hit formidable bumps with the school prayer decisions of the early 1960s,[25] and came to an unceremonious halt with the infamous abortion decisions of 1973.[26] This is the context of the Court's poignant appeal in *Casey* for popular ratification of the abortion regime that it has unilaterally imposed upon the nation.[27]

In *We Hold These Truths*, religious leaders responded to that appeal in a manner both decorous and firm: "Moreover, in *Casey* the Court admonished pro-life dissenters, chastising them for continuing the debate and suggesting that the very legitimacy of the law depends upon the American people obeying the Court's decisions, even though no evidence is offered that those decisions are supported by the Constitution or accepted by a moral consensus of the citizenry. If the Court is inviting us to end the debate over abortion, we, as Christians and free citizens of this republic, respectfully decline the invitation."[28]

I think that puts the matter rather nicely. The statement goes on to note an ominous parallel with another great dispute in the history of the American experiment:

> The crisis created by *Roe* and its legacy is not without precedent in our national life. Our present circumstance is shadowed by the memory of the infamous *Dred Scott* decision of 1857. Then, the Court, in a similar act of raw judicial power, excluded slaves of African descent from the community of those possessing rights that others are bound to respect. Abraham Lincoln refused to bow to that decision. It was in devotion to our constitutional order that Lincoln declared in his First Inaugural Address that the people and their representatives had not "practically resigned their government into the hands of that eminent tribunal." Today we are again in desperate need of political leaders who accept the responsibility to lead in restoring government derived from the consent of the governed.[29]

Are there political leaders prepared to meet the present challenge? I have no idea. Certainly in the last year there has been lively discussion among politicians, both at the national and state levels, about the need to check the usurpations of the courts. This concern may be motivated in part by the jealousy of legislators who wish to protect their own prerogatives. While not the most edifying of motivations, it should not be scorned. In a fallen creation and a constitutional order designed for men and not for angels, the desire to protect one's own power has a worthy and necessary part in the right ordering of things.

Also noteworthy is that in the last year, some courts, and the Supreme Court in particular, have taken cognizance of the agitation over judicial usurpation. Notable in this connection was the decision on doctor-assisted suicide.[30] In both the oral argument and the decision itself, the Court expressed a rare and refreshing caution about usurping the legislative function and about the dangers of court-made law.[31] A careful reading of the unanimous opinion and its concurring opinions, however, is not entirely encouraging. It seems evident that a majority of the Court still believes that the question of a constitutional right to assisted suicide is for the Court to determine at a politically propitious time in the future. In *City of Boerne v. Flores,*[32] which overturned the Religious Freedom Restoration Act, the Court actually strengthened its insistence that it has a monopoly on constitutional interpretation. In short, while we may welcome the outcome of the decision on assisted suicide, we should not be deceived that it resolves, or is even a step toward resolving, the crisis of judicial usurpation. It does demonstrate that the Court reads the election returns and did not want to spark another firestorm comparable to the controversy over its abortion regime. We may be grateful when the Court is cautious in exercising the power it has usurped, but we should not forget that it is still usurped power.

As we continue to ponder and discuss this crisis, we need to remember that the question of legitimacy, in theory and practice, is theological. By this I mean we are faced by a challenge that goes to the heart of this or any other regime: By what authority does it rule?

In addressing this question, I share the sound conservative instinct—the Burkean instinct—that questions of political theory should not be pressed more than necessary, and that there is a certain prudence and honor in

just muddling through the messy ambiguities of any political order. Unfortunately, the Supreme Court will not
permit us to do that. In recent decades, and especially
in recent years, it has forced the question of the legitimacy of the regime. Especially in the *Casey* decision, but
not only there, it has thrown down the gauntlet, and citizens who care about the future of this constitutional order have no choice but to respond. In so doing, we should
recall that short of the Kingdom of God, no form of
government is unambiguously legitimate. The question
is whether ours is still the form of government constructed
by the Founders and, if not, how that circumstance might
be remedied.

President Washington said in his First Inaugural
Address, "we ought to be no less persuaded that the propitious smiles of Heaven can never be expected on a nation that disregards the eternal rules of order and right
which Heaven itself has ordained; . . . preservation of the
sacred fire of liberty and the destiny of the republican
model of government are justly considered, perhaps, as
deeply, as finally, staked on the experiment intrusted to
the hands of the American people."[33]

The question is whether we, in our putative sophistication, can now dismiss such a claim as no more than
a rhetorical flourish. In his Farewell Address, Washington declared, "Of all the dispositions and habits which
lead to political prosperity, religion and morality are indispensable supports. In vain would that man claim the
tribute of patriotism who should labor to subvert these
great pillars of human happiness—these firmest props of
the duties of men and citizens."[34] Religion and morality
are not alien intrusions upon our public life, but the foun-

dation of our pursuit of the common good. Those who sneer that Washington's words are the words of a dead, white, male slave owner have the duty, it seems to me, to explain why we should adhere at all to a constitutional order constructed by such flawed and limited human beings—people so unlike our very superior selves!

Again, the question of legitimacy is a question of theology, and the Court itself has framed the question in such terms. In its own intellectually bumbling way, the notorious mystery passage of *Casey* and the accompanying opinion pose the radical proposition that our polity has but two players. On the one hand is the autonomous, unencumbered individual, and on the other is the Court, the sole source of governmental legitimacy and ultimate authority. *Casey* asks the American people to ratify this radically new political order. I do not think that is going to happen. But those of us who decline to give our consent to this new order are obliged to explain the reasons for our dissent.

Our dissent understands that *Casey* and other recent decisions are part of the judicial pattern of the last several decades that has increasingly excluded the deepest convictions of the sovereign people from the deliberation of how we ought to order our life together. The root of our difficulty, I suggest, is in the abuse of the religion clause of the First Amendment.[35] As I have discussed at length elsewhere, the two provisions of the religion clause (and there is only one religion clause, not two religion clauses) have been pitted against one another.[36] The goal and end of the religion clause—the free exercise of religion—has again and again been subordinated to the means that is to serve that end, the nonestablishment of religion.

Nonestablishment, in turn, is taken to mean that religion be confined to the strictly private sphere of life; that wherever government advances, religion must retreat. And today government advances almost everywhere.

The novelty and audaciousness of the American experiment was chiefly in the religion clause, in which, for the first time in history, a government declared that it had no authority to determine the sovereign people's definition of whatever higher sovereignty they might acknowledge. This most crucial factor in the American understanding of limited government is the greatest safeguard against what Pope John Paul II calls "open or thinly disguised totalitarianism."[37] The state is limited by its accountability to the sovereign people, and the sovereign people, in turn, are free to name the sovereignty to which or to whom they hold themselves accountable. This novel and intricate arrangement is expressed in phrases such as the "Laws of Nature and of Nature's God"[38] and the affirmation that "ours is a nation under God."

The alternative to the theology of the Court is not theocracy. The alternative to the naked public square is not the sacred public square: it is the civil public square. The alternative is democratic governance through republican institutions. Nobody should seek a confessional state. With the Founders, we seek to preserve a constitutional state within a confessional society. Whether the society continues to be confessional is the business of the institutions of religion, not the business of the state. In its hostility to the robust, persistent, and apparently increasing religious vitality of American society, the Court has come very close to establishing in law its own functional religion of relentless secularism, creating a different form of confessional state that is radically antithetical to the confession of the sovereign people. Not all share the confession of the majority, of course, a confession that in public terms takes the form of what is broadly defined as the Judeo-Christian moral tradition. The Court has pursued its unhappy course in the name of protecting minorities that dissent from that tradition, and, too often, it forgets that the rights of minorities can be secure only when they are secured by the beliefs of the majority.

Judicial usurpation is no doubt driven by many factors, but the most notable is the judiciary's all but explicit declaration that the American people are incapable of self-government. The actions of the Court deny the competence of the people as citizens to give political effect to the commanding moral truths by which we ought to order our life together. Judicial usurpation is, in other words, based on contempt for the sovereign people and rejection of the constituting maxim that just government is derived from the consent of the governed. We must hope that our present crisis, once it is clearly understood, can be remedied by constitutional means. We have no choice, however, but to entertain the possibility that we may be wrong about that. If it cannot be remedied, we are indeed discussing the end of democracy—this time without the question mark.

GOVERNMENT BY
THE "THOUGHTFUL PART"

Russell Hittinger

Y CONTRIBUTION to the original *First Things* symposium was entitled "A Crisis of Legitimacy." I explained why the Supreme Court has brought about a crisis of legitimacy, not just for the Court itself, but for the entire constitutional order. I argued that this crisis is marked by two things: first, by a long train of court rulings that constitutionalize principles contrary to rightly-formed conscience; second, by a train of decisions which remove from the political order the ability of citizens to remedy the Court's errors. Citizens and their elected representatives are required to obey, or at least comply with, rulings that express principles contrary to conscience, and they are required to believe that those rulings are the law of the Constitution and must remain so short of an amendment. This double bind—an objectionable decision, then constitutionalized—is exactly what Abraham Lincoln objected to in the case of *Dred Scott v. Sandford*[1]: "Its language [is] equivalent to saying that [slavery] is embodied and so woven into that instrument that it cannot be detached without breaking the constitution itself."[2]

Many of our critics did not appreciate the aim of the symposium, which was not merely to quarrel with particular decisions of the courts, but to call attention to the double bind. As Lincoln understood the problem, no constitutional regime is undone by a stupid or even by an illegal use of power by a particular branch of government. Whether judges should be more or less "active" in their interpretation of the Constitution, indeed whether judges ought to be more or less considerate of traditional moral principles, are questions of politics and policy debates as well as questions of law. They are not trivial issues, but neither do they threaten the regime. The regime is threatened or changed when specious principles, to use Lincoln's words, are "so woven" into the fundamental law that those principles cannot be dislodged without "breaking the constitution itself."[3]

David Brooks suggests that a "return to first principles is the antithesis of the Conservative Temper."[4] The *First Things* symposiasts, in giving "fealty to abstract ideals and beliefs," are tempted to favor them over the concrete conventions, pieties, and ongoing conversations which constitute society.[5] Brooks makes a Burkean point: a healthy polity, indeed, a polity in which political conversation is at all possible, does not constantly or lightly revert to abstract discussions of first principles.[6] Yet Brooks implicitly regards the symposium as trying to move abruptly from disputes over policy to metaphysical, moral, and religious questions.[7]

Gertrude Himmelfarb makes a similar criticism. Questioning the legitimacy of the *regime*, Himmelfarb says, distracts from the humdrum of the ordinary political process, where conservatives have won significant victories: "We have, in this respect at least, accomplished something like a major reform, if not a revolution. It has been confined largely to the arena of social policy and achieved through the normal workings of the political process. It has not even required any constitutional amendment, which makes it all the more commendable. Other areas, however—the culture, the media, academia, and, most notably, the judiciary—have resisted the conservative trend."[8]

Himmelfarb suggests that the *First Things* symposiasts ignore the constraints of policy debates and allow their frustration over the state of the *culture* to spill over into questioning the legitimacy of the *regime*.[9] Arguing in the same vein, Midge Decter observes that the rhetoric of revolution whether by the New Left or the 1994 Republican Congress inexorably confronts the "stolidity and. . . contentment of the general populace" and the "sluggishness and obduracy of democratic society."[10]

Still other critics, again on the political Right, accuse the *First Things* editors and symposiasts of religious intemperance, perhaps intolerance. Walter Berns asserts that the symposium confirms the opinion "that religious conservatives are extremists."[11] Francis Fukuyama suggests that by raising the issue of legitimacy of the regime, Christian conservatives are liable to be viewed as "a somewhat nutty and out-of-touch interest group."[12] Peter Berger goes further, alleging that the religious right has fixated upon and absolutized the issue of abortion, suggesting "[it] seems to me . . . that for most of the *First Things* contributors, and for the magazine's editors, the driving concern has been not so much the power the courts have improperly assumed but rather what they have done with this power."[13] Interestingly, Berger agrees that the courts have usurped power, but insists that "time and again, the other two branches of government have usurped power in constitutionally dubious ways."[14] In other words, the symposiasts are not really concerned about the routine misdemeanor of usurpation of authority, but with the felony of the judicially imposed policy on the matter of abortion.

These critics make good points. For my part, I should not wish to dispute their wisdom. A healthy polity requires of its citizens patience and prudence in addressing the imperfections of government. In a democracy, all factions, including religious and other partisans of *First Things*, must learn how to be good losers. The virtues of civic life are distinct from the virtues of religious obedience. In any case, ordinary political conversation presupposes the legitimacy of the regime.

Yet these critics miss the most salient point of the symposium: It was not the editors or symposiasts of *First Things*, but the Supreme Court itself, in *Planned Parenthood v. Casey*,[15] that supplied the premises for the question of the legitimacy of the regime. For the Court self-consciously staked its own legitimacy, and indeed the legitimacy of the constitutional "covenant" on the principles which it discovered and applied in that case. The Court proposed a Lincolnian double-bind situation. Take away *Casey*, and the *First Things* symposium would be vulnerable to just the kind of criticisms made by Himmelfarb. If, however, we took the right measure of *Casey*, the charge of radicalism should be aimed at the Court, not at the symposium. So it is necessary to return to *Casey*, and to reconsider the regime-threatening doctrine announced by the Court.

Before turning to *Casey*, two points are in order. First, I pick my words carefully when I say that a doctrine is "announced." The Court appeared to understand that it was proposing something new. It evinced an unusual degree of candor and anxiety about the response of the polity to its handiwork in this case. Gerard Bradley has put the question in this way: "We need not know whether the doctrine of *Casey* is not yet law but a proposal—a judicially drafted bill—awaiting final approval."[16] Perhaps the Court will silently or explicitly relinquish its doctrine of the social contract in *Casey*. At this point, however, it will not do to interpret away the *Casey* doctrine as incautious dicta which reflect the Court's rather anxious response to a crisis. In the first place, all of the great cases where the Court has defined its own authority and the nature of the social contract [17] have been rendered in moments of crisis. Moreover, students of American constitutional law know that judicial dicta have a life of their own at law. Justice Brandeis's dictum in *Olmstead v. United States,* that the framers of the Constitution "conferred, as against the government, the right to be let alone—the most comprehensive of rights and the right most valued by civilized men,"[18] has become virtually a self-evident axiom of constitutional law. For good or ill, the interpreting community of constitutional law (judges, scholars, and activists) take judicial dicta seriously. When one side dismisses an argument as a mere dictum, everyone knows that this is a point of rhetoric. Finally, the Court's dicta in *Casey* represent the most recent statement of its view of the social contract and the authority of the Court. To my knowledge, the majority of the Court has not repudiated the principles proposed in *Casey*.[19]

Second, it might be useful to define the word "regime," for our use of this word in the *First Things* symposium was criticized. The word "regime" is the translation into Latin *regimen* of the Greek word *politeía*—the constitution or form of the civic life. The *politeía* includes the ruling element or class (*políteuma*) and the common education (*paideía*).[20] The ancients did not distinguish as sharply the social and institutional facets of the *politeía*. The regime is more like the soul of a body politic, making it both a political community (rather than a tribe, family, or economic corporation) and individuating it as a particular kind of political community (aristocratic rather than monarchical). This is not the place to speculate how the ancient meanings of *politeía* or *regimen* correspond to modern institutions. Here, it is enough for us to note that a regime changes when the ruling powers are reallocated. The change from a parliamentary democracy, where many individuals and groups hold ruling shares, to rule by a single party is a change of regimes. As I read it, in *Casey*, the Court announces precisely this kind of change in regime and holds it out for approval or disapproval by the people. Moreover, the proposed change in the *políteuma* implies a profound change in the *paideía*—in the civic education respecting what or who is to be honored. In *Casey*, we catch a glimpse of that new *paideía*: the honoring of unbounded individual liberty and the superintendence of the judiciary in distributing the loaves and fishes of that right.

Judicial Exemplarism

In *Planned Parenthood v. Casey*, the authors of the joint opinion write that "the reservations any of us may have in reaffirming the central holding of *Roe* are outweighed by the explication of individual liberty we have given combined with the force of *stare decisis*."[21] There are at least two grounds for their decision: first, a constitutional ground, which concerns the substantive due process right of a woman to procure an abortion; second, "a series of prudential and pragmatic considerations designed to test the consistency of overruling a prior decision with the ideal of the rule of law, and to gauge the respective costs of reaffirming and overruling a prior case."[22]

To complicate matters, in at least two places the triumvirate takes note of yet a third consideration, namely, the Court's legitimacy. The authors write that overruling *Roe v. Wade*,[23] "would not only reach an unjustifiable result under principles of stare decisis, but would seriously weaken the Court's capacity to exercise the judicial power."[24] Enumerating the grounds of their decision, the authors write: "After considering the fundamental constitutional questions resolved by Roe, principles of institutional integrity, and the rule of stare decisis, we are led to conclude this: the essential holding of *Roe v. Wade* should be retained and once again reaffirmed."[25]

This floating third principle—call it institutional integrity or authority—is the most important feature of *Casey*. We will return to it after considering the first two grounds of the decision.

Even on a cursory reading, one is perplexed by the fact that the answer given to the first question (whether there is a constitutionally protected right to procure an abortion) is at odds with the answer given to the question of stare decisis, for stare decisis is only intelligible if one has reason to suspect that the first issue was erroneously decided. But Justices O'Connor, Souter, and Kennedy vigorously defend, and indeed extend, the jurisprudence of individual rights running from *Griswold v. Connecticut*[26] through *Roe v. Wade*.[27] The authors of the joint opinion write: "It is a promise of the Constitution that there is a realm of personal liberty which the government may not enter"[28] Then, they rather crisply set forth the constitutional issue: "The underlying constitutional issue is whether the State can resolve these philosophic questions . . . such . . . that a woman lacks all choice in the matter, except perhaps in . . . circumstances in which the pregnancy is itself a danger to her own life or health, or is the result of rape or incest."[29] Finally, after explicitly adopting the substantive due process method of privacy cases, they resolve the issue: "At the heart of liberty is the right to define one's own concept of existence, of meaning, of the universe, and of the mystery of human life. Beliefs about these matters could not define the attributes of personhood were they formed under compulsion of the State."[30]

Why, then, go through the hand-wrenching of a stare decisis analysis? According to their own principles, the woman has a fundamental constitutional right to procure an abortion without undue burden. And this is only the species of a broader genus of liberty, gathered from the case law on matters of privacy and autonomy.[31] Thus, *Roe* does not stand to *Casey* as *Plessy v. Ferguson*[32] stands to *Brown v. Board of Education*[33] or as *Lochner v. New York*[34] stands to *West Coast Hotel Co. v. Parrish.*[35] In short, there is no need to explain why *Roe* was not overturned if *Roe* was essentially correct on constitutional grounds. Even more curious is that, in the stare decisis section of the opinion, the Court avers that for an entire generation abortion has become a form of birth control, and that overturning *Roe* would disturb the settled expectations of those who use abortion for that purpose.[36] But in the section devoted to the constitutional question—to the issue of the rights of the woman—the Court does not make the fundamental right depend upon these contingent social facts. Rather, the right is grounded in the very nature of the liberty at stake. There is no reason to think that, were only a small fraction of women to use abortion for purposes of birth control, rather than some other means of "self-definition," the Court could reverse *Roe* without undermining a fundamental principle of the Constitution.

What can we conclude from the Court's opinion? We might conclude that there was a difference of opinion among the triumvirate, and they decided to include, on the one hand, the strongest argument in favor of the constitutional right, and on the other, the strongest argument in favor of stare decisis. The reason that I raise the incompatibility of the first and second grounds is to address those who would diminish the problems presented by *Casey,* either by reducing the rights analysis to mere dictum, or by so focusing upon the stare decisis analysis that the opinion is construed as a derogation from the principles of *Roe v. Wade.* The true story is that the right is augmented and made less dependent upon contingent social facts and that stare decisis is invoked with respect to contingent social facts. One might suppose that this conjunction of incompatibles reflects the dilemma of American opinion on the subject of abortion.

The most remarkable novelty of *Casey* is neither the alleged right to invent the meaning of the universe nor the application of stare decisis to the question of whether to overrule *Roe*, but rather the Court's proposal that its own legitimacy is a principle for settling the dispute over abortion. After explaining the nature of the liberty right to be upheld, the Court states that "it is necessary to understand the source of this Court's authority, the conditions necessary for its preservation, and its relationship to the country's understanding of itself as a constitutional Republic."[37] At this juncture, the Court begins to develop a position that is without precedent in our constitutional history: "The Court's power lies . . . in its legitimacy, a product of substance and perception that shows itself in the people's acceptance of the Judiciary as fit to determine what the Nation's law means and to declare what it demands."[38]

Were an executive officer to define his power in this fashion, we might suspect it was Mussolini. It is a doctrine not merely of supremacy in law, but of what I shall call *exemplarism*.[39] An organ of government is legitimate insofar as it is able to speak the voice of the whole people, and insofar as the people are able to hear their own voice in it. Consider the following declarations of the triumvirate in *Casey:*

> To all those who will be so tested by following, the Court implicitly undertakes to remain steadfast, lest in the end a price be paid for nothing. . . . So, indeed, must be the character of a Nation of people who aspire to live according to the rule of law. Their

belief in themselves as such a people is not readily
separable from their understanding of the Court
invested with the authority to decide their constitutional cases and *speak before all others* for their constitutional ideals. If the Court's legitimacy should
be undermined, then so would the country be in its
very ability to see itself through its constitutional
ideals. The Court's concern with legitimacy is not
for the sake of the Court but for the sake of the Nation to which it is responsible.

. . . .

Where, in the performance of its judicial duties, the
Court decides a case in such a way as to resolve the
sort of intensely divisive controversy reflected in Roe
and those rare, comparable cases, its decision has a
dimension that the resolution of the normal case does
not carry. It is the dimension present whenever the
Court's interpretation of the Constitution calls the
contending sides of a national controversy to end
their national division by accepting a common mandate rooted in the Constitution.[40]

The metaphor of roots or rooting is interesting because
the triumvirate go on to say that "the *root* of American
governmental power is revealed most clearly in the instance of the power conferred by the Constitution upon
the Judiciary of the United States and specifically upon
this Court."[41]

The meaning conveyed by this language is unmistak-
able. The root of the ruling power is revealed most clearly
in the judiciary. The judiciary is not a co-equal branch,
but a branch that enjoys some legitimate claim to more
fully exemplify the "root." This notion is given further

weight by the Court's insistence that it does not merely decide the case, but issues a "common mandate." Thus, the Court in *Casey* speaks beyond the parties to the case to the entire nation, and argues that the people could not understand themselves as a political or constitutional entity except through the rulings of the Court. As Bradley puts it, the Court announces "We will be your Court, and you will be our people."[42]

Beyond Judicial Review

It is important to distinguish this bid to change the *políteuma* from previous expressions of judicial authority. Let us take two cases which are defining moments of Article III powers, *Marbury v. Madison*[43] and *Cooper v. Aaron.*[44] In the first, the Court defined its power in reference to other branches of the U.S. government[45]; in the second, it defined its power in reference to state governments.[46] I do not intend to examine these decisions at the level of detail they deserve. Rather, I wish to contrast them with *Casey* in order to show that *Casey* appears to cross a threshold that had not been crossed before.

Notice that the *Casey* Court does not merely reiterate the important, but relatively modest, point about judicial review made by Justice Marshall in *Marbury v. Madison*:

> Those who apply the rule to particular cases, must of necessity expound and interpret that rule. If two laws conflict with each other, the courts must decide on the operation of each.
>
> So, if a law be in opposition to the constitution; if both the law and the constitution apply to a par-

ticular case, so that the court must either decide that case conformably to the law, disregarding the constitution; or conformably to the constitution, disregarding the law, the court must determine which of these conflicting rules governs the case. This is of the very essence of judicial duty.[47]

Justice Marshall makes no reference to the legitimacy of the Court's power beyond the written Constitution; he makes no assertion of judicial authority beyond the case at hand. No doubt, Justice Marshall's understanding of judicial authority implicitly contains the idea of the Court policing the boundaries of the people's conversation through the institutions of the U.S. government. For all of that, however, Justice Marshall's articulation of the principle of judicial review does not hint at a doctrine of judicial exemplarism. Marshall refused to issue a writ of mandamus delivering a governmental post to Mr. Marbury; yet he did not issue a "common mandate" to the people.

In *Dred Scott*, the Court tried to make a bid to issue a mandate to the entire body politic on the subject of slavery. That bid was clearly and decisively rejected by Lincoln in his First Inaugural Address:

I do not forget the position, assumed by some, that constitutional questions are to be decided by the Supreme Court; nor do I deny that such decisions must be binding in any case, upon the parties to a suit, as to the object of that suit, while they are also entitled to very high respect and consideration, in all parallel cases, by all other departments of the government. And while it is obviously possible that such decision may be erroneous in any given case, still the evil effect following it, being limited to that particular case, with the chance that it may be over-ruled and never become a precedent for other cases, can better be borne than could the evils of a different practice.

At the same time the candid citizen must con-fess that if the policy of the government, upon vi-tal questions affecting the *whole people,* is to be irrevocably fixed by decisions of the Supreme Court, the instant they are made in ordinary litigation be-tween parties, in personal actions, the people will have ceased to be their own rulers, having, to that extent, practically resigned their government into the hands of that eminent tribunal.[48]

The key in this passage is Lincoln's phrase—"ques-tions, affecting the whole people." He denied that the whole of common good is exemplified and governed by Article III judicial power. He understood that were the Court's authority to exemplify and reach the whole of the common good, it would be a change of regimes—indeed, a change as startling and novel as the effort by Justice Taney to declare that an unbounded natural right of slavery exists in, and was intended by, the Constitution.

If we turn to *Cooper v. Aaron*, we find some incau-tious remarks about judicial authority, which, if not quali-fied, would amount to a new doctrine of judicial supremacy. Immediately after *Brown*, a school board in Little Rock, Arkansas was delaying implementation of desegregation, and the Governor of Arkansas threatened to use National Guard units to block desegregation of schools. After citing *Marbury v. Madison*, Chief Justice Warren wrote:

It follows that the interpretation of the Fourteenth Amendment enunciated by this Court in the Brown

case is the supreme law of the land, and Art. VI of
the Constitution makes it of binding effect on the
States "any Thing in the Constitution or Laws of
any State to the Contrary notwithstanding." Every state legislator and executive and judicial officer
is solemnly committed by oath taken pursuant to Art.
VI, cl. 3, "to support this Constitution."

. . . .

No state legislator or executive or judicial officer can
war against the Constitution without violating his
undertaking to support it.[49]

Responsible constitutional scholars are aware that these
sentences cannot stand without qualification because, so
far, they conflate the Constitution and the Court's occasional case law. If *Cooper* is read in a flat-footed way, the
Constitution is nothing more nor less than the status quo
of the Court's interpretation—an idea that would hardly
reassure minorities.

Although *Cooper* seems to cross a threshold into a novel
doctrine of constitutional order, it can be grabbed by its
coattails and brought back. The main holding in *Cooper*
is that state authorities cannot unilaterally nullify rights
won in a federal court under the Fourteenth Amendment.
At stake here is not the exclusive supremacy of the judiciary, but of the federal government in matters reached
by the Fourteenth Amendment. In his concurring opinion, Justice Frankfurter seemed to realize that the remark
about judicial supremacy had to be put in such a context:

Every act of government may be challenged by an
appeal to law, as finally pronounced by this Court.
Even this Court has the last say only for a time.

Being composed of fallible men, it may err. But revision of its errors must be by orderly process of law. The Court may be asked to reconsider its decisions, and this has been done successfully again and again throughout our history. Or, what this Court has deemed its duty to decide may be changed by legislation, as it often has been, and, on occasion, by constitutional amendment.[50]

Looking at it from Justice Frankfurter's perspective, *Cooper* is not an apt precedent or analogue for the doctrine spelled out in *Casey*. First, there is no root and branch metaphor identifying the people's grant of power with the judiciary. Second, although desegregation was a national controversy, the Court in *Cooper* does not address itself to the entire nation, but rather to state officials in Arkansas who were attempting to nullify rights won in a federal court. Third, in light of Justice Frankfurter's concurring opinion, other governmental actors are not bound by their Article VI oath to conflate the Constitution with the voice of the Court in a particular case. Rather, they are required to correct a judicial error through an orderly process of law. In sum, despite two sentences which seem to conflate the Constitution with the case law, *Cooper* on the whole preserves the ideal that our constitutional order consists of many ruling shares and many voices. Although *Cooper* does represent an aggressive policing of boundaries by Article III courts, it does not change the *políteuma*.

To Speak Before All Others

Such cannot be said for *Casey*. In no more than a stray dictum or two, the Court claims to have settled a national controversy and asks for the obedience of the nation precisely on the ground of the Court's competence to do so: "Their belief in themselves as such a people is not readily separable from their understanding of the Court invested with the authority to decide their constitutional cases and *speak before all others* for their constitutional ideals. If the Court's legitimacy should be undermined, then, so would the country be in its very ability to see itself through its constitutional ideals. The Court's concern with legitimacy is not for the sake of the Court, but for the sake of the Nation to which it is responsible."[51]

Plainly, the Court here goes beyond the judicial duty to speak the law in the case at hand; it claims to speak constitutional ideals and to be the primary voice in that regard. Had Lincoln been faced with that doctrine of judicial supremacy and exemplarism in connection with *Dred Scott,* he could not have taken his Article vi oath; or, he could have taken the oath only on the condition of rejecting the Court's view of its authority.

If we take Lincoln's perspective, the *First Things* symposium raises exactly the right questions with regard to *Casey.* For us, as for Lincoln, there are two issues. First, there is the question of whether a right is protected by the fundamental law of the Constitution; second, there is the question of the scope of the Court's jurisdiction over that question. In *Casey,* the Court declares an unbounded right of liberty, and it declares its own plenary authority to exemplify the voice of the people—so much so, that were the Court resisted the people would lose their regime, their *politeía.*[52]

No one knows how far the present Court is committed to this new doctrine, or even whether it perceives it as a new doctrine; it can be only a matter of speculation whether the Court has considered the implications of *Casey*. On its face, however, this is a regime-changing doctrine. Whereas the Court once invoked the Constitution to protect rights and ruling shares against the will of transient majorities, *Casey* claims to speak for a supermajority of the entire people—it speaks for the collective will, or at least the "thoughtful part."[53] (One can only imagine the status of the "unthoughtful part" with regard to its share in the common good.) If this expression of power were put in the mouth of an executive officer of government, or in the mouth of a French-style Committee for Public Safety, we would see it for what it is: the reduction of the *políteuma* to one voice. Between the declaration of the Court and the common good, no place remains for the operation of public reason except in obedience to the Court. To the extent that this radical reconfiguration of the regime goes unchecked, the Court will continue to shut down any ruling voice other than its own. To the extent that other branches and departments of government comply with, or tacitly approve, the doctrine of judicial supremacy and exemplarism, the regime changes. And with each tacit approval, season after season, a new *paideía* inexorably emerges: To honor what the Court honors, and to honor it precisely because the Court so demands.

Take, for example, the decision in *Boerne v. Flores*.[54] The Court contended that Religious Freedom Restoration Act[55] (RFRA) was a usurpation of power by Congress.[56] In this decision, the Court abstained from the exemplarist language of *Casey*, but the reduction of ruling voices to that of the Court is evident. Five decades ago, the Court (not Congress) incorporated the religion clauses of the First Amendment against the states. In its evolving jurisprudence of religious liberty, the Court generally took an expansive view of free exercise. State laws that impaired the free exercise of religion were held to a high standard of scrutiny. Free exercise of religion was protected not merely by an anti-discrimination principle, but by the positive principle that the people's discharge of their religious duties (prayer and good works) should not be significantly impaired, even when the law is one of general applicability neutral on its face with respect to religion. States had to show compelling interest and narrowly tailored means.

In the *Employment Division v. Smith* [57] ruling, the Court changed its own standard of review, reducing the free exercise clause to an anti-discrimination principle.[58] Despite severe impairment of the people's religious practices, states only need to show that they did not discriminate against the religion so affected. In response, by a virtually unanimous vote, Congress enacted RFRA, which was signed by the President in 1993.[59] In *Boerne*, the Court ruled RFRA unconstitutional on the ground that Congress's authority to enforce the Fourteenth Amendment extends only to those rights whose scope have been defined by the Supreme Court. In other words, the protections guaranteed by the Fourteenth Amendment are no more and no less than what the Court decrees in its occasional case law—even when the case law changes from term to term and those changes embody completely contrary principles. Framed only a decade after *Dred Scott*, the enforcement clauses of the three Civil War amendments were intended to prevent the Court from hijacking the amendments.

Suppose the Supreme Court were to rule that resegregation of schools comports with the equal protection clause of the Fourteenth Amendment. Then suppose that Congress tries to remedy that mistake by passing a law pursuant to its section v powers—a law that in effect restores the higher standard articulated by the Court itself. According to the *Boerne* opinion, Congress would be usurping authority. At any given moment, the Constitution is coincident with the Court's pronouncements.

Seen against the background of *Casey,* the Court in *Boerne* has swatted down perhaps the only remaining power capable of checking abuses of judicial power. The *Boerne* holding allows the Court to act unilaterally and to render important clauses of the Constitution immune from the conversation of other branches and departments of government. By a kind of judo, Justice Kennedy makes it look like Congress is defining its own powers when it tries to hold the Court to the Court's own standard in previous cases. After citing Justice Marshall in *Marbury,* Justice Kennedy concludes:

> When the political branches of the Government act against the background of a judicial interpretation of the Constitution already issued, it must be understood that in later cases and controversies the Court will treat its precedents with the respect due them under settled principles, including *stare decisis,* and contrary expectations must be disappointed. RFRA was designed to control cases and controversies, such as the one before us; but as the provisions of the federal statute here invoked are beyond congressional authority, it is this Court's precedent, not RFRA, which must control.[60]

The upshot is that, while the Court is free to change its case law at will, and thus to make the Constitution a mere byproduct of its shifting opinions, the other branches and departments must submit to the case law as though it were the Constitution. This is not Justice Marshall's understanding of judicial review. It is the *Casey* doctrine.

It is true, of course, that the Supreme Court has not yet disallowed the people's right under Article v to amend the Constitution. But amendment is virtually the only route left for correcting a judicial error. This situation follows logically from *Casey*. For in its understanding of itself as the root of governmental power, the Court presumes that it holds a plenary grant of authority to speak in the name of the entire polity—a presumption that can only be gainsaid by amendment. All other constitutional voices are silenced. The polity must submit to the Court's definition of its power, or the polity has to commit itself to a never ending plebiscite. Indeed, a constant plebiscite tacitly admits the claims made by the Court about its own authority. Either way, we find ourselves approaching something like "the end of democracy."[61] (Once again, to respond to critics like David Brooks,[62] it is necessary to understand how it has come to pass that the table of civic conversation has been reduced to abstract discussion of the first principles of a regime.)

One of the lessons of this century, which nearly everyone claims to have learned, is that unlimited executive force in human government is dangerous. Throughout the civilized world in the 1920s and 1930s, people became dissatisfied and contemptuous of legislatures and parliaments. In Spain, Italy, Germany, Russia, Japan, and even to some extent in the United States (during the Great

Depression), people wanted public conflicts and crises to be resolved by strong executive action. The multi-voiced, polycentric model of political authority was abandoned in favor of exemplarism. Executive powers were thought to exemplify the common good, not to mention the "thoughtful part."[63] After World War I, the civilized part of the world beat its breast with so many mea culpas, and resolved never again to retreat from the civil conversation of constitutional democracy, and never again to hand over power to unbounded executives. Interestingly, even during the Cold War, Americans vigilantly guarded against executive power that would arrogate to itself the right to be the only voice and the only power that speaks for the people.

But the very generation that learned the lesson about the hard despotism of unbounded executive power, failed to learn the lesson about the soft despotism of courts. In the case of contemporary America—and, increasingly, in both Canada and in Europe as well—courts, rather than executive officers, claim to be the final and exclusive voice of the people. Courts tell us when to stop talking and when to obey. The emerging doctrine of judicial supremacy and exemplarism is alien to our institutions; it has a very bad track-record when expressed through executive organs of government; and it makes the fundamental law a theater of constant dispute over authority and first principles of the regime.

3

Prudent Warnings
and Imprudent Reactions

Hadley Arkes

A CONGRESSMAN, getting ensnarled in his own syntax, declared, "A friend of the farmer . . . one of whom I am which." I would say: a participant in that symposium of *First Things*, one of whom I am which. But I should say at once that even I was startled by the resonance that the symposium managed to generate in the land—and I was even more astonished by the adverse reactions of some of our friends, from people, you might say, within our family. The symposium was arranged for the purpose of sounding a warning, and we certainly produced our effect if some people were in turn alarmed by the alarm we had sounded. Burke once remarked that the seasoned political man, "who could read the political sky will see a hurricane in a cloud no bigger than a hand at the very edge of the horizon, and will run into the first harbor."[1] "Head for a harbor," said one of our friends, "not start a revolution"—not urge people to the threshold of insurrection.

But we had sought, in several ways, to direct people away from a course of lawlessness, and of our own prudence I will have more to say in a moment. Yet I was struck in contrast with the notable want of prudence shown by our erstwhile allies: Their reactions seemed to me out of scale, for they seemed to be taking far more offense at us than at the offenses that we had sought, in detail, to describe. They professed to share our judgments, in the main, about the wrongs produced by judges, but they gave us ample reason to doubt that agreement. It might be said more accurately that they reached the same conclusion about the wrongness of certain decisions produced by the courts, but it became clearer now that they did not share the understandings that lay behind our judgments. At several levels, they did not understand the deep wrongs of these cases as we understood them, and therefore they could not see, in the same way, that these cases were describing a genuine "crisis in the regime" itself.

For our own part, we never thought that we were repudiating the American regime. Quite the reverse: We were seeking to vindicate the principles of the regime, to restore them in the face of a political class that was artfully replacing that regime with something else. Our friends seemed to take as gravely serious the threat that we writers were posing, and yet they could not take with the same seriousness the understanding that Lincoln had sought to convey in his "House divided" speech,[2] namely, that a regime quite republican in its outward forms could be converted, in its substance, into something else, something radically different. Which is to say, our friends were curiously failing to take seriously the classic understanding that even decent regimes may fall into a certain corruption, even while they retain their outward forms.   We were told that certain crazies in the 1960s—I think the technical term would be "meshugenas"—because certain meshugenas railed against America and declared a crisis in the regime, that there could not be, in America, a crisis in the regime, and that anyone who cast up a warning had to be a meshugena.

Announcing Tyranny

Let me start, then, with the simplest things, with a sense of our current situation, and I mean here a sober estimate, and not a flexing of interpretive genius. My dear friend Mary Ann Glendon tells me that she steals from me, and I am going to reciprocate by stealing from her—from a story she has used deftly, in recalling that scene from the film *Young Frankenstein*, with Gene Wilder. Dr. Frankenstein is led into his castle by Igor the hunchback, played by Marty Feldman. Frankenstein gently touches Igor's back and says, "I may be able to help you with that hump." And Marty Feldman replies, "What hump?"

Mary Ann Glendon then observed, with Tocqueville, that "tyranny need not announce itself with guns and trumpets. It may come softly—so softly that we will barely notice when we become one of those countries where there are no citizens but only subjects. So softly that if a well-meaning foreigner should suggest, 'Perhaps you could do something about your oppression,' we might look up, puzzled, and ask, 'What oppression?'"[3]

Flash back, for a moment, to an evening, in Washington, D.C., in 1986, the day after the Supreme Court refused to strike down the laws on sodomy in the states.[4]

It left that judgment then in the hands of legislatures. At a party in town, an old friend, a seasoned lawyer in Washington, asked me, "Do you really want *politicians* making decisions on matters of this kind?" And I said, "Consider what you are saying: that as people are drawn to office through the process of elections, they are rendered less fit to address questions of justice or matters of moral consequence." It was the most damning thing to be said about a democratic regime. It was also clear that my friend was part of a growing class of people who would readily prefer to be ruled, on the matters of the highest consequence, by people in judicial office who do not have to suffer the rigors of running for election. Those judges would be drawn, of course, from the best law schools, the schools that people like my friend had attended—in short, they would be people rather like himself.

This is not a fiction, or a fable of the future: I take this to be a mark of our present situation and the understanding of a considerable number of the people who form our political class. Indeed, without this understanding it would be hard to account for the intensity that was focussed on defeating the nominations of Robert Bork and Clarence Thomas. Those nominations became freighted with a larger significance because either man was understood to be, potentially, the fifth vote in favor of overruling *Roe v. Wade*.[5] But for both men, overruling *Roe v. Wade* meant returning the question of abortion to the political arena, to legislatures in the states. Both Bork and Thomas have been far from the point of finding, in the Constitution, the ground for protecting unborn children against the decisions of legislators who would withdraw the protections of the law. But if there was really a constituency now behind the "right to abortion," if that right commanded the depth of support that Joseph Biden and Edward Kennedy claimed for it, then there was no threat presented by Bork and Thomas. The issue of abortion would merely have been taken out of the cloistered arena of the courts and returned to the domain of a public politics. And there the public sentiment might have insisted on retaining the right to abortion—if that sentiment was as unequivocal, as unshaded with exceptions, as the law created by the Supreme Court.

But of course it was not, as Biden and Kennedy must have known. They probably knew that even people who described themselves as pro-choice thought that some abortions were unjustified and wrong and could be restricted rightly in the law. The public could not be depended on to install again a regimen of abortion in which abortions would be permitted for any and all reasons, throughout the entire length of the pregnancy. That kind of a regimen was the only arrangement that the radical feminists, and the Left in the Democratic party, would now regard as tolerable, and that kind of arrangement, produced by the courts, could be sustained only by the courts. What has to be understood about the Democratic party is that, in the aftermath of *Roe v. Wade*, the party had become, in effect, the party of the courts. The party would take it as one of its central missions to protect the authority and insulation of the courts—to protect the courts from political interference—and the courts in turn could be counted on to enact certain parts of the agenda of the Democratic Left that the party could not declare in public or make the ground of a public campaign. Most of the Democrats would vote, in 1996, for the Defense of Marriage Act, a bill that rejected same-sex marriage.[6] And Mr. Clinton, in the dead of night, would quietly sign the bill. But Mr. Clinton would continue to appoint to the bench the kinds of judges who could be counted on, in the long run, to undermine that Act.

I take it, then, not as a speculation, or a bit of science fiction, that we have an important part of the political class that is quite willing to remove certain matters of moral consequence from the sphere of popular government, or common deliberation, and be ruled on these matters by a corps of lawyers, who will reflect in their rulings the ethic that now prevails in the law schools and the universities.

In my own contribution to the symposium,[7] I had written on the case of *Romer v. Evans*[8] and gay rights, and the way in which the sentiments articulated by the Supreme Court were making their way from legal institutions into private settings. The Court declared that a tradition of Jewish and Christian teaching on sexuality and homosexuality can be dismissed, as Justice Kennedy said, as nothing more than an "animus," an aversion that could annex to itself no reasoned grounds of support. And once the Court has declared, from the highest levels, that moral reservations about homosexuality reduce to nothing more than a blind, unreasoned prejudice, it becomes all the easier for professional associations of all kinds— bar associations, associations of law schools, universities— to incorporate in their procedures an avowal that one will not discriminate on the basis of "sexual orientation." And so, in one major law firm in New York, a senior partner, a serious Catholic, had opposed in public certain regulations on so-called "sexual orientation." This senior lawyer was suddenly, discreetly, dropped from the recruitment committee of his firm. For his presence on a committee engaged in hiring would invite the charge that the process of hiring was biased at the outset by the presence of a man who bore what the Supreme Court itself has pronounced a "prejudice." But that problem would be the same if this senior partner merely exercises his franchise as a partner to vote on the tenure, or retention, of young associates. That is to say, his very presence in the firm begins to constitute the immanent ground of a grievance and of litigation. Law firms are nothing if not sensitive to incentives, and they will quickly come under an incentive to forestall the problem at the threshold through the simple expedient of not hiring people who are—shall we say?— "overly religious." But in this way, a new orthodoxy makes its way outward; it moves from public laws to rules governing private firms, corporations, universities, until it begins to affect the things that people will find it safe to say to another even in private settings. As my former professor, Leo Strauss, taught years ago, the notion of the "political regime" extends beyond the formal institutions of government to the ethic that pervades the way of life of a community.[9] What we are seeing, in the movement on gay rights, is a movement that is promising to alter the political regime itself.

But that movement can be seen even more fully, even more deeply, on the issue that almost all of us, gathered in *First Things*, regard as the central, or architectonic question right now in our politics, the question of abortion. And I would put the weight of my own remarks on that point, for it illustrates more than anything else the real change that has already taken place in the nature of our political regime. That issue brings out, even more dramatically, the classic problem of a crisis in the regime, the problem that seems curiously to have eluded the sight of political friends who would ordinarily stand among the most politically acute.

A Litmus Test?

In my business, as we used to say, I see a lot of the public, and my travels bring me into touch with audiences that have not been uniformly sympathetic on the matter of abortion, to put the matter mildly. I have usually broached the problem to them by noting, right away, that in the absence of any extended argument, I would not expect them to share my position on abortion. But I ask them simply to flex their imaginations in this way for the sake of understanding their fellow citizens who cannot regard this issue as anything less than overriding: Imagine that some people think that abortion involves the taking of human life. They understand that they are not indulging fancies about leprechauns or centaurs; they know they can summon a substantial body of evidence from embryology to confirm that this is not some odd, religious opinion on their part. These convictions are not at all, then, like emphatic views on the Hale-Bopp comet. In that event, if these people have reason to think that human lives are taken in these surgeries, they look out and see that 1.3 million lives are being taken each year—as though the government had withdrawn the protections of law from a whole class of people in this country—as though 1.3 million members of a minority could be lynched without restraint and without the need even to render a

justification. Again, I do not ask people to share this judgment, but to encompass merely this recognition: If other
people did look out at the country and see these things
taking place, where would you expect these people to rank
this concern within the overall inventory of things political? Would it rank just below the concern for interest rates or unemployment? Once we understand what
people see, how could we react with outrage or bafflement
if we find that these people cannot see that issue as anything other than central—if they cannot see it merely as
peripheral?

Some of our friends reproached us for making the issue
of abortion a kind of litmus test of the regime. Their
complaint then was that we were, on balance, making too
much of abortion. But we were not making this a litmus of the regime exactly, and we wondered in turn
whether the issue did not come down to this: that in their
heart of hearts, some of our friends really were not possessed by a lively sense that there were real human beings getting killed in these surgeries. If they thought we
were making altogether too much of abortion, we raised
the question in response of whether they had been making altogether too little. Here we are not thrown back
upon idle speculations; one could do a very precise content analysis of the number and length of articles devoted
to the problem of abortion in the leading journals of neo-
conservative opinion. And here too I speak as "one of
whom I am which," since I have sprung from those circles
myself. When I raised this point with one editor, he waved
aside my "interpretation" of *Commentary* and other journals. But I was not offering an interpretation; I was offering
testimony, bolstered in some cases with correspondence

saved over twenty years. In that correspondence, and the conversations they reflect, editors of our leading neo-conservative journals, devoted to distinctly "public interests," explained that they wished really to avoid any dealing with this vexing issue, which divides and inflames their readership.

Our friends then, among the neoconservatives, have treated this issue of abortion guardedly, with caution and reserve. They have never treated it as an issue of central or urgent importance, and they would impart a false sense of things if they suggest that they had been in steady alliance with us, until we had suddenly jolted far ahead and treated this issue with a new salience. For us it has ever remained the same. What is jolting now for our friends is that we have drawn, to a new level of explictness, our explanation as to why this matter has entered a new phase of gravity that marks nothing less than a crisis in the regime.

Our sense of the crisis was arranged, one might say, in tiers, but what was curious is that our friends did not recognize, in the first instance, just where we were holding back and showing forbearance. In our indictments of the regime in its current state we hardly said anything more severe than could have been said of the regime in the middle of the nineteenth century, the republic that made its accommodation with slavery. The presence of slavery marked a corruption or a flaw running deep to the very root of a polity founded on the principle that human beings deserved to be ruled only with their consent. And yet, as Lincoln understood, the opponents of slavery could not have been justified in taking up arms to overthrow an elected government that sustained slavery. They could not have done that without violating the very principle they were seeking to vindicate. But the same problem in principle would have to constrain us today. As long as elections are open, and we are free to persuade our fellow citizens, we could not be warranted in using force outside the law. Some of us have been careful also to be guided by the teaching in Plato's *Crito*, a work that offers some powerful instruction in prudence for holding back even when we are utterly persuaded that the cause of justice lies on our side.[10] One mystery here is why some of our oldest friends did not assume that Fr. Neuhaus and the rest of us were as anchored in these understandings—or as tutored in the canons of prudence—as they were.

For on their own part, our friends should have been alert to the fact that the same constraints would have come into play even if we had a democratic government that was presiding over an Auschwitz and shipping people to killing centers. And yet, what if someone asked us, under these conditions, "Would it be wrong to rescue the innocent victims, who are about to be killed unjustly?" Could we honestly tell them that it would be wrong, even when it means running counter to the law?

But the same problem in principle must come into play, even in a muted form, with the matter of abortion. It bears recalling here that many of our friends among the critics would not really contest us on the question of abortion taking human lives. On that point, they would concede our premise. But in that event, what could they honestly say to the person who now asks, "Would it be wrong, or unjustified, to rescue the innocent human beings who are being killed in these surgeries?" Our friends do not seem to recognize, in Lincoln's words, just how

much we have had to bite our lips and "crucify [our] feelings"[11] for the sake of urging people to obey the law in
these instances. When people ask us earnestly—as I have
been asked—about the rescue of the innocent, we turn
away from offering encouragement. Without surrender-
ing the argument, we try, decorously, to change the subject, or we simply counsel them to obey the law. I fear,
though, that for many of our friends collected in the symposium in *Commentary*, Lincoln's words could be adapted
again: Nothing may satisfy them until we cease calling
abortion wrong, and begin calling it right.[12] Nothing else
may ease their minds or quiet their angers.

A Crisis in the Regime

Given what was at stake, it seemed to me that our severe
critics among our friends were themselves showing the
most pronounced want of prudence, for their reactions were
out of scale, and they were lingering on the surface of
things without tracing matters, in a serious way, to the
core of principle. And by that I do not mean simply that
they had not thought through the matter of abortion, but
that they had not treated with a sufficient seriousness the
notion of a genuine crisis in the regime. As I suggested
earlier, they did not seem to take seriously the depth of
the issue that Lincoln framed for us in the crisis of the
"house divided": Was it possible that the outward forms
of the regime may remain the same, even while the moral
substance was decisively changed, and the regime was
converted in substance, into something else? Lincoln used
to point up Senator Pettit of Indiana, who insisted that
the self-evident truth proclaimed in the Declaration of

Independence—that "all men are created equal"—was nothing less than a "self-evident lie."[13] As Lincoln understood, of course, the American republic did not begin with the Constitution, but with the Declaration, and that "proposition," as he put it, on which the nation was founded and dedicated. But evidently, there were portions of the American political class that were no longer committed to that proposition. They would vote to sustain a regimen of slavery, and they would acquiesce in every alteration of the laws, every abridgement of constitutional freedom, that was necessary to preserve those arrangements of slavery. In other words, men who filled the office of Senator might nevertheless be *acting on premises that were incompatible, at the root, with the premises that underlay their offices.* In classic terms, this was a case of the "corruption" of the political order, and as the ancients understood, this kind of corruption had to be an immanent possibility even in the best of regimes. Why should we suppose, then, that this country should be exempt from these dangers, inherent in political life? The American regime was, without question, a republic and a constitutional order. But within the framework of that regime, the need to keep reinforcing the system of slavery was imparting to the law an authoritarian character. Slave codes, sentinels, passports, curfews—the system of slavery was made all the more explicit as slavery moved from the plantation into the cities. Frederick Law Olmsted, visiting the South, remarked that he had seen "more direct expression of tyranny in a single day and night in Charleston, than in Naples in a week."[14] And in this way, a government that remained outwardly a republic could be transmuted into something strikingly different in its substance.

Even now it is not appreciated just how penetrating was Lincoln's argument here, or just how sobering was the lesson he was trying to convey. No book has presented Lincoln as clearly on these matters as Harry Jaffa's classic book, *Crisis of the House Divided*,[15] for no other writer has treated, with the eye of a trained philosopher, the substance of Lincoln's thought. I have taught often from that book, but teaching it recently, and teaching it more fully, I found myself shaken a bit in catching finally Jaffa's sense of the depth of the problem. I suspect that I was more alert to it this time precisely because it connected so directly with that argument we have engaged. Some of us have argued for years that Lincoln's arguments on slavery, and the crisis of the republic at the time, were the closest analogies to the questions we were facing with abortion and our recent crisis. But it has become ever clearer to me that Lincoln's argument was not merely analogous: He was dealing with the same problem. Or to put it another way, our problem, today, radiates from the same questions in principle, which is why the problem of abortion has held such a grip on us.

In his debates with Stephen Douglas, Lincoln sought to warn off those Republicans and Free-Soilers who were drawn to Douglas and his scheme of "popular sovereignty" in the territories of the United States. That scheme was offered for its pragmatic appeal, as it promised to deliver some territories to the side of freedom, while preserving the civic peace. Douglas's plan would preserve the peace by striking a posture of neutrality in regard to slavery. As Douglas said in that famous phrase, "I don't care" whether slavery is voted up or down; that moral question would be left for the people of a territory, or a state, to decide for themselves. But as Lincoln would point out, there was nothing neutral in the "don't care" policy. As Lincoln put it in the debate at Quincy, Illinois,

> when Judge Douglas says he "don't care whether slavery is voted up or down," . . . he cannot thus argue logically if he sees anything wrong in it; . . . He cannot say that he would as soon see a wrong voted up as voted down. When Judge Douglas says that whoever, or whatever community, wants slaves, they have a right to have them, he is perfectly logical if there is nothing wrong in the institution; but if you admit that it is wrong, he cannot logically say that anybody has a right to do a wrong.[16]

Aquinas and John Stuart Mill remind us that, when we say something is wrong—that it is wrong, say, for parents to torture their children—we mean that it is wrong for everyone, for anyone; that anyone may rightly be restrained from torturing infants, that anyone may rightly be punished for performing that act. If someone told us then that he would leave parents to their own judgment on these matters, that he "doesn't care" whether they torture their children or not, he has not taken a position of neutrality. He has decided, in effect, that the torturing of infants stands in the class of those things "not wrong."

Lincoln's charge against Douglas was that the very object of his policy was to break down the sense, in a democratic people, that there was something "wrong" in slavery. His device was to treat the matter persistently, in Lincoln's words, as a "morally indifferent thing." And so Douglas would say that certain states, in their economy, feature oysters, certain of them feature cranberries, and others use slaves. As Lincoln pointed out, Douglas grouped slaves with cranberries and oysters—morally indifferent things. Or he encouraged us "to speak of negroes as we do of our horses and cattle."[17] But if the American people backed themselves in that state of mind, their indifference to slavery in the territories would readily spill over into the states as well. If they came to think that this was, in the end, a legitimate form of property, they would have to agree more readily that citizens of the United States should not be dispossessed of their ownership of this property in slaves when they entered a territory of the United States. But in that event, why should they be deprived of that legitimate property when they entered another state? The "privileges and immunities" of citizens of the United States describe a body of rights that may be portable for citizens as they travel from one state to another. Why will it not be discovered that this right to own slaves is part of that body of rights, carried from one place to another, and protected then in the states as well? And why should other citizens object to any of these claims—if they have talked themselves into the notion that they may be quite indifferent on the question of whether one human being may rule another without his consent?

I would earnestly put before you, then, two passages drawn from Harry Jaffa, trying to explain Lincoln, and I would make those passages the ground of our further reflections, as we try to explain or judge them. It was Lincoln's charge that Douglas was reshaping the climate of opinion and reshaping, at the same time, the American soul. Jaffa sought to condense Lincoln's understanding here in this way: that "a free people cannot disagree on the relative merits of freedom and despotism without ceasing, to the extent of the difference, to be a free people."[18] And in a related passage, Jaffa remarked, again construing Lincoln, that "if the majority favors despotism, it is no longer a free people, whether the form of the government has already changed or not."[19] I used to think that Jaffa was waxing metaphoric, but what was jarring for me recently was that I came to see that, on these points, he and Lincoln were being *quite literal*. That is the shocking thing, if true, and it has to be explained.

The beginning of the explanation is to be found in that crisp summary Lincoln provided when he said that the "sacred right of self government" was so perverted in Douglas's construction that it would amount to just this: "That if any *one* man, choose to enslave *another*, no *third* man shall be allowed to object."[20] Lincoln spoke of men, not black men, for his point was that the argument in principle for slavery could not, would not, be confined to blacks. On this matter, there is no statement more penetrating and decisive than that famous fragment Lincoln had written for himself, when he imagined himself engaged in a conversation with the owner of black slaves and put the question of how that white owner could justify this enslavement of the black man:

> You say A. is white, and B. is black. It is color, then: the lighter having the right to enslave the darker? Take care. By this rule, you are to be slave to the first man you meet, with a fairer skin than your own.
>
> You do not mean *color* exactly?—You mean the whites are *intellectually* the superiors of the blacks, and therefore have the right to enslave them? Take

care again. By this rule, you are to be slave to the first man you meet, with an intellect superior to your own.

But, say you, it is a question of interest; and, if you can make it your *interest*, you have the right to enslave another. Very well. And if he can make it his interest, he has the right to enslave you.[21]

In this fragment, Lincoln was also reflecting the understanding of his political idol, Henry Clay. In one of the debates with Douglas, Lincoln recalled that someone had pressed on Clay the argument that blacks were an inferior race, drawn from an uncivilized land. And Clay responded, in a remarkable passage, that

> Whether this argument is founded in fact or not, I will not now stop to inquire, but merely say that if it proves anything at all, it proves too much. It proves that among the white races of the world any one might properly be enslaved by any other which had made greater advances in civilization. And, if this rule applies to nations there is no reason why it should not apply to individuals; and it might easily be proved that the wisest man in the world could rightly reduce all other men and women to bondage.[22]

With this ground, Jaffa was moved to suggest that the very willingness of certain Southerners to affirm the inferiority of black people, as the condition that justifies their enslavement, was sufficient to prove that these Southerners were themselves unfit for self-government. Or, it might establish that they were no longer a democratic people, even when they were voting and mimicking the acts that describe citizens in a republic. That may sound implausible and a bit far-fetched, but that is the point that gets us closer to what I am more and more disposed to treat as the literal truth of the matter.

I would make my approach to it in this way: People may go into voting booths and cast votes, and for all we can see, they are acting in the familiar modes of citizens in a republic, engaged in the act of voting, or manifesting a government by consent. But we know of course that we cannot always give a moral account, or even an accurate descriptive account, of what people are doing when we merely describe their outward behavior. Smith is trying to open the window to the house on the second floor: Is he trying to break in, or he is on a commission to clean the windows? Smith goes to the garage of his next door neighbor and takes the hose on the wall. But from that outward act alone we cannot say that he is engaging in a theft. He might have had permission to use the hose, or he might not have permission, but there is a fire in his house and he is seeking to borrow the hose for a moment for a justified end. Before we can give an account of the act, or its moral significance, we need to know something about the purposes animating the actor, or his own understanding of the reasons that inform his action.

Now, if you will follow me a bit further, I would ask you to imagine an election, in Germany, in 1932. There are some good Germans concerned about the Versailles Treaty and drawn to Hitler and his program for dealing with the Depression. They know that he has a severe program, shall we say, in dealing with the Jews. They know, too, that there is a risk that Hitler and his Nazi party may remove this government by consent and replace it with a dictatorship of some kind. This German voter may doubt that Hitler is fully serious in following through on his threats about the Jews, or that he would really act upon his expressions of contempt for the Weimar republic; but in his willingness to vote for Hitler, he marks his willingness to take a chance on these things. In that respect, he would separate himself from the people who think that the avoidance of genocide, and the preservation of constitutional government, are things so important that they cannot be placed in the basket of things "we are willing to take a chance upon." On the other hand, this voter may indeed think that Hitler means it about the Jews, and the voter is quite willing, for his own part, to vote now to dispossess the Jews of their property and redistribute their businesses to deserving Aryans. The question then is: When this man casts a vote, is he affirming, with that vote, the principle of government by consent? When he engages in the act of voting, is he affirming the rightness in principle of a government that rules people only with their consent?

Apparently not, for he is not really concerned to preserve a regime of elections as absolutely necessary condition of politics. Nor is he concerned to protect the right of his neighbors to enjoy an equal claim to that goverment by consent, a government that would protect their rights and their lives. The voter is acting to assert his interests, or his passions, quite apart from the form of the regime. If he is counting on a majority of Germans to vote with him in dispossessing the Jews, then he is merely affirming, through the ballot, the principle of the Rule of the Strong. If that is the case, the question then is:

Does he have any ground of complaint when Hitler moves to suspend constitutional government after the Reichstag fire? For wouldn't Hitler merely be asserting now the same principle that the voter was acting upon in the voting booth? That voter would have no ground of complaint, for he was not in a position to offer a moral account, or a moral justification, for a "government by consent."[23] He had overthrown, or discarded that principle already, in his understanding, even as he was casting his vote. He had gone through all of the outward acts, quite familiar to citizens voting in a democracy; but in point of fact, in literal truth, he had not been acting, in the voting booth, as a citizen in a democracy. And if a majority of the electorate had acted in the same way, with the same understanding, it could indeed be said that the outward forms of a republic had been present, but that this group of voters had ceased being a democratic people. As Jaffa put it, "in choosing to enslave other men it is impossible not to concede the justice of one's own enslavement." Or again, the voters no longer composed "a free people, whether the form of the government has already changed or not."

A Private Right to Kill

Let me bring the matter back then to our current situation, our present discontents. The doctrine of slavery, said Lincoln, meant that if one man sought to enslave another, a third man may not object. And my friend Russell Hittinger summed up our own situation in this way a few years ago: We have now created a private right to use lethal force, a private right to kill, for wholly private reasons.[24] One person may now claim to kill a second person, a

second being, for reasons that may not rise above convenience, and under those conditions a third person may
not object. That third person, or the rest of the community, may not object, because this is now, as we are told,
a matter of "privacy." As Hittinger put it, imagine that
a farmer in Vermont was told in the 1850s that if he objected to the prospects of slaves around him, he should
not buy one. But he is also informed at the same time
that he may not join with his fellow citizens in Vermont
in deliberating about the question of whether the political community, in its laws, will recognize or honor this
form of property. That is a matter of privacy, he is told,
and it forms no part of the legitimate business of the polity.
And now, in our own day, he is told that if he objects to
abortion, he should not choose one for the women in his
life; but the choice of abortion remains a private matter,
outside the laws. That is to say, whether the laws on homicide will be extended or contracted, to protect children
in the womb or leave them unprotected, is no longer part
of the legitimate business of the polity. But if the laws
on homicide, or the protection of life, are not part of the
purpose of a polity, or central to its legitimate business,
what purposes on earth could be more apt or central?

We can readily anticipate the argument that would
be offered in protest or resistance: Surely, it might be said,
the claim for abortion is not as broad as Hittinger and I
have stated it. Surely it would not be a claim that a person has a franchise, or right, of homicide in regard to *any*
other person, and that the rest of us have been rendered
powerless to object. Lincoln had sought to show that the
argument for slavery, when cast in a principled form, could
not be cabined, or confined to black people. But surely,

the argument would go, this claim over abortion is more readily and evidently cabined. And yet, is it? In the first place, we should take note of the obvious point that not everyone could be enslaved. One person could choose to enslave another, but only from that class of beings who were marked off as *available*, a class of beings who would not be protected from enslavement. In our own case we begin with a class of beings who are not protected from the private killing or this private homicide. And if that claim were so readily cabined, to what would be it be cabined, the right of a woman to kill the offspring contained in her own womb?

But we quickly learned, in the *Baby Doe* cases in the early 1980s, that the doctrine in *Roe v. Wade* would have to carry over to certain newborns.[25] They might come out with Down's syndrome or spina bifida, and we were told then, by jurists such as Thurgood Marshall, that the same rights of privacy contained in *Roe v. Wade* entailed now the exclusive, private right of the family to determine whether their newborn child had a life worth living, or a life worth preserving.[26] If the baby was slated for abortion, but in one of those rare cases, survived, then there were doctors and jurists ready to argue that the right to abortion entailed the right to an "effective abortion," or a dead child.[27] After all, if a woman thought she could bear giving up a child that was hers, she would have brought the baby through to birth and given the child up for adoption. Very recently, of course, we have seen the case of the grisly "partial-birth abortion," with about 70 percent of the child outside the birth canal. The head is kept in the birth canal so that it may be collapsed and the baby killed, only inches from emergence and live birth, so that the fiction could be preserved that the child is not yet born.[28]   But once again we are told, quite explicitly, by partisans of abortion, that any yielding on this matter will imperil the whole corpus of rights articulated in *Roe v. Wade*. We do not invent these connections in principle: the other side *insists* upon them.   Ms. Kate Michelman insists, for the National Abortion Rights Action League, that the rights articulated in *Roe v. Wade* cannot be confined to the treatment of the child in the womb.[29]

But as I say, there was no doubt about the connection, earlier on, between *Roe v. Wade* and the right to dispose of infants born with serious handicaps or medical problems.   And there has been no attempt to disguise it by confining the doctrine to infants in the womb. We have been told, by many of the same people, arguing from the same book, that the right of privacy in *Roe* should entail the "right to die," or the right then to assistance in dying for adults who lack the means, or the competence, to end their own lives.[30] Who were the candidates for this right?   First it was people in a supposedly terminal state, but who were not dying at a decorous enough speed.[31]   Then it was comatose patients, who were not exactly terminal, but living in a state, we were told, that could hardly be called "living."[32]   In a flight of metaphor, their condition was often described as "vegetative," as though a person in a diminished state had suffered a shift in kingdoms, from animals to plants.   As the argument advanced another step in the train, it was applied to people who were not comatose, but conscious some of the time, but who were not "what they used to be," people who were so impaired that their lives were wanting in fullness or in the vigor that marked human flourishing.[33]   In the case of Dr. Kevorkian, the candidates may now include people who are simply depressed and have no wish to live. And indeed, as Michael Uhlmann has shown, the decision of the Ninth Circuit in the *Glucksberg* case had quite well established a right to die, or "assisted suicide," that would extend simply to the patient who was so depressed, or so weary of life, that he simple wished to be quit of it.[34]

By the time we have moved along this route, the right to die entails the obligation of certain doctors to act as agents, or accomplices, in inflicting death. That is what a "right" to die means in its hard, operational side, or in its moral logic. If it is rightful for a patient to end his life, he should not be deprived of this good, or this "right," merely because he is incapable of effecting his own death. If he has a right, another person with the competence and means may have the obligation to minister to him. The patient may also be too comatose to announce his own intentions or execute a formal will. And yet, why should patients in those conditions suffer discrimination and be deprived of a "good" made available to others? Once we establish the class of people who should not be deprived of this right, and establish that doctors or administrators in a hospital have the responsibility to administer this right, why should it not be available to orphans or people without families? Why should it not be granted to them through the helpful intervention of strangers who happen to be doctors and administrators?

Again, I offer no fictions or speculations. I merely note the train of cases we have already seen and the arguments that have been brought forth already to show how the doctrine of privacy in *Roe v. Wade* should be extended, in mercy and liberality, to cover these cases. We move from children in the womb to newborns out of the womb, and from there to aged, or even middle-aged, people, with conditions terminal, but then not so terminal, unconscious but then partially conscious, or conscious but depressed. And then finally we arrive at a new "right" in the law for strangers to administer death to adults, well outside the womb, who have neither ordered nor consented to their deaths. When we view the sweep of this movement, and the rather astounding propositions that have been put in place, we must wonder: Why has this recent development not caused even deeper tremors in the public than the arguments put forth by the symposium in *First Things*? So the question may be put again, How would this claim to kill, for private reasons, be cabined any more readily than that principle of enslaving other men, whose reach and dynamic Lincoln saw with an unsettling accuracy? And Lincoln managed to see the direction of that tendency precisely because he saw the principle that lay at the heart of the thing.

I return then to that final, sobering connection: that a people who have made themselves suggestible to these things have ceased to be a democratic people. In regard to slavery, I think that argument, offered by Lincoln, can be understood as literally true. And if that argument at the core is the same thing, could the same charge be levelled today? Can we take it, not as a sweeping metaphor, but as a literal truth: that we are in danger of ceasing to be a democratic people, and that a regime, outwardly a republic in its forms, has been converted, in our lifetimes, into something radically different?

As the measure of things, I ask you earnestly to consider, from what you have already seen and heard, whether the most educated people in this country have not in fact grasped hold of this right to abortion as though it were now the central right, the touchstone of our liberties, because it is the guarantor of sexual freedom, and sexual freedom has become the most fundamental freedom of all. And in taking hold of abortion as a fundamental right, a constitutional right, a right now bound up with the regime itself, have they not been moved then to affirm one or both of the following propositions:

(1) "I have a 'right,' anchored in the Constitution, to kill another human being, a child in the womb, if the advent of that being would adversely affect my interests, disrupt my plans, or cause me embarrassment." That is, do we not find among some of our people an unashamed claim right now of a right to kill for their own convenience? If so, that must be a novelty in our tradition, and could it be anything other than sobering or terrifying? Still, there is enough of a lingering moral reflex in our people that most of them, I think, would recoil from that kind of a claim. To their credit, they seek to avoid that way of framing the principle. But in trying to avoid it, I submit to you that they usually back into a second proposition, even more portentous yet.

(2) "The being I would kill is *not* a human being, and it is not yet a real person. But any evidence from embryology or genetics would be quite beside the point, for the decisive question is whether *I myself* regard the being as human. Or to put it another way, my right here is the right to decide just who is a human being, on the strength of my own beliefs, and as it suits my own interests." I may not have a right to kill any other human being, but I have a right to decide who is a human being when

it comes to killing or disposing of that being. Either that claim reduces to the same thing, or it announces a principle, as I say, even more radical and unsettling yet.

I can report to you, from my own experience, that a surprising number of people, products of the best colleges and universities in the country, are indeed willing to affirm one or both of these propositions as part of their defense of the right to abortion. I submit to you that a right to kill, cast in these terms, will not be cabined, any more than the claim to enslave could be cabined. And a people who have incorporated in their understanding these principles—absorbed them, you might say, in their understanding of their lives and their rights—cannot be a democratic people. They cannot count themselves as part of an association devoted to the end of securing the constitutional rights of other members of the community, for they cannot give an account any longer of why other human beings have a claim to be the bearers of rights secured under the laws and the Constitution.

In the course of defending this new "right" to abortion, they have talked themselves out of the notion of "natural rights" held by Lincoln and the American Founders. But that understanding was absolutely necessary to the Constitution in the sense that, without it, one could not give a coherent account of the Constitution or the "rights" it was meant to secure. The partisans of abortion have meant to establish an expansive notion of rights; but the requirements of their own argument have compelled them to evacuate from the logic of "rights" its deepest meaning. In all strictnesss, then, the partisans of this new, diminished "right" cannot protect my life, my freedoms, my rights, against the most arbitrary takings and restrictions, for they have utterly removed the moral ground for the definition and defense of those rights. Under these conditions, I would state anew, and state even more forcefully what we stated last year: We are in the gravest crisis of my lifetime in the understanding of our people—nothing less than a crisis in the regime itself.

THE RESTORATION OF POLITICS

Several years ago I innocently inflamed an audience of philosophers when I suggested that the rules of baseball were merely conventional rules, and they could be altered, even reversed in some places, in a way that we could not alter or reverse the axioms of justice. But some people in the audience insisted that the "infield fly rule" was really a fragment of "natural law" on the matter of fraud. In this, I think my colleagues were mistaken, but I was charmed by their effort to make the argument. Either way, it was evident that many infielders, waiting under pop-ups, are quite distant from comprehending the deeper principles that sustain them as they wait for that ball to come down. And happily, they can put on their gloves and uniforms and go out on the field every day, preserving the game of baseball, without being able to offer an account of the principles underlying their vocations. We are reminded here of the blessings that may be wrought for us by institutions: They envelop our daily, prosaic acts, with a significance that may run beyond our own understanding. People may be going to work every day in a society framed by the principles of a free economy and a constitutional order without having much awareness of the principles that shaped these institutions that now frame their everyday lives. And so, within the space created by those institutions, we may indeed be free for a long while to make the case in public against abortion and euthanasia. It is also a melancholy and curious fact that the United States seems to be the main place in the West where there is anything like a vibrant pro-life movement, proclaiming its principles in public and commanding votes in legislative assemblies.

How long that will last is uncertain, and it is by no means something to be expected enduringly. As I have already pointed out, the fix already seems to be in as far as gay rights are concerned: the sentiments and machinery are coming into place to penalize even those words said in private that would call into question the rightness of homosexuality. On the matter of abortion, the skittishness of people like Newt Gingrich and other Republicans reflects a sentiment abroad in the public that politicians, with sensitive antennae, can neglect only at their peril. What Gingrich and other politicians are reflecting is the sense that the audiences they encounter do not want to hear about this question of abortion. It is too vexing, too agitating, and more members of the public seem to be coming to the view that these moral questions are not the business of government and legislators. In that respect, the sentiments of the public have indeed been shaped by the regime marked by the rule of the judges, as Felix Frankfurter warned us years ago. Over a train of cases, Frankfurter cast up warnings about judges venturing into "political" questions, and his teaching may be put in this way: Let judges stand in the place of politicians in dealing with hard questions, and we will soon bring forth a class of politicians who are quite willing to stand aside and leave those vexing, controversial questions, to those other politicians in robes, the political men and women who do not have to run for re-election.[35] Under these conditions it should not surprise us that politicians wish to avoid the kinds of questions that agitate their voters, questions like abortion or even the raising of taxes. And what is produced then is a breed of politicians with the reflexes of civil servants: They would prefer to serve under conditions of permanent tenure, as a career, and they would be pleased to secure that career in office by running errands for their constituents, or delivering services in a decidedly apolitical fashion.

The rule of judges has begotten a class of politicians quite willing to affect a belief in their own incompetence to address the most serious moral questions, the questions that have ever been at the heart of politics. And with the tutoring of the judges, the conviction has been fostered in the public that matters of moral consequence should not be legislated by politicians, but left in a sphere of privacy protected by judges. More and more, the public shows a certain unease, or distaste, in dealing with these matters, and that mood has deepened, in turn, the inclination of the politicians to steer away from these unsettling questions. The politicians do not offer now the dramatic examples offered, say, by a Lincoln and Douglas, as they staged a serious argument for three hours at a stretch. And a public deprived of those examples seems less and less capable of engaging itself in these questions in the manner of the audiences that gathered for Lincoln and Douglas.

But if this sense of the matter is correct, our problem would not be treated readily by any change overnight in the laws. Of course, some modest changes in the jurisdiction of judges could produce some wholesome effects. Staying the hands of judges could indirectly shift some decisions back to the hands of politicians, and in that way we could return to the political arena some critical argument over these moral questions. But no change overnight in the laws, say, on abortion would provide a fix, or a solution, to the problem we have described. As I have remarked before, even if the elves could come in the middle of the night and overturn *Roe v. Wade*—even if we could awake the next morning and find that all of the laws in the States, cancelled by *Roe*, were in force once again—our situation would not be changed. The problem now is that a whole generation has grown up with the slogans of *Roe v. Wade* and "choice" and "a woman's right," as though they were woven into the Constitutioin itself. An abrupt change in the laws would have the appearance of a *coup d'état*, a simple imposition of power. And a change sprung in that way, without preparation, could hardly be sustained if those laws are detached from the moral understanding or the moral sentiments of the public.

This matter of abortion has been ruled now so thoroughly by judges that there would be a need for a conversation before the public could be put in the frame of mind to begin legislating again. And one of the benign purposes of that conversation would be to reveal that the public is not as gravely divided on this question as it has pleased many people to assume. In fact, a conversation could help to bring out some of the broad, remarkable agreements on this matter. Even people who describe themselves as pro-choice think that some abortions ought

be restricted. They think that abortions should not be
ordered up for casual reasons, especially late in the pregnancy, and majorities of the public, in surveys, have rejected the notion of abortions performed to avoid financial
strain or allow a woman to finish school.[36] The points of
agreement in the public would readily come out if there
were a proposal on the table, something that legislators
and the public could act upon as a matter of the public
business. The prospect of a serious bill would draw people
into a conversation; and the points of consensus could be
brought out rather clearly if we could begin at the places
where even people who are "pro-choice" would readily enact
restrictions on abortion.

The bill on partial-birth abortions seems to have
sprung in part from this kind of understanding. But my
own proposal was the most modest of all: that we simply
agree to preserve the life of the child who survives the
abortion.[37] Even the judges seem to agree that the child
may be protected, but the judges have never been asked
to settle the reasons, or the ground, on which the child
may be protected. We would suggest that the Congress
offer this construction: that the child has an intrinsic
dignity in herself as a rights-bearing being; that her claim
to receive the protections of the law should not pivot on
the question of whether anyone happens to *want* her.
Grant us those premises, and we can unravel the so-called
"right to abortion," step by step. That sense of the matter seems to be amply confirmed by the other side, for
they too see where the dynamic would move once these
questions in principle have been planted. And so they
have been willing to put themselves in the most awkward
position: For the sake of resisting even the slightest re-

striction on abortion, they have been willing to resist any
effort to restrict the grisly partial-birth abortions, which
cannot claim, in their defense, any medical rationale. They
cannot claim, that is, that they bear any relation to the
health of the pregnant woman. Their rationale is simply to make it possible to have an abortion up to the minute
of birth by claiming that the child, with its head remaining
in the birth canal, is not yet "born." And so, to preserve
the abstract "right of abortion" in its purity, unqualified,
unimpaired, the partisans of abortion have been willing
to avert their eyes from a prospect that appalls the rest
of the country, namely, crushing the head of a child,
moments before birth, and sucking out her brains.

My own political friends and I would stand right now
against the current of modern liberal jurisprudence—the
jurisprudence put in place over the past twenty-five years.
But if we are insurrectionaries, the insurrection we have
in mind would be constituted simply by pressing a conversation with people on the other side. It begins by
crediting the notion that our adversaries are not bereft
of moral judgment, and that even people who describe
themselves as pro-choice would end up agreeing with us
on 90 percent of the cases. Or they would discover that
level of agreement if only they would detach themselves
from that "heresy" they have been asked to absorb over
the past quarter century: that matters of moral consequence
cannot be addressed through the deliberations of citizens
in the politics of a republic.

When we offer, in relation to the current crisis, a "conversation" about the meaning and the requirements of the
Constitution, we are offering, as a remedy, an approach
that was quite consistent with Lincoln's understanding of

the American Constitution. It might be said that, by the very arrangement and logic of the Constitution, disputes over the Constitution unfold through an ongoing conversation among the branches. By the terms of the Constitution, none of the branches has been assigned a final or sole authority in settling the meaning of the Constitution.

And yet, some of our friends who shared our understanding of the current crisis have flown off toward schemes that are quite different from Lincoln's approach—schemes that are rather untethered, and rather bound to set off more tremors among the American people. One legislator out West actually introduced legislation, not only to restrict the judges, but to repudiate *Marbury v. Madison*. Lincoln did not think it necessary to repudiate *Marbury v. Madison* in order to make his argument about the limits on the courts, and the authority of the political branches to act as interpreters of the Constitution. He did not have to make that argument because Chief Justice Marshall's argument in *Marbury* was quite consistent with it. Marshall had never claimed for the judges the final or sole authority to interpret the Constitution. He made the unexceptionable point that, in the matters that come before the judges in the form of cases, the judges would be obliged to consider the Constitution as well as the statute. Even the severest critics of the Court could hardly reject Marshall's critical lesson here in jurisprudence, namely, that there is a critical distinction between the ordinary law and the basic law, or the law that tells us how we make laws. In that event, as Marshall explained, the fundamental law claims a logical preeminence over any statute, and in a collision between a statute and the fundamental law, the judges would be obliged to honor the Constitution over the statute.[38]

But so too would any legislator or executive. If a President were confronted with a bill, enacted by Congress, that provided for conscription into the military but only for members of a minority race, would the President be confined only to questions of *utility* as he weighed the question of whether to sign or to veto? Would he be obliged, that is, to consider only the question of whether this measure would "work"? Or would he be free—but more than that, obliged—to consider whether this measure was also compatible with the principles of the Constitution?

In another proposal, and another, understandable recoil from the Court, our friend Robert Bork offered another reform: that the decisions of the Supreme Court, on a constitutional matter, may be overruled by a two-thirds vote in both houses of Congress.[39] I gather that Judge Bork has since thought better of that scheme. His second thoughts have been quite prudent, for he must be aware that a proposal of that kind is likely to be seen as threatening and radical by most of the public. And yet this casting about for a solution, on the part of an accomplished conservative jurist, simply highlights a deeper paradox: Why do so many conservatives fly to remedies of this kind while passing by something already embedded in the Constitution and confirmed in notable precedents—namely, Lincoln's teaching on the authority of the political branches to interpret the Constitution and limit the powers of the courts. As Lincoln complained, it was bizarre to think that the policy for the whole government could be fixed simply through one case, an adversary proceeding, involving the interests of two private parties.[40] If those two parties also happened to be in collusion, they could conceivably join with a bare majority on a Court of nine members. Seven men, then, in effect, could impose a policy on the whole nation.

The alternative offered by Lincoln was clearly drawn, and borne out in some telling precedents; yet it still comes as a surprise to many lawyers, even conservative lawyers, and for that reason it bears restating. As Lincoln remarked during the debates with Stephen Douglas, if the Court pronounces Dred Scott to be a slave, the rest of us will not form a mob to free him and overthrow a decision of the Court.[41] Under the proprieties of the Constitution, we will respect the judgment handed down by the Court in *that case*. But if we bear the most serious reservations about the *principle* of law articulated in that case, there is no obligation for the Executive and the Legislature to take up that principle, absorb it as their own, and adopt it is as a "political rule of action": they could not be obliged, that is, to legislate only on that principle and on no contrary principle. As Hamilton had observed in *The Federalist*, Number 78, the Court has neither the power of the sword nor of the purse; its power depends on the force of its reasons, on its capacity to persuade.[42] If the President and the Congress were not persuaded, then they could confine their respect for the decision to the judgment that was handed down in the case of the two litigants. But there would be no obligation to apply that principle to any persons or case beyond that litigation.

The Lincolnian understanding was tested and exemplified in the clearest way in two cases that arose early in the Lincoln Administration. I took up these cases years ago in my book *First Things*, and I would refer people back to that book; but I would mention the cases in a compressed way right now. One involved a black student in Boston, who was denied a passport to study in France. And in another, also coming out of Boston, a black inventor had been denied a patent. Both decisions were rendered, in the Buchanan Administration, on the basis of the holding of the Court in the *Dred Scott* case. If black people could not be citizens of the United States, then these two agencies of the federal Executive reasoned along these lines: that blacks could not carry abroad the passports of American citizens or hold patents under the American law. I would merely point out then that two branches of the Administration, facing practical judgments, applied the *principle* of *Dred Scott* to circumstances quite remote from any facts that arose in that case. There were, here, no instances of black people contesting their deliverance from slavery and litigating over their freedom. The situation perfectly exemplified Lincoln's understanding of the problem—and the remedy he would apply. The Lincoln Administration quashed both of those decisions. Orders were given to grant the passport and the patent, and the Attorney General came out with an official opinion that, in the understanding of this Administration, any free black man born in the United States was a citizen of the United States. And in the decisions that came under the hand of the Executive, that was the principle that would govern the judgment.[43]

Hence the surprise among a few of us, about ten years ago, late in the Reagan Administration, when some of our people were surrounded on a committee, with appointees of the Congress, dealing with the National Institutes of

Health and the issue of fetal tissue. The question was whether experiments with that kind of tissue should be confined only to fetuses killed in spontaneous abortions, or whether it was legitimate to use the tissue collected from fetuses killed in elective abortions. If we thought that there was something wrong with the latter, then an ancient maxim of the law advised us that it may be wrong to profit from wrongdoing. And yet, even among the people on the committee who rejected *Roe v. Wade* there was a lingering belief that the Executive department, nevertheless, was obliged to absorb as its own the ruling in *Roe v. Wade*. There seemed, then, no getting out from under that arrangement. Some of us, however, made the argument that it was legitimate for the Reagan Administration to speak with a Lincolnian accent: It should have been possible to say that this Administration does not accept the principle articulated in *Roe v. Wade*, and therefore it does not accept, as the materials fit for a legitimate experiment, the tissues drawn from innocent children killed in the womb in wrongful abortions. The Administration might then have insisted on confining the experimental work of the NIH to the tissues drawn from spontaneous abortions. But we had sought to make here a deeper point about the Constitution: that this construction of the law could not have been wrong unless Lincoln's understanding was wrong; and I would submit to you that, under the logic of the Constitution, there is no way in which Lincoln could possibly have been wrong.

Some of our political friends have reproached us—or thought they were reproaching us—when they said, "You would not be offering up complaints if the judges had cast the protections of the Constitution around unborn children. At that moment you wouldn't be complaining about an activist judiciary." But again, they are right for the wrong reasons. Our complaint against the judges was never cast in those terms, like "activism," that are abstracted from any sense of the principles of moral judgment. As people in the founding generation might have put it, our complaint was that the judges were placing the construction of rights on principles that were deeply wrongful. Our friends managed to miss a large portion of our critique precisely because they too have detached themselves from the understanding held by Lincoln, Jackson, and Jefferson about the limits on the judges under our constitutional system. There is not the least inconsistency between our complaints and a willingness to have judges act in the most vigorous manner as judges: they should indeed devote themselves, in a scholarly, disciplined way, to the task of extracting the implications contained in the principles of the Constitution. When those principles collide with any measure of the positive law, they should use all of their arts of judgment and prudence to convey that understanding and possibly strike down those measures. Judges should indeed be free to be judges. But we can confer on them this wider, stronger mandate, and do it with more serenity, if we understand that the judges are in fact hedged in by the benign restraints and interplay of the Constitution. Their mistakes may be confined and challenged by other branches and officers who bear a comparable responsibility to articulate the principles of the Constitution. And so we can say, with a certain confidence and good temper, let the conversation go on.

Justice Scalia has found it necessary of late to remind us that what was new under the sun in 1776 and 1787 was

the prospect of a people governing itself.[44] The decision
was made for popular government, with a restricted set
of things held back from the reach of the majority. From
the reactions of some of our critics, it would appear that
the Preamble of the Constitution had been improvidently
drafted. In this construction, it might have read: "We the
judges of the United States do ordain and establish this
Constitution . . . and we shall occasionally delegate to the
people of the United States some limited, legislative powers, which we think they may exercise without damaging
their sensibilities." But this was a regime, rather, that
promised to live through a process of citizens deliberating together in public even, and especially, on matters of
moral consequence. Still, no one who views the American public in its current, diminished state, with its moral
reflexes growing dimmer, can possibly be beamish about
the prospects. Yet, on the other hand, if we are tutored
by Aristotle and John Stuart Mill, we may have reason
to suspect that the moral reflexes of our people have been
dulled precisely because they have lost the practice of
reflecting, in public, on moral questions as part of the
discipline of reaching a judgment on the laws. We suspect that they have lost that practice in large part because
the politicians have fallen out of practice on these matters. And the politicians have fallen away from this cul-
tivation of the legislative art because the judges have made
them an offer they cannot refuse: they have delivered the
politicians from the responsibility to cast judgments on
matters that divide and agitate their constituents. The
project of limiting the judges is a project, then, in restoring
to the public its capacity to deliberate again on questions
of moral consequence as though it really matters—as

though practical arrangements in the law will hinge upon the judgments of citizens, refined through elections and legislatures. But bumbling or not, artful or not, there is something in principle good about people putting these questions to themselves and facing this exercise. Perhaps it was, finally, Chesterton who caught the sense of this matter long ago, when he remarked that governing oneself is rather like blowing one's nose or writing a love letter: it is something that a man ought to for himself even if he does it badly.

4

Justice, Legitimacy, and Allegiance

Robert P. George

M Y CONTRIBUTION to the *First Things* symposium
was a commentary on the encyclical letter,
Evangelium Vitae ("The Gospel of Life"), by
Pope John Paul II.[1] That letter, which had been issued a
year and a half earlier, forcefully reasserted the Catholic
Church's firm and constant teaching regarding the value
and inviolability of human life.[2] Thus, it condemned
abortion and euthanasia as "crimes which no human law
can claim to legitimize."[3] Moreover, the encyclical argued against use of the death penalty, stating that criminal punishment "ought not go to the extreme of executing
the offender except in cases of absolute necessity: in other
words, when it would not be possible otherwise to defend society."[4] The print and broadcast media duly recorded the pope's vigorous reaffirmation of the Church's
teachings on the moral wrongfulness of abortion and
euthanasia and took particular note of what Joseph Car-
dinal Ratzinger, Prefect of the Congregation for the

Doctrine of the Faith, described as the Pope's development of the Church's doctrine in opposition to capital
punishment.[5] What received scant attention, however, was
the Pope's philosophical analysis of legally sanctioned injustice and its implications for the authority of laws and
the legitimacy of political regimes.[6]

Although the Pope did not address the question of
judicial authority in relation to the authority of legislators and other elected officials, much less address the scope
and limits of constitutional judicial review in the United
States (or anywhere else), the editors of *First Things* commissioned my essay for the symposium precisely because
Evangelium Vitae addressed so directly, and with such a
high degree of philosophical sophistication, the issues of
legal authority and political legitimacy in modern constitutional democracies. The editors believed, as I believe,
that the Pope's teaching on these issues is highly perti-
nent to circumstances in which a judiciary, charged to
interpret and apply the fundamental law of a democratic
republic, has, under the pretext of performing that function, usurped the authority of the people to act through
the institutions of representative democracy to protect the
unborn and other potential victims of injustice and to
secure the overall common good.

The first thing to notice about the Pope's teaching is
that it is pro-democratic.[7] Perhaps it goes without saying that not every pope has been an admirer of democracy. Critics of democracy, including some popes, have
worried that belief in the superiority of democratic institutions in some sense presupposes or entails the denial
of objective moral truth. Even some who sympathize with
democracy as an ideal have been concerned that, in practice,

democratic institutions subtly inculcate in the people living under them the spirit of moral relativism or subjectivism. Certain critics of the subjectivist or relativist spirit of this age suggest that the sources of society's pathology are precisely in the democratic institutions bequeathed to the public by the nation's founders.[8] Throughout his pontificate, however, John Paul II has robustly defended the principles and institutions of democratic governance.[9] And his defense of these principles and institutions has been neither half-hearted nor merely pragmatic. John Paul II enthusiastically promotes democracy not as some sort of "lesser evil," "but as a system which more perfectly than any other embodies the great moral truth of the fundamental dignity of each human person." [10] It is for this reason, the Pope says in *Evangelium Vitae*, that the "almost universal consensus with regard to the value of democracy is to be considered a positive 'sign of the times.'"[11]

At the same time—and this is the second thing to notice about the teaching of *Evangelium Vitae*—the Pope warns against making a fetish of democracy, or "idoliz[ing] [it] to the point of making it a substitute for morality or a panacea for immorality." [12] After all, democratic institutions are *procedures* for making political decisions; they cannot guarantee substantive justice. As the Pope reminds us: "Fundamentally, democracy is a 'system' and as such is a means and not an end. Its 'moral' value is not automatic, but depends on conformity to the moral law to which it, like every other form of human behaviour, must be subject: in other words, its morality depends on the morality of the ends which it pursues and of the means which it employs."[13]

What is interesting about human positive law, from

the moral point of view, is not merely that laws enforce obligations that already exist as a matter of moral law, but that laws sometimes create moral obligations that would otherwise not exist.[14] The moral obligation to obey the law is, however, conditional and, as such, defeasible.[15] The injustice of a law or a system of laws can destroy its power to bind the consciences of those ostensibly subject to it. This is the central core of truth in the oft-misunderstood statement *lex iniusta non est lex* ("an unjust law is not law")—a proposition taught not only by St. Augustine[16] and St. Thomas Aquinas,[17] but also in substance by Plato,[18] Aristotle,[19] and Cicero.[20] And, as the Pope affirms, the democratic provenance of a law does not render its obligation-imposing power indefeasible.[21] Even a law enacted by impeccably democratic procedures can be unjust, and insofar as it is unjust it can fail to create an obligation to obey.[22]

Indeed, certain sorts of unjust laws may not licitly be obeyed. For example, it is morally wrong to comply with laws requiring people to perform actions that are themselves unjust or otherwise immoral. From the moral point of view, people subject to such laws do not have the option of obeying them. The fulfillment of their moral responsibilities requires people to disobey the laws. So, for example, a conscientious physician would simply refuse to comply with a law requiring him to administer a lethal injection to any patient whom he diagnoses as carrying HIV. Not only is there no moral obligation to obey such a law, there is a strict moral obligation not to obey it. It matters not whether the law in question was put into place by a military junta, a judicial oligarchy, or a democratically elected legislature.

But what of laws, such as those permitting abortion and euthanasia, which do not require anybody to do anything, but are, rather, *permissive* of gravely unjust actions? The Pope says that such laws are "radically opposed not only to the good of the individual but also to the common good; as such they are completely lacking in authentic juridical validity."[23] The wholesale legal permission of evils such as abortion and euthanasia constitutes a failure of government to fulfill its primary responsibility, that is, to protect the weak and vulnerable against unjust physical assaults. Moreover, such a permission is gravely unjust inasmuch as it denies the unborn, the handicapped, the frail elderly, and other vulnerable persons their rights to the equal protection of the laws. Where such a denial of equality is worked by democratic means, as with the abortion license in most European countries for example, it damages the integrity of democracy itself—for, as the Pope has so clearly seen, the principle of equality is itself central to the democracy's moral justification.[24] By the same token, where the denial of equal protection is worked by a judicial oligarchy, as in the United States, it reflects not only a usurpation of democratic authority, but as an assault on democracy's core principle.

Certain critics of the *First Things* symposium have alleged that the symposium was driven not by a concern about judicial usurpation as such, but by opposition to abortion and euthanasia. Peter Berger argued that the concern of the editors of *First Things* and most of the contributors to its symposium on judicial usurpation "has been not so much the power the courts have improperly assumed but rather what they have done with this power. And at the center of this concern is the issue of abortion."[25] To illustrate what he referred to as "the problem here," Berger proposed a thought-experiment: "Imagine that abortion in the United States had achieved its present legal status through an act of Congress rather than a Supreme Court decision. Imagine further that the Supreme Court had then ruled this action to be unconstitutional. I doubt very much that most of the *First Things* contributors would have viewed the latter action as a serious usurpation of power. . . ."[26]

Berger is correct that I and, I suspect, others involved in the *First Things* symposium (with the possible exception of Robert Bork, despite his firm pro-life convictions[27]) would have applauded a decision by the Supreme Court invalidating an act of Congress or, to make Berger's point more sharply than he did, acts of state legislatures to deprive the unborn of legal protection against abortion. But, if we attend to the Pope's analysis of democracy and its moral presuppositions in *Evangelium Vitae,* we can see that this is not the "problem" for the *First Things* symposiasts that Berger thinks it is.

I had occasion in my contribution to the symposium to contrast the Pope's analysis of the moral presuppositions of democracy with extracurial remarks by Justice Antonin Scalia.[28] Scalia, of course, is a passionate and relentless critic of *Roe v. Wade*[29] who has long argued that the Court's invalidation of state laws restricting abortion was a gross usurpation by the judicial branch of democratic legislative authority.[30] He is also firmly committed to the pro-life cause.[31] Yet, Scalia's view is that the Constitution commits the nation to neither pro-life nor "pro-choice" principles; rather, he maintains, abortion is a "political" and not a constitutional issue.[32] And the

Constitution leaves such issues entirely to democratic resolution by Congress or the state legislatures. So, Scalia declared to an apparently scandalized audience at the Pontifical Gregorian University in Rome, "if the people want abortion, the state should permit abortion in a democracy."[33]

But if, as I think, and as the Pope teaches, and as Justice Scalia agrees, abortion is the unjust killing of innocent human beings who, as a matter of right, are entitled to the equal protection of the laws, then there is a problem for a democracy in permitting abortion. (Of course, whether it is a problem that judges in any particular democratic society are empowered to do anything about is another question.) Since it is the principle of equality which provides the moral justification for democratic rule in the first place, the denial of equality, even if effected by democratic means, is inconsistent with democratic principles. In this sense, democracy is not a morally "neutral" mechanism for deciding disputed questions. Its own moral presuppositions exclude certain outcomes—even where these outcomes represent the preferences (or, for that matter, the considered, but gravely mistaken moral judgments) of a majority.

EQUAL PROTECTION

As I suggested a moment ago, to understand the moral basis of democracy in this way is not, by itself, to decide in every or any particular case that judges should invalidate legislation (including permissive abortion legislation) which conflicts with their views—however sound—of what equality requires. The existence and scope of judicial power to invalidate democratically enacted laws, including laws whose injustice compromises the principles of democracy itself, is settled not by natural law (i.e., the moral law), but by the positive constitutional law of a given democratic polity.[34] On this particular point, Justice Scalia is plainly correct. But to adopt this understanding is to begin to see the dubiousness of the simple symmetry presupposed by Berger's criticism of the *First Things* symposium. And we can go much farther toward undermining belief in this alleged symmetry if we consider the commitment to the principle of equality concretely embodied in the Constitution of the United States.

The Fourteenth Amendment expressly forbids the states from denying to any person within their jurisdiction the equal protection of the laws.[35] So, a court exercising judicial review of abortion laws must decide the following two questions: (1) Are the unborn "persons" within the meaning of that term as it is used in the Fourteenth Amendment? and, if so, (2) Does the abortion law under review deny to unborn persons the "equal protection of the laws"?

Justice Harry Blackmun, in his opinion for the Court in *Roe v. Wade*,[36] purported to deal with the question of whether the unborn are persons within the meaning of the Fourteenth Amendment, noting that if the unborn are persons then their right not to be killed is specifically protected by the Fourteenth Amendment.[37] Thus, the Court's duty would be to strike down permissive abortion laws as violative of the constitutional rights of unborn persons.[38] In the end, however, Blackmun effectively dismissed the question by simply observing that in places in the Constitution outside the Fourteenth Amendment where the term "person" is used (as, for example, in the provision that says that "persons" must have attained the age of thirty-five in order to serve as President of the United States[39]) it applies only postnatally.[40] He also argued, famously, that the Court could not, and therefore need not, "resolve the difficult question when life begins" given that the matter is "at this point in the development of man's knowledge" disputed by scientists, philosophers, theologians, and other experts.[41] Of course, Blackmun went on implicitly to resolve precisely this question quite against the proposition that "life begins" anytime prior to birth. Yet this is absurd from the scientific viewpoint, and indefensible philosophically.[42] And it set Blackmun up for precisely the criticism he received, namely, that *Roe* was an utterly unprincipled decision, an exercise, as Justice Byron White said in dissent, of "raw judicial power" in which the Court merely substituted its own policy preferences for the contrary judgment of the elected representatives of the people.[43]

Could the matter have been decided otherwise? Can a principled argument for the outcome in *Roe* be constructed? Blackmun's manifest failure to identify a principled ground for the decision has sparked a massive industry, now in its twenty-fifth year, of "rewriting *Roe*" to put it on an intellectually secure constitutional footing. Many of the best and brightest in the legal academy have joined in this effort—all to no avail. It is not merely that there is no specifically enumerated constitutional right to abortion. It is that there simply is no principle in the Constitution by whose affirmation the American people have committed themselves to a regime of abortion-on-demand. The matter is not even close.

The best that plausibly can be said for the cause of abortion as a constitutional matter is what Justice Scalia says, namely that, though the Constitution does not forbid the states to restrict abortion, it does not require them to do so.[44]

By contrast, a far stronger case—a genuinely principled argument—can be made that the American people have, by ratifying the Fourteenth Amendment's guarantee of equal protection, committed themselves to a proposition which is incompatible with the regime of abortion-on-demand. One way of stating the argument is to observe that "person," in ordinary language, connotes what logicians call a "substance sortal," that is to say, an essential property, which implies that whatever has it *has it necessarily* and never exists without it. Human beings come to be and become persons at the same time; they do not become persons at some point after coming to be (nor do they cease being persons without ceasing to be).[45] The thirty-nine (or so) year-old person who is now, say, Dean of the Loyola School of Law is indistinguishable from the being (or, in philosophical terms, the "substance") who was at an earlier stage of his life a twenty-three year-old law student, an eighteen year-old undergraduate, a thirteen year-old adolescent, a six year-old child, a one year-old infant, a five month old fetus, a four week old embryo, and a newly conceived human being. The Dean progressed from his conception through the embryonic, fetal, infant, and adolescent stages of his life into his adult stage as a distinct, unified, self-integrating organism without undergoing substantial change, that is without ceasing to be one kind of being or substance (possessing one kind of nature) and becoming a different sort of being.[46] Of course, there was a time when he did not exist. But when he came into existence, he came into existence as a person. There was no stage in his life at which he existed but was not yet a person. Just as *he* was once an adolescent and before that an infant, the very same *he* was once a fetus and before that an embryo. And this is one respect in which deans are just like the rest of us.

John Finnis summed up the matter nicely in his critique of John Rawls's argument that restrictions on abortion violate the liberal principle of public reason which, according to Rawls, ought to govern legislative decision-making on questions of constitutional essentials and matters of basic justice.[47] Any justification for denying unborn human beings the right to the equal protection of the laws, Finnis argues,

> will have to have abandoned the one real basis of human equality and equality rights, namely the fact that each living human being possesses, actually and not merely *potentially,* the radical capacity to reason, laugh, love, repent, and choose *as this unique, personal* individual, a capacity which is not some abstract characteristic of the species but rather consists in the unique, individual, organic functioning of the organism which comes into existence as a new substance at the conception of that new human being and subsists until his or her death whether ninety minutes, ninety days, or ninety years later—a capacity, individuality and personhood which subsists as real and precious even while its operations come and go with many changing factors such as immaturity, injury, sleep, and senility.[48]

But someone may object: Is it not possible that the framers and ratifiers meant something very different by "person" when they used that term in the Fourteenth Amendment? Indeed, it is possible. Whether the framers really did have something very different in mind is certainly relevant to whether a court would now be justified in striking down a legislatively enacted regime of abortion-on-demand as a violation of the equal protection rights of the unborn. Important questions of the proper understanding and role of "original intent," for example, would immediately be put into play. As yet the argument has not been made. Although the ratifiers of the Fourteenth Amendment did not have the question of abortion in mind—what they were concerned about, rather, was racial bias against the recently freed slaves—they very deliberately framed the Equal Protection (and Due Process) Clause(s) in general terms to forbid the denial of equal protection (and due process) to any person or class of persons, and all the evidence from the ratification debates is consistent with the proposition that by "persons" the framers and ratifiers meant (and meant to protect) all living members of the species *homo sapiens*.

In any event, I am not here arguing that Justice Scalia is wrong to suggest that courts could not be justified in striking down liberal abortion laws. To make that argument, I would have to address the panoply of reasons militating in favor of judicial restraint when it comes to an issue such as abortion.[49] I am here interested merely in showing that, unlike the Court's decision in *Roe*, a decision outlawing or substantially restricting abortion could be supported by a plausible and truly principled constitutional argument. Thus, the symmetry presupposed by Berger's criticism of the *First Things* symposium does not in fact exist.

The conception of democracy, and the understanding of America's democratic institutions, which the symposiasts had in mind when expressing their concerns about the possible "end of democracy" and offering their criticisms of "the judicial usurpation of politics," were not conceptions according to which democracy is (as Justice Scalia supposes) a simple, morally neutral mechanism of majority rule, whereby fifty-one percent of the people do as they please. Rather, it is a conception of democracy which, as the Pope's analysis in *Evangelium Vitae* brings to light, is shaped by its own justifying moral principle of the equality-in-dignity of all human beings—a conception which, I and others connected with *First Things* believe, was operative in the central proposition of the Declaration of Independence ("all men are created equal") and enshrined in our Constitution (particularly, though not exclusively, in the Equal Protection Clause of the Fourteenth Amendment). Under our conception of democracy, the function of democratic institutions is to serve as the mechanisms by which the people act to fulfill their moral-political responsibilities to protect the weak and innocent, preserve and promote public health, safety, and morals, and secure the overall common good.

A Profound Dilemma

In engaging the question of the legitimacy of the regime of judicial rule, a point that I and other participants in the *First Things* symposium should have made more explicitly is that apart from the most tyrannical regimes (which conscientious citizens may rightly—and where possible should—work to subvert), the question of legitimacy is a matter of degree, rather than an either-or proposition. Consider the case of non-tyrannical but authoritarian regimes. Because democracy, as the Pope teaches, embodies the principle of human equality, a regime that fails to adopt, or move in the direction of, democratic rule will necessarily implicate itself in a measure of injustice. And insofar as a regime implicates itself in injustice, it weakens the citizens' reasons for giving their loyalty or allegiance to the regime. In a word, it weakens, even if it does not destroy, a regime's legitimacy. However, no regime this side of God's sovereign rule in the kingdom of heaven is perfectly just, utterly free of injustice. But that certainly does not mean that every regime is simply illegitimate and may rightly be subverted. Even non-democratic regimes can deserve the allegiance of their citizens. Citizens of non-democratic regimes are certainly justified in working by peaceful means toward the goal of democratic rule; if their government is not a tyrannical one, they even now have reasons for obeying the laws enacted by their rulers, serving in the military, and treating the official acts of government as politically authoritative. In short, they have reasons for giving the regime their allegiance.

So, even if we are correct in arguing that the regime of judicial rule in the United States is doubly unjust—first, in its usurpation of democratic authority and, second, and not unrelatedly, in the wicked ends it has sometimes, as in *Roe*, set for itself—that does not mean that we should support revolutionary action against the government of the United States. While these injustices weaken the legitimacy of the regime they do not render our whole government simply illegitimate. The unjust and unconstitutional acts of the judiciary should be resisted; loyal citizens of the United States should work to restore those aspects of constitutional self-government that have been undermined by usurping judges. But the means used to resist judicial usurpation and restore democratic rule must themselves be constitutionally and morally sound. The identification and use of such means will itself require careful democratic deliberation—what Mary Ann Glendon, writing in response to the *First Things* symposium, called "the hard work of citizenship."[50]

But the courts, and the Supreme Court in particular, should recognize the profound dilemma in which their usurpations have placed many conscientious and loyal American citizens. It would be bad enough for citizens who recognize the equality-in-dignity of unborn human beings to find themselves on the losing side of a democratic debate over the question of abortion. (This is the position in which pro-life citizens of the United Kingdom or Sweden find themselves.) Even worse, it further weakens the legitimacy of the regime for such citizens to be deprived of any right to work through normal democratic processes to preserve or restore legal protection for the unborn. It is not merely that the judicial manufacture of a constitutional right to abortion-on-demand makes the political task of protecting the unborn especially difficult, but that the institution claiming the ultimate authority to specify the meaning of the nation's fundamental moral-political commitments, namely the Supreme Court, tells the nation that the Constitution to which citizens are asked to give their allegiance includes so grave an injustice as the abortion license. Thus, citizens are asked to be loyal to a constitution that not only fails to protect the basic

right to equality of the unborn, but also one which denies them any democratic means to effect the protection
of that basic right short of amending the Constitution.

Even prior to the *Dred Scott* decision in 1856,[51] the
legitimacy of the regime of government in America was
weakened by the grave injustice of slavery. Still, conscientious citizens such as Abraham Lincoln, who opposed
that monstrous evil, could, he and many others believed
(and I believe), honestly swear to uphold the Constitution because, whatever its inadequacies, it did not contain a strict right to own slaves. True, it failed to secure
the moral right of every human being not to be enslaved,
but it did not remove the authority of democratic institutions to abolish slavery and secure the moral right against
it. The people in their states retained the authority to
act through democratic means to effect abolition within
their jurisdictions, and the people of the northern states
chose to exercise this authority. Congress, in its exercise
of general jurisdiction in the federal territories, had (or
so it was thought) the authority to act against slavery, albeit
in a limited way, and did so act. Of course, inasmuch as
the southern states permitted slavery, they were guilty of
grave injustice, and insofar as the United States Constitution permitted slavery in states that chose to retain "the
peculiar institution," it failed to protect the right of those
enslaved to the equal protection of the laws.[52] But as bad
as this situation was, no citizen was asked to pledge allegiance to a regime whose basic constitutional principles
included something so unjust as a right of some human
beings to buy, sell, use, and use up other human beings.

Then came *Dred Scott*.[53] According to the understanding of the Constitution by which Roger Brooke Taney and

those justices joining him sent Dred Scott back into slavery, the American people, acting through the constitutionally established institutions of democracy at the federal
level, had no authority to interfere with the right of slaveholding, even where, as in the territories, general jurisdiction was in the hands of the federal government.[54] This
was, in effect, to manufacture a constitutional right to
slaveholding.[55] Indeed, it is difficult to see how the practical
import of this decision was not to deprive even the free
states of their effective power to prohibit slavery within
their borders. So not only was *Dred Scott's* central holding unjust, but it was also a gross usurpation of the people's
authority to act through their democratic institutions to
prohibit, or, at least, contain slavery. And, in these respects, *Dred Scott* resembles nothing so much as *Roe v.
Wade*,[56] and it created for many morally conscientious citizens of the antebellum era precisely the dilemma which
Roe creates for many such citizens today.

When it comes to cases such as *Dred Scott* and *Roe*,
there seem to be but two options available to citizens who
recognize the profound injustices these decisions work:
Either citizens are to treat the legitimacy of the Constitution as gravely weakened, or they are to deny that the
Court has the authority to settle definitively the meaning of the Constitution—in other words, either the Constitution is illegitimate or the Court is behaving
illegitimately. In reaction to the *Dred Scott* case, a not
so insignificant number of abolitionists chose the former
option—some going so far as to denounce the Constitution as a "covenant with death and agreement with hell"[57]
and even to burn copies of it. Lincoln, however, chose
the latter option. While recognizing the authority of the

Court to resolve the particular case (despite the incorrectness and injustice of its ruling), he refused to concede to the justices the right to lay down a rule permanently binding the other branches of government to recognize a constitutional right of slaveholding.[58] Plainly referring to the decision in *Dred Scott*, Lincoln stated:

> I do not forget the position assumed by some that constitutional questions are to be decided by the Supreme Court, nor do I deny that such decisions must be binding in any case upon the parties to a suit as to the object of that suit, while they are also entitled to very high respect and consideration in all parallel cases by all other departments of the Government. And while it is obviously possible that such decision may be erroneous in any given case, still the evil effect following it, being limited to that particular case, with the chance that it may be overruled and never become a precedent for other cases, can better be borne than could the evils of a different practice. At the same time, the candid citizen must confess that if the policy of the government, upon vital questions affecting the whole people is to be irrevocably fixed by decisions of the Supreme Court, the instant they are made in ordinary litigation between parties in personal actions, the people will have ceased to be their own rulers, having to that extent practically resigned their government into the hands of that eminent tribunal.[59]

I would suggest that the proper response of pro-life citizens to the call by Supreme Court Justices Sandra Day O'Connor, Anthony Kennedy, and David Souter in *Casey* to end the debate over abortion and "[accept] a common [pro-abortion] mandate rooted in the Constitution,"[60] is to reassert Lincoln's argument in response to judicial usurpation and injustice in *Dred Scott*. We should say, in effect, that while we could not in conscience give our unfettered allegiance to a regime committed in its very constitution to abortion-on-demand, any more than we could give wholehearted allegiance to a regime constitutionally committed to chattel slavery, we do not accept the authority of judges to read into the Constitution a right to abortion. On the contrary, we reject the justices' claim to have their ruling treated as a legitimate and authoritative interpretation of the Constitution. And we will resist their usurpation of our authority, as a people, to act through the institutions of representative democracy to protect the rights of the unborn. In other words, our response to judicial usurpation and injustice in our own time should not be to denounce the Constitution or to withdraw our allegiance to the United States, but rather to reassert the true principles of the Constitution and to reaffirm our allegiance to this nation, under God,[61] in its aspiration to secure true liberty and justice for all.

PART II

Lessons from the Past

5

THE VENERABLE ARGUMENT
AGAINST JUDICIAL USURPATION

Gary D. Glenn

F OR ONE HUNDRED AND FIFTY YEARS, distinguished
American statesmen of widely differing political
positions have persuasively criticized the Supreme
Court for usurping politics under the guise of enforcing
the Constitution. For over one hundred of those years
this criticism came from liberals and Progressives like
Abraham Lincoln, Theodore and Franklin Roosevelt, and
FDR's Attorney General (and later Supreme Court Justice) Robert Jackson. It is only during the last generation that judicial usurpation has been contested by
conservatives like Ronald Reagan, Attorney General Edwin
Meese, Justice Antonin Scalia, and most recently, the *First
Things* symposiasts.

The "politics" usurped is what Lincoln at Gettysburg
called "government of the people, by the people, and for
the people," that is, democratic politics, through elected
and removable representatives. The "judicial usurpation
of politics" takes place when the Supreme Court acts upon

four related claims: 1) "the Constitution" is not the text
of 1789 as amended according to the provisions of Article
v; 2) the Constitution of 1789 is not the supreme law of
the land as Article VI says it is; 3) on the contrary, decisions of the Supreme Court are the supreme law of the
land; and 4) it is therefore impossible for the Court to
act unconstitutionally because every Court decision is, by
definition, *constitutional* law.

   In 1958 the Court made this position its "settled doctrine": "the federal judiciary is supreme in the exposition
of the law of the Constitution . . . [i]t follows that the
interpretation of the Fourteenth Amendment enunciated
by this Court in the *Brown* case is the supreme law of
the land."[1] If Supreme Court decisions are the supreme
law of the land, then it is impossible for the Court to act
unconstitutionally, since the Constitution has no meaning apart from what the Court says it means. From this
it follows that whatever the Court says the Constitution
means is not only what the Constitution *means*, it *is* the
Constitution. In this way, what ordinary citizens call "the
Constitution" is wholly absorbed into the Court's interpretation and thus disappears as a standard for judging
the validity of Supreme Court decisions.

   The history and political diversity of the criticism of
this doctrine is instructive. Those with liberal inclinations should understand that it is not "conservative" to
believe that the judiciary usurps politics. It may be true
or false, but it is not conservative. Moreover, openness
to criticisms of judicial usurpation will help contemporary liberals perceive the tension between their commitment to government by the people and their desire for
the political results which government by the people may

not give them—but which government by unelected and unremovable justices may. For the last two generations, liberals have been able both to profess belief in government by the people and to accept as legitimate the policy decisions which frequently flow from the judicial usurpation of that government. The time will come when this will no longer be possible, and liberals will need to decide which is the deeper commitment—to constitutional democracy or to progressive policies.

Those with conservative inclinations, for their part, should know both that "the judicial usurpation of politics" is not essentially a conservative idea and that conservative ends are not necessarily served by opposing it. In fact, the judicial usurpation of politics began with conservative, nineteenth-century justices who wished to preserve slavery in particular and later private property generally. That judicial power has been abused so long and so effectively by their political opponents might tempt conservatives to wish that conservative justices would abuse it for conservative ends. Yet if conservatives are committed to the Constitution, they will be hostile not to judicial power as such but only to its abuses.

The core argument of the *First Things* symposiasts is so old that it is "venerable" and allows liberals and conservatives alike to reflect on the danger to their country, not to mention their souls, of wanting both to have and eat their constitutional cake.

The Beginnings of Judicial Usurpation

In 1857, the Supreme Court ruled in *Dred Scott v. Sandford* that the Constitution prohibits Congress from outlawing slavery in the territories of the United States. Previous Congresses and presidents had interpreted the Constitution to *permit* what the Court now said it *prohibited.* The constitutional provision which they thought authorized the outlawing of slavery is Article IV, section 3: "Congress shall have Power to . . . make all needful Rules and Regulation respecting the Territory . . . belonging to the United States."

Lincoln publicly criticized the Court's decision on both political (policy) and constitutional grounds in the famous 1858 debates with Judge Douglas. The nerve of his constitutional criticism he stated in his First Inaugural Address in 1861: "[I]f the policy of the government, upon vital questions affecting the whole people, is to be irrevocably fixed by decisions of the Supreme Court, the instant they are made, in ordinary litigation between parties in personal actions, the people will have ceased to be their own rulers, having to that extent practically resigned their government into the hands of that eminent tribunal." This begins what was later called the "progressive" objection to the Court's usurpation of politics by its abuse of judicial review. Lincoln does not object to the constitutionally legitimate *use* of judicial power to nullify acts of Congress; he objects to the *abuse* of that power.[2]

The problem then and now is how to distinguish the constitutionally legitimate *use* from the constitutionally illegitimate *abuse* of the Court's power. Justice Curtis set forth the previously established judicial solution to the problem in his *Dred Scott* dissent. Congress and the President, Curtis argued, have a right to interpret the Constitution in the act of legislating, and after some time has passed, *their interpretation becomes binding on the Court.*

This theory was called "practical construction" or "practical interpretation." According to Curtis, this had been the living constitutional law from its first formulation in *Stuart v. Laird* (1803) until *Dred Scott*.[3] Including the First Congress (1791), eight Congresses and presidents, "beginning with General Washington, and coming regularly down as far as Mr. John Quincy Adams, thus including all who were in public life when the Constitution was adopted,"[4] had made a "practical construction" of the Constitution that permitted Congress to outlaw slavery in the territories. Such "practical construction nearly contemporaneous with the adoption of the Constitution, and continued by repeated instances through a long series of years, may always influence, and in doubtful cases, determine the judicial mind on a question of the interpretation of the Constitution."[5] Curtis adds that to abandon "interpretation of the Constitution, according to the fixed rules which govern the interpretation of laws" means "we have no longer a Constitution; we are living under the government of individual men, who for the time being have power to declare what the Constitution is," according to their own views of what it ought to mean.[6]

Curtis defends what the *Dred Scott* majority attacks, namely, the view that the people's representatives have, at least under certain circumstances, as good a claim to interpret the Constitution as do the courts. But we must be precise in this matter. Curtis's defense does not imply that the people's representatives cannot violate the Constitution.[7] But in invalidating legislation the Court exercises its power legitimately only when the Constitution and an act of Congress are at "irreconcilable variance," that is, cannot "by any fair construction be reconciled to each other."[8] It was *this* exercise of judicial power that the Founders defended publicly during ratification as necessary to preserve the democracy that the Constitution establishes. The Court must recognize the right of the people's representatives to interpret ambiguous constitutional language in giving effect to popular will. Constitutionally, justices are *not* the people's (that is, the current generation's) representatives. This understanding is manifest in the text itself: Unlike members of Congress and the President, justices do not stand for election or reappointment.

The "judicial usurpation of politics," according to the Founders, Lincoln, and Curtis, occurs when the Court nullifies Congress' long-standing, previously-unchallenged interpretation of ambiguous constitutional language. Having stood for a period of time, Congress' interpretation ought to be fixed beyond the Court's power to change it. For an unaccountable Court later to challenge Congress' interpretation is judicial usurpation, not democracy.

The Constitution frees justices from accountability to the people so they can protect the Constitution, not from any contested act of the President and Congress, but from *abuse* by the President or Congress: "The standard of good behaviour for the continuance in office of the judicial magistracy is ... [a]n excellent barrier ... to the encroachments and oppressions of the representative body."[9] The Constitution, though it establishes government by the people, presumes that the most likely inspiration for such abuse in a popular government will come from the people themselves.[10] Hence, the Court is insulated from popular control so that it can control popular abuse of the Constitution.

From the point of view of the Constitution, the *Dred Scott* majority asserted a new judicial power not found in any founding document, not previously found in any Court opinion (in particular not that judicial power defended by Marshall in *Marbury v. Madison*), and incompatible with the idea of government by the people.

The judicial power defended by the Founders in the famous and authoritative *Federalist,* Number 78 is, on the other hand, quite different. There, Hamilton defends Congress' right to decide the meaning of ambiguous passages in the Constitution, while explaining what we must now call "original judicial review."[11] Against the charge that judicial refusal to uphold legislative acts means unelected justices are superior to elected representatives, Hamilton argues that this is not true as long as the justices uphold the will of the people contained in the Constitution against the will of the people's representatives contained in ordinary legislation. In other words, the will of the people contained in the Constitution is superior to both the Congress and the Court.[12] This view, *and only this view,* makes any kind of "judicial review" consistent with government by the people's elected representatives. Moreover, it makes a certain kind of judicial review an ally—even an indispensable ally—of the *enduring,* hence presumably more sober and thoughtful, will of the people contained in the Constitution, as against the *transient,* hence presumably less considered and less moderate, will of the people or their representatives contained in ordinary legislation. In contrast, *Dred Scott*'s novel doctrine substitutes the Court's will for that of the people.

It should now be clear that the judicial doctrine of "practical construction" is an application of the Founders' "irreconcilable variance" principle. As such, it is indispensable to reconciling, commensurate with the Constitution, government by the will of the people with legitimate "original judicial review." *Dred Scott*'s abandonment of "practical construction" began "the judicial usurpation of politics."

THEODORE ROOSEVELT AND THE HEIRS OF ABRAHAM LINCOLN

Lincoln, of course, lived before the term "progressive" appeared in our political vocabulary. Still, I provisionally connect him to the Progressives on this matter because they did so. In a 1913 speech delivered on Lincoln's birthday, entitled "The Heirs of Abraham Lincoln," Theodore Roosevelt asserted that "We Progressives and we alone are today the representatives of the men of Lincoln's day who upheld the hands of Lincoln and aided him in the great task to which he gave his life, and in doing which he met his death . . . Lincoln and Lincoln's supporters were emphatically the Progressives of their day."[13] Roosevelt then endorsed a proposed constitutional amendment that would "give to the people the right themselves to decide the policy of the government upon vital questions in cases where they do not agree with decisions rendered by the Supreme Court." He said such an amendment, which would subject Supreme Court decisions to popular referenda, would merely "[carry] out the principles set forth by Lincoln in this his First Inaugural Address."[14]

Roosevelt believed that the courts (not only the Supreme Court) had usurped politics by finding unconstitutional such Congressional acts as the income tax, workmen's compensation, and health and safety regulations and foiling state attempts to protect working people, small businessmen, and farmers from monopolies and exploitation by employers.

Roosevelt's remedy was based on "the power which Abraham Lincoln claimed for the people, the power of being master over the courts exactly as they are master over the legislative bodies and executive officers." The remedy "is that when two of the agencies established by the Constitution for its own enforcement, the legislature and the courts, differ between themselves as to what the Constitution which created them means, or what it is to be held to mean, then that the people themselves, the people who created the Constitution, who established, whom Abraham Lincoln said are masters of both court and legislature shall step in and after due deliberation decide what the Constitution is or is not to permit."[15]

Although the Progressives succeeded in amending the Constitution to elect senators directly, permit an income tax, and to grant women the right to vote, their amendment to establish popular control of the judiciary failed.

New Deal Progressives and "Effective" Government

A generation later, Franklin D. Roosevelt rejoined the battle, taking his bearings from the same Lincolnian position as had Theodore Roosevelt: "[T]he people of these United States are the rightful masters of both congresses and courts, not to overthrow the Constitution, but to overthrow the men who pervert the Constitution."[16] Roosevelt was concerned because the Court had spent several years declaring unconstitutional his Administration's efforts to deal with the Depression. These decisions "cast a deep shadow of doubt upon the ability of the Congress ever at any time to protect the Nation against catastrophe by squarely meeting modern social and economic maladjustments." Roosevelt was not much concerned with the Constitution itself, but rather with the country's very real and very serious economic problems. He cared about the Constitution only inasmuch as it is a grant of powers to a government "which the Founding Fathers sought to make strong enough to meet new national problems."[17] He went so far as to dismiss as "academic" criticisms that the Court was not intended by the Constitution to have the power to declare acts of Congress unconstitutional.

Roosevelt's attorney general, Robert Jackson, in *The Struggle for Judicial Supremacy* (1941),[18] revealed a great deal about the New Deal view of the relation of the Supreme Court to democracy. The Constitution, Jackson claimed, establishes the Court as "an overriding legal authority completely independent of popular will." By 1933, the Court had "largely controlled the economic and social policy of the country . . . on principles found nowhere in the Constitution." Moreover, it "had not only established its ascendancy over the entire government as a source of constitutional doctrine, but it . . . sat almost as a continuous constitution convention which, without submitting its proposals to any ratification or rejection, could amend the basic law."[19]

One must pay careful attention to see that Jackson's objection is *not* based on the absence of constitutional warrant for the Court's anti-New Deal decisions. Like FDR, Jackson did not much care about the Constitution. His objections to the Supreme Court were political, not constitutional: "The basic grievance of the New Deal was that the Court has seemed unduly to favor private economic power and always to find ways of circumventing the efforts of popular government to control or regulate it . . . Our struggle has been one to restore effective government— the only means through which the will and opinion of the people can have any expression."[20] Jackson would have objected to the Court's anti-New Deal decisions quite as much if the Constitution has contained a clause saying "The New Deal is unconstitutional." His concern was "effective," not constitutional, government, because "liberal-minded lawyers also recognized that constitutional law is not a fixed body of immutable doctrine. We knew its rules had their beginnings and endings, . . . in the checkered history of the Court. We saw that those changes were identified with the predominant interests or currents of opinion of past epochs, though they were often made in the name of the Constitution itself."[21]

Jackson's emphasis on predominant interests appears to exclude any interest in what the Constitution itself means. He speaks as though the Constitution has no fixed meaning: All previous decisions of the Court are equally valid or invalid, and constitutionally it does not matter which. What does matter is whose political interests predominate in constitutional law at any given time.

The upshot of Jackson's claim is that the Court was wrong, not because it ignored the Constitution but because it permitted "a past that was dead and repudiated in the intellectual and political world" to maintain a "firm grip on the judicial world." This progressivism with a vengeance recognizes no *Constitution* in the sense of a permanent structure of ends, standards, powers, rights, and forms. Our Constitution was formerly thought to bind judges until properly amended. But Jackson's progressivism replaces the Constitution so understood with a perpetually changing constitutional law. The result is that the *Constitution* as such no longer protects any one. Only those who control *constitutional law* can do so.[22]

It followed that, for New Deal Progressives, the remedy for the judicial usurpation of politics was not, as it was for Lincoln, a return to government supported and restrained by what we must now call "the Founders' Constitution" as amended according to its own provisions. Instead these Progressives "demanded for our generation . . . the right consciously to influence the evolutionary process of constitutional law, as other generations had done."[23] Thus, "government of the people, by the people and for the people," justified by the principles contained in the Declaration of Independence and given form and effect in the Founders' Constitution as amended, is reinvented by the will of each generation.

The New Deal abandonment of the distinction between the Constitution and constitutional law was made explicit in John Mabry Mathew's *The American Constitutional System*. (1940): "By its very nature, the Constitution of the United States is a constantly developing body of law."[24] Similarly, Rexford G. Tugwell, a leading member of the New Deal "braintrust," described the Constitution as "a product of Court interpretation," and he added, "The pretense that a body of agreed higher law [i.e. the Constitution] exists is a kind of national conspiracy, maintained because of need. A Constitution is necessary to the American system. That it no longer exists is an intolerable thought."[25] He did not publish these thoughts until 1976.

The New Deal's absorption of the Constitution into constitutional law replaced the Founders' understanding of what a constitution is with that which Thomas Jefferson expressed privately but never (as far as I know) publicly:

> [N]o society can make a perpetual constitution or even a perpetual law. The earth belongs always to the living Generation. They may manage it then, & and what proceeds from it, as they please, during their usufruct. [But] . . . The constitution and the laws of their predecessors extinguished then in their natural course, with those who gave them being. . . . Every constitution then, & every law, naturally expires at the end of 19 years [Jefferson's calculation of the average life span of a majority of those now of age]. If it be enforced longer, it is an act of force, & not of right.[26]

By adopting this theory of the sovereignty of each generation, New Deal Progressivism found a way to have its constitutional cake and eat it too: Continue to refer to the constitutional text, so the people will think judicial decisions made in its name actually follow it, while simultaneously justifying the government of each generation in giving the words whatever meaning it pleases.[28]

This progressivism abandons Lincoln's ground for opposing *Dred Scott*, namely that the Constitution has a meaning independent of what the Court says it means. This ground had enabled Lincoln to distinguish Court decisions that are valid constitutional law from those which are unconstitutional law. For New Deal Progressives, this distinction does not exist. For them, only Congress, the President, administrators, and state governments could make unconstitutional laws. The Court could not.

WILLIAM BRENNAN AND THE
PROGRESSIVE USURPATION OF POLITICS

What the progressive replacement of the Constitution by constitutional law eventually came to mean is made clear in a 1985 speech by Justice William Brennan: "[T]he genius of the Constitution rests not in any static meaning it might have had in a world that is dead and gone, but in the adaptability of its great principles to cope with current problems and current needs. What the constitutional fundamentals meant to the wisdom of other times cannot be their measure to the vision of our time."[28] That is, justices should not be bound by *finding* meaning in the Founders' Constitution. Rather the Justices should *give* it meaning for our time: "[J]udicial power resides in the authority to give meaning to the Constitution."[29]

Two generations before Brennan, Jackson had defended allowing "each generation" to form constitutional law in its own image, thereby abandoning the Founders' Constitution in the name of the sovereignty of "each generation." But for Jackson, "each generation" still meant government by the people through their elected and removable representatives. Jackson intended only to justify the Court's getting out of the way of "the government." Notice, however, that New Deal Progressives did not regard "the Court" as part of "the government." This is apparent from Roosevelt's introduction to the 1935 volume of his *Public Papers and Addresses*: "For nearly a half century the tendency of *the Supreme Court* arising from these economic and social predilections has unfortunately been to place a narrowing construction on the powers of *the Government. The rights of Government* to protect individual citizens from aggregations of private economic power were being gradually whittled away." There are fourteen such explicit juxtapositions of "the Court" and "the Government" in this fourteen-page introduction.[30]

In contrast to New Deal Progressives, for Justice Brennan "each generation" means neither the sovereignty of the people (as it meant to Jefferson), nor of their elected and removable representatives (as it meant to the New Deal Progressives), but the sovereignty of the Supreme Court. The Supreme Court *is* the government to the extent it chooses to be. In Brennan's progressivism, the Constitution explicitly disappears into the Supreme Court's interpretation, and government of and by the people's elected representatives explicitly disappears into government by an unelected judiciary.[31]

Brennan's progressivism guts "consent of the governed" by reducing it merely to the right to impeach justices or amend the Constitution to correct judicial usurpation.[32] But these remedies are constitutionally designed to be all but impossible in practice. And experience shows that the design works, for no Supreme Court justice has ever been successfully impeached. Similarly, amendments are virtually useless to remedy judicial usurpation of simple majority rule because the Constitution makes simple majorities insufficient to amend. Minorities are deliberately given a veto over all majorities of less than two-thirds in both houses of Congress and less than 50 percent plus one in two-thirds of the state legislatures. This system of minority veto is so effective that, in 210 years, only four Supreme Court decisions (including *Dred Scott,* which took a civil war) have been overturned by amendment.

THE EVOLUTION OF PROGRESSIVISM

Progressivism "reinvents" itself in each generation. It emerged by name late in the nineteenth century as a critique of the Constitution as undemocratic. Professor Woodrow Wilson, as he then was, thought the Constitution's purpose was to prevent tyranny and establish not democracy but liberal (limited) government. But now that democracy has been established, our constitutional structure is outmoded. The progress of history guarantees that the problem of tyranny has been solved once and for all. Since history is inevitably a progress towards ever greater freedom and democracy, we no longer need constitutional restraints to prevent "regressing" to tyranny. Institutions like separation of powers are now merely obstacles to the effective implementation of the popular will.[33]

In the early twentieth century, Theodore Roosevelt sought to restore government by the people through the Constitution by making the people masters over the Court directly. This failed remedy would have abolished the Founders' distinction between the *permanent* will of the people embodied in the Constitution and their *transient* will as expressed in referenda.

In the late 1930s, New Deal Progressives Franklin Roosevelt and Robert Jackson thought democracy meant only the will of the people as reflected in the outcome of elections. They disdained the Constitution's limits on the powers of each generation.

Justice Brennan, a late twentieth-century progressive, taught that the Court should promote "human dignity" and that justices should "give" meaning to the Constitution accordingly. Unlike Theodore and Franklin Roosevelt, Brennan did not regard this as usurping the right of the people to govern themselves, for he believed that neither the Constitution nor "government by the people," but rather Progressive courts, secure our rights. But Brennan's Progressive constitutional law excludes all understandings but its own of "the will of each generation" and "human dignity."[34]

LESSONS FROM THE PROGRESSIVE EXPERIENCE

Lesson 1. Lincoln campaigned in 1860 to elect Republicans committed to appointing new justices who would overturn *Dred Scott.* His election led the South to choose secession and civil war rather than live under a Constitution controlled by the Republicans. *Dred Scott* was overturned by the Civil War and the Fourteenth Amendment. But civil war is not a constitutional remedy for judicial usurpation. It is a sign of constitutional failure, to say nothing of being humanly costly. Those committed to the Constitution cannot reasonably look to remedies which presuppose the Constitution's failure.

Lesson 2. Theodore Roosevelt failed to secure democracy, through constitutional amendment, against the Court's usurpation. There was no precipitating event, like a civil war, to produce the kind of consensus that had existed on the Fourteenth Amendment.

Lesson 3. Franklin Roosevelt showed that an overwhelmingly popular President, confronted with an unprecedented economic crisis, just reelected by the largest landslide in history, with a two-thirds majority in both houses of Congress, could bully *one* member of the Court (and hence the Court itself) into submission. Each of these circumstances, not to mention their coincidence, is so rare that they cannot be considered solutions to judicial usurpation. The normal condition of American politics is that the people and the government are divided, in which case the Court has *carte blanche.*

Lesson 4. Overall, the Progressive experience shows that on rare occasions, epoch-making events, like the Civil War and the Great Depression, permit the overcoming of judicial usurpation. However, such epochal events require unusual combinations of circumstances.

Lesson 5. The Progressive experience shows that it is rarely practical to rely on constitutional amendments to overcome judicial usurpation. Indeed, the theoretical possibility of such a remedy serves more frequently to enable Congress to appear to do something while actually avoiding doing anything. It permits representatives to vote for an amendment to overturn a particular Court decision, satisfying public outrage, while knowing the chances are negligible than any amendment will pass on which the people are divided. Thus experience confirms constitutional theory: Amendments cannot be a remedy with the frequency with which the Court has usurped politics.

Lesson 6. The Progressives never attempted one potential solution to judicial usurpation. Article III, section 2, of the Constitution states that "The Supreme Court shall have appellate jurisdiction . . . with such Exceptions and under such Regulations as Congress shall make." Congress has exercised this "exceptions power" only once, when it withdrew the Court's right to review the Civil War Reconstruction Acts. In *Ex Parte McCardle* (1869) the Court recognized the constitutionality of this power. "We are not at liberty to inquire into the motives of the legislature . . . the power to make exceptions to the jurisdiction of this Court is given by express words."[35]

Through disuse, this solution has now been forgotten even by the politically informed. It is, however, still alive in law reviews and even in recent testimony before Congress.[36] Defenders of judicial usurpation argue both that the Court could simply declare any such Congressional act unconstitutional and that such restrictions would be useless because they would not invalidate Court decisions already made. It would require a major effort once again to bring this democratic means of controlling the Court into the public debate.

Lesson 7. Perhaps the most sobering lesson from the past is that the Progressive triumph merely replaced pre-1937 conservative usurpation with post-1937 liberal-progressive judicial usurpation.

Lesson 8. The Progressive experience suggests that there is no feasible short-term solution to the judicial usurpation of politics, because correcting judicial usurpation is likely to be practical only in circumstances so extreme that decent people would not try to bring them about even if doing so might give an opportunity to restore democracy.

The Restoration of Government by the People

The earlier progressive experience mirrors the recent failure of conservative attempts to correct judicial usurpation. The judicial appointments of Republican presidents, from Richard Nixon to George Bush, have produced a moderating of the usurpation in one or two areas, but nothing more.[37] Indeed, it is instructive that all the decisions decried by the *First Things* symposiasts took place *after* attempts to appoint a more conservative judiciary began with Richard Nixon in 1968. The usurpations of the post-New Deal and Warren Courts,[38] some of which Nixon opposed and pledged to appoint justices to undo, are not the symposiasts' concern. Yet those usurpations remain in place with some moderation, for instance, in church-state matters, racial gerrymandering, and concerning rights of criminal defendants.

Nevertheless, the recent conservative failures do not mean there will never be a solution. The experience of Lincoln and Franklin Roosevelt shows the need to be prepared to propose improvements when a crisis arises. We do not know whether the crisis will be political or constitutional, like the Civil War, or economic, like the Great Depression. To the extent that the progressive experience is a guide, it tells us that we will have to wait for crisis of some kind to overturn the usurpations which are the subject of the *First Things* symposium. At the present time, our situation more closely resembles that of Theodore Roosevelt in 1913 than of Franklin Roosevelt in 1937.

In preparation for times of crisis, we should keep "the judicial usurpation of politics" argument before the thinking public so that when things turn bad there will be publicly available a well-developed and intellectually serious body of thought making clear what needs to be done. But while keeping this argument alive, we also need to think about what we should do when events avail themselves. If we take seriously the symposiasts' stated objections that the Court has usurped politics by violating the Constitution, then we should aim to restore *constitutional* democracy. That would mean we should not simply replace justices whose usurpations we deplore with justices whose usurpations we approve.

But suppose circumstances do not give us that choice. What if we are forced to choose between usurpations which we approve and those we disapprove? Suppose, in other words, that restoring constitutional restraints on the judiciary continues to be impossible. This is more than a theoretical possibility, as suggested by its having been the case since the Civil War. It would suggest that "government by the people," as the Founders' Constitution conceives it, had proved to be impossible. We would then be forced to choose between continued usurpation, but of a kind whose substance we approve, or continued usurpation of a kind we disapprove. If we would then choose the former, that would tell us that our present objection is fundamentally not to judicial usurpation but only to the kind of judicial usurpation.

Arguments against judicial usurpation are not merely pragmatic objections to the unjust substance of policy. They are a constitutional objection, aimed at restoring government by the people, in which the judiciary obeys the law of the Constitution, in contrast to the law-unto-itself government by judiciary that has replaced it. Usurpation is bad because constitutional government is good.

But usurpation is the worst evil only if constitutional government by the people is the greatest good. But is it? What if judicial usurpation produces substantively more just results than does constitutionally legitimate government by the people? Arguably, the progressive Court did that when it declared racially segregated schools unconstitutional in *Brown v. Board of Education* (1954). The usurpers have a great tactical advantage in this struggle, for they are interested only in results, not in legitimacy.

The *First Things* symposiasts place their argument on the high-minded ground of legitimacy. Yet, if constitutionally legitimate government was somehow restored, the usurpation argument would require them to accept as constitutionally legitimate a future Court's refusal to overturn immoral but constitutional acts of the people's representatives. For example, if legislatures recognized same-sex marriages, protected the right to abortion, or the like. Granted that this is not the present problem, still integrity requires that we face the high price of the symposium's high-mindedness. Would we not need the fortitude of a Thomas More to accept such a victory for judicial law-abidingness?

> **More:** And go he should, if he was the Devil himself, until he broke the law!
>
> **Roper:** So now you'd give the Devil benefit of law!
>
> **More:** Yes. What would you do? Cut a great road through the law to get after the Devil?
>
> **Roper:** I'd cut down every law in England to do that!
>
> **More:** (Roused and excited) Oh? And when the last

law was down, and the Devil turned around on you—
where would you hide, Roper, the laws all being flat?
This country's planted thick with laws from coast
to coast . . . and if you cut them down—and you're
just the man to do it—d'you really think you could
stand upright in the winds that would blow then?
(Quietly) Yes, I'd give the Devil benefit of law, for
my own safety's sake.[39]

That it might be necessary to defend the devil for the sake
of preserving even defective law is a sobering lesson in
the limits of politics and a timely reminder that our battle
is not ultimately against the Court's abuse of its power
but "against the principalities, against the powers, against
the world rulers of this present darkness, against the spiritual hosts of wickedness in the heavenly places."[40]

Nevertheless, the symposiasts (Bork perhaps excepted)
object to the Court's usurpation not merely because it is
constitutionally illegitimate but because it serves morally
reprehensible ends. Perhaps they emphasize the usurpation rather than the moral reprehensibility because they
think the people are morally healthier than the judicial
elites and hence judge that the people's representatives
would be less likely to adopt the morally objectionable
policies which the justices have and will continue to impose. In these judgements they are probably right. But
it is questionable how much help the people will be in
achieving the symposiasts' ends. For liberal relativism has
corrupted the people as it has the judicial elites. Although
the people's superior decency makes their representatives
less likely to vote to permit the slaughter of innocents,
the people's relativism makes them less willing to con-
demn that slaughter by others and to vote out of office

representatives who do not oppose it. That relativism appears to have convinced the American people as a political whole that they can live in a sea of blood shed by the hands of others, and not be implicated in the shedding of it; to live amidst sexual dissolution, and not be affected by it; to live in a moral sewer, and not smell.

CONCLUSION

Since the symposiasts appeal from the judiciary to the people and the Constitution, they must assume that the people are up to self-government under the Constitution. But even aside from the problem of popular relativism,[41] we must consider what qualities the people would have to have to be fit for such self government.

I have argued that, for the people to be so fit, certain ideas must be restored to their minds. They must understand "irreconcilable variance" as the only principled grounds ever articulated for making government by the people, that is, by representatives of the people, consistent with the Court's constitutional power to declare acts of the people's representatives unconstitutional. They must be reminded that the Court is constitutionally obligated to uphold the constitutionality of a legislative act so long as "it can by any fair construction be reconciled with the Constitution." They must be taught that this principle was adopted by the Marshall Court (1803) and remained the living constitutional law until *Dred Scott* and that it was then rejected by the Court in favor of a new but unconstitutional claim to declare legislative acts unconstitutional even if such acts *could*, by a fair construction, be reconciled with the Constitution. In other words, the

Court now claims the constitutional right to strike down a law if it can find an interpretation of the Constitution with which the act is inconsistent. The people must be taught that this kind of "judicial review" is unconstitutional because it usurps politics. It does so both by making government by the people incompatible with judicial review and by replacing government by the elected and removable representatives of the people with government by unelected and unremovable justices.[42]

But the theoretical soundness and historical legitimacy of "irreconcilable variance" may be only necessary and not sufficient to restore government by the people. That this may be so is suggested by the fact that, for seven generations, our constitutional law has sanctioned *Dred Scott's* judicial wilfulness over the self-abnegating judicial obedience to the Constitution which the Founders' Constitution required of justices and which was uniformly followed by the Court until the Taney Court overthrew it in 1857.

Do not the anti-democratic thinkers of antiquity teach that self-abnegation and law-abidingness are not likely to be found in democratic leaders and that the more democratic a democracy becomes, the less likely such qualities are to exist? Does not the history of our constitutional law confirm that these might well be too much to any longer expect of justices? Did not Lincoln warn us before *Dred Scott* that there will arise among us "men of ambition and talents" who "scorn to tread in the footsteps of my predecessor, however illustrious"; men who "thirst and burn for distinction" and who find no "gratification of their ruling passion . . . in adding story to story, upon the monuments of fame, erected to the memory of others."[43] Does not this prophecy both fairly characterize and adequately explain the attitude of those justices for whom the Founders' Constitution, as understood by the Founders, represents "a world that is dead and gone" and who seek distinction in usurping "the authority to give meaning to the Constitution"?

If these things are so, more will be needed to restore government by the people than sound ideas and adventitious circumstances. After all, the sound ideas of "irreconcilable variance" and "practical construction" were judicially overthrown after being established for seventy years. Obviously, sound ideas are not enough even to preserve, let alone restore, constitutional democracy. Lincoln himself thought in terms of preventing such usurpation. Prevention, he thought, "will require the people to be united with each other, attached to the government and laws, and generally intelligent." A tall order, that. But if a pound of cure equals an ounce of prevention, then restoration requires something more.

The something more required to restore the Founders' Constitution is something which the Founders themselves tended to deprecate, namely, political leadership. They deprecated it because it was both unnecessary and dangerous to their Constitution.[44] Since they provided a good Constitution, they thought, what it needs are administrators to maintain it, not leaders to change it. Hence, we call what we have the "Clinton administration" not the "Clinton government." The "Administration" administers the Constitution and in doing so preserves it. Leaders, on the other hand, are oriented not to preservation but to change. If you want change, then you need leaders, not administrators. But the need for change signifies there is a problem that the Constitution cannot remedy. What is wrong now is that the Constitution no longer governs. It took leaders like Roosevelt, Jackson, and Brennan to displace the Constitution. It will take leaders to reinstate it.

Restoration of a democratic constitutionalism requires the coming together of sound ideas like "irreconcilable variance" and "practical construction," favorable circumstances in the form of a great crisis, and leadership equal to the task. But we cannot either predict or control that coincidence. While we wait on events, we can continue the symposium's work. We do that by seeking the common ground on which thoughtful and honest liberals and conservatives could meet, if both were willing to learn once again how to live under the Constitution which secures government of, by, and for the people. That ground is understanding the Constitution as limiting the Court to enforcing the law of the Constitution and condemning the Court when it uses the Constitution's symbolic legitimacy to exclude political opponents' views from a place in the constitutional order. For that is what it does when it interprets ambiguous constitutional language[45] to impose one policy on the country by claiming it is the only one permitted by the Constitution, instead of leaving constitutional ambiguity to be resolved in the democratic process.

6

Democracy in America

Carson Holloway

PRACTICALLY ALL AMERICANS are more or less committed to democracy. Few of us, of course, would naïvely hold that democracy is unproblematic. But most of us confidently assert, with Churchill, that democracy is the worst form of government—except for all the others that have been tried. We like to think that we possess an unflinching awareness of our regime's defects, while simultaneously reassuring ourselves that no other regime can in practice hold a candle to it. We therefore see no need to examine the foundations of democracy too deeply. What would be the point, if we know (or think we know) in advance that it is superior? Yet isn't a possible result of such a commitment to democracy that we will have a much less clear-eyed appreciation of its disadvantages?

Perhaps, then, we should not be surprised that the debate sparked by the *First Things* symposium was spirited, even angry, and revealed important differences between

liberals and conservatives—and even among conservatives—on such fundamental questions as what tends to
preserve and what threatens to destroy democracy. The
editors of and contributors to the symposium, having
warned that democracy was in danger of being lost and
having reflected on how it might be saved, were accused—
not only by the usual opponents on the left, but also by
traditional allies on the right—of having advanced an
argument that was un-American or anti-American and
hence, presumably, antithetical to democracy.[1]

One hundred and sixty years before the *First Things*
symposium was published, Alexis de Tocqueville, too,
voiced the fear that democracy might degenerate into
despotism. We are compelled to admit that he was in a
better position to do this issue justice than we are. Tocqueville, after all, spoke from the privileged perspective of
an intellectual outsider: He is not committed to democracy. To be sure, he is resigned to its triumph and therefore committed to making the best of it. But when an
opportunity arises to declare his friendship for the new
order, he foregoes it. Instead, he merely says that he is
"no enemy of democracy."[2] Tocqueville, it seems, is not
so convinced as we Americans are of the superiority of
democracy. In the closing paragraphs of *Democracy in
America*, he asserts that "No man on earth can affirm, absolutely and generally, that the new state of societies is
better than the old." Indeed, he confesses that as he con-
templates the democracy that has just emerged he is
"tempted to regret that state of society which has ceased
to be."[3] Thus are we directed to the ground of Tocqueville's
lack of commitment to democracy: his familiarity with,
and genuine though qualified admiration of aristocracy.

Tocqueville's experience of and sympathy for the aristocratic alternative is the source of a more profound understanding of the nature of modern democracy, its inclinations and aversions, than we can have, committed as we are to a belief in democracy's superiority. Tocqueville's acquaintance with aristocracy's strengths gives him a keen eye for democracy's weaknesses. The result is a more penetrating account of the developments that the *First Things* symposium addresses, an account from which both the symposium's participants and defenders, as well as its critics, can learn.

The Tendency to Despotism

The point of departure of the *First Things* symposiasts is the fear that America may have ceased to be truly a democracy, and certainly will cease to be one, if the Supreme Court is not somehow brought under control. It may be, the editors' introduction gravely warns, that America has "betrayed" the "democratic idea" and that our system of government has "become something else" besides democracy.[4] The editors do not shrink from using the term "despotism" to describe the government they see emerging.[5]

The system that has supplanted, or soon will supplant, American democracy is undemocratic, it seems, in two respects. First, its political decisions are not made by the people or their elected representatives, but by a tiny minority of unelected officials. The editors argue that politics is the activity of "free persons deliberating the question, How ought we to order our life together?" and that democratic politics exists when the people "deliberate and decide that question."[6] Democratic politics, however, has largely ceased to exist in America. Instead, the editors see an "entrenched pattern of government by judges" which adds up to "nothing less than the usurpation of politics."[7] Today, they suggest, "the judiciary," not the people, "deliberates and answers the really important questions entailed in the question, How ought we to order our life together?"[8]

Other contributors to the symposium express similar views. Charles Colson, for instance, writes that "we have very nearly reached the completion of a long process I can only describe as the systematic usurpation of ultimate political power by the American judiciary."[9] Similarly, Judge Robert Bork suggests that we are ruled by a judicial "oligarchy" and holds that the "most important moral, political, and cultural decisions affecting our lives are being removed from democratic control."[10]

Second, America's new governmental arrangement is undemocratic in that the decisions the judges reach are very often at odds with what the people would have decided had they been allowed to do so. Put simply, the new regime has no respect for, and hence no hesitancy about flouting, the widely- and long-held moral convictions of the people. In cases involving abortion, physician-assisted suicide, homosexuality, state-supported same-sex education, and state support of religion, the courts have imposed policies that most people find deplorable and have struck down policies that most people find praiseworthy.

Bork complains, therefore, that currently the Supreme Court is, "despite the moral objections of most Americans," legislating the "fads" of the "cultural elite" to which most of the judges belong.[11] Russell Hittinger argues that the Court's right to privacy jurisprudence—which began in *Griswold v. Connecticut* (1965) as a "judicial attempt to stretch the Constitution to make it better reflect the traditions and conscience of the people"—quickly evolved into "a reason for constitutionally invalidating those very traditions as the ground for public policies and laws."[12] Today, any attempt on the part of the people to "address legislatively common concerns in terms of traditional morality must pass through a gauntlet of judge-made law." And the effect in many cases is "to place public expressions of traditional morality outside the new political order."[13] To sum up, in the words of a sympathetic commentator on the symposium, James C. Dobson, "On the most essential matters of human life and conscience, the courts have systematically invalidated the will of the people."[14]

Over a century and a half ago, Tocqueville, having examined modern democracy in its infancy, perceived its tendency to degenerate into just such a despotism as the *First Things* symposium describes. He recognized that effective political control could fall into the hands of a minority, and in *Democracy in America* teaches that under certain circumstances "even the smallest party need not give up hope of becoming master of public affairs." Moreover, he recognized the likelihood that such a ruling minority will seek to impose its own moral and cultural "fads" upon an unconvinced public. Thus his book says of this faction that "their caprice controls everything, changing laws and tyrannizing over moral standards."[15]

Tocqueville's project, however, is more comprehensive than that of the *First Things* symposiasts. While the latter describes, draws out the implications of, and asks how we should respond to the nascent despotism with which we are faced, the former is nothing less than the search for full knowledge of the "shape of democracy itself . . . its inclinations, character, prejudices, and passions."[16] Tocqueville, then, offers an account of the possible causes of democracy's transformation into despotism and in the process confronts us with an uncomfortable but crucial question: Is the ultimate cause of that transformation rooted in the very nature of democracy? He forces us to face the disquieting possibility that America's apparent slide toward judicial tyranny is not the result of accidental historical causes—say, for example, the mistaken appointment of misguided individuals to the Supreme Court, or even the mistaken adoption of misguided constitutional traditions like judicial review—but rather the working out of tendencies necessarily present in democracy. Thus, we draw from *Democracy in America* a more profound and more profoundly disturbing account of the usurpation upon which the symposium comments.

The immediate cause of the rise of despotism is, according to Tocqueville, an apolitical public, a lack of interest in public affairs on the part of the people. The "few" come to dominate politics, he writes, because the "crowd" is "absent or inattentive." The former "alone are on the move while the others rest."[17] Indeed, Tocqueville would perhaps hold that the symposium misidentifies the primary problem, which is less the "judicial usurpation of politics" than the public abdication of politics.

To be fair, some participants in the symposium notice the connection between the Court's assertiveness and the public's indifference. Bork, for example, observes that in the face of judicial oligarchy "the public appears supine, willing to watch democracy slip away."[18] Similarly, Hadley Arkes laments the lack of any serious public reaction to the courts' "novel and portentous" steps on issues such as "abortion, euthanasia, and 'gay rights'."[19] Of all the parties to the debate, however, William Bennett, writing in response to the symposium, addresses this connection most clearly. Observing that the people have so far declined to resist the courts by the available legal means, he suggests that "the problem is not simply with the Court" but also "with the citizenry itself." Indeed, he argues that "the heart of the matter" is "a culture of acedia" that "has taken deep root in the soil of late twentieth-century America," and "which has led to acquiescence and passivity."[20] Bennett's analysis, insofar as it points to the character of the people as the primary problem, is certainly more Tocquevillian than those offered by most of the other commentators.

Nevertheless, from Tocqueville's perspective Bennett has not yet penetrated to "the heart of the matter." For the Frenchman argues that the sloth that opens the door to despotism grows naturally in the soil of equality. That is, the "culture of acedia" that Bennett rightly identifies, the "complacency" and "servility" he rightly deplores, have their roots, according to Tocqueville, not merely "in the soil of late twentieth century America" but in the soil of democracy itself. This insight into the character of democracy is made possible through a comparison of democracy and aristocracy.

Tocqueville observes that Americans are powerfully inclined toward an excessive concern with material comforts. The "taste for physical well-being," he contends, dominates American society: It is "felt by all," and although it "is not always exclusive" of every other serious concern, "[e]veryone is preoccupied caring for the slightest needs of the body and the trivial conveniences of life."[21]

Moreover, this materialistic tendency is no accident. Rather, it is an expression of the very nature of democracy; it is not a peculiarity of the American temper but a necessity of the democratic temper. Tocqueville notes that this tendency is increasingly visible in an increasingly democratic Europe, but that in aristocracies one does not encounter this trait but rather its opposite: "[O]ne finds many people in the enjoyment of the comforts of life without their developing an exclusive taste for them."[22]

What accounts for this tendency? Tocqueville does not contend that democracy simply gives rise to the longing for material comfort. On the contrary, that desire is "universal, natural, and instinctive," and therefore is present in all societies, including aristocracy.[23] Rather his position is that the democratic state greatly intensifies this natural desire. His knowledge of this democratic vice is a result of his knowledge of aristocracy's opposite virtue.

Because an aristocracy has fixed social classes, aristocrats are born, and expect to die, rich. They have "never experienced a lot different from their own" and "have no fear of changing it."[24] As a result, they simply take physical pleasures for granted. For them, the "comforts of life" are not "the aim of their existence" but rather "just a way of living. They take them as part of existence and enjoy them without thinking about them."[25]

The peasants of an aristocracy are equally indifferent to material comfort, but for different reasons. Just as nobles grow accustomed to their wealth, the people grow accustomed to their penury: They do not think about physical comfort "because they despair of getting it and because they do not know enough about it to want it." And the social conditions of both nobles and peasants, beyond merely detaching them from material comforts, actually drive them to a positive attachment to more elevated things. With the natural longing for physical well-being "satisfied without trouble or anxiety," the aristocrats' "turn elsewhere and become involved in some grander and more difficult undertaking that inspires and engrosses them." Similarly, "the poor are," by their irremediable material deprivation, "driven to dwell in imagination on the next world."[26]

In a democracy, however, the absence of fixed social classes and the concomitant possibility of upward economic mobility emancipates the taste for physical comfort. "In America," Tocqueville observes, "I never met a citizen too poor to cast a glance of hope and envy toward the pleasures of the rich or whose imagination did not snatch in anticipation" at those pleasures. More than merely releasing this natural desire, however, democracy actually exacerbates it. If aristocracy calms the passion for physical comfort in the few by providing them with effortless satisfaction and in the many by foreclosing any expectation of satisfaction, democracy agitates this passion by providing all with a tantalizingly incomplete satisfaction. Tocqueville argues that with the abolition of privilege, the division of inheritances, and the spread of freedom and education, a great many "middling fortunes are established," which provide "enough physical enjoyments" for their owners "to get a taste for them, but not enough to content them." And since the heart is most agitated not by "the quiet possession of something precious but rather the imperfectly satisfied desire to have it and the continual fear of losing it again," the result is that everyone is "continually engaged in pursuing or striving to retain these precious, incomplete, and fugitive delights."[27]

It is this fixation on material comforts, so natural to democracy, that gives rise to the political apathy that in turn opens the door to the very despotism lamented by the *First Things* symposium and foreseen by Tocqueville. "There is," Tocqueville contends, "no need to drag their rights away from citizens" who are "[i]ntent only on getting rich," for "they themselves voluntarily let them go." Those bent on material gratifications, he continues, "find it a tiresome inconvenience to exercise political rights which distract them from industry. When required to elect representatives, to support authority by personal service, or to discuss public business together, they find they have no time. They cannot waste their time on unrewarding work."[28]

Faced with such hedonism-induced political somnolence, an ambitious individual or faction will find "the way open for usurpations of every sort." Such a tyrannical individual or group will "get away with everything else" so long as "material interests" continue to "flourish."[29]

This, it seems, is a remarkably prescient account of the rise of judicial oligarchy lamented by the participants in the *First Things* symposium. Tocqueville's argument about how democracy tends to succumb to despotism fits remarkably well with the history of how democracy has in fact tended to give way to rule by judges in modern America. The aspiring despots have behaved more or less as Tocqueville would have predicted. The judges, guided perhaps by an instinctive grasp of the democratic character's materialistic bent, have safely confined their usurpations largely to questions of social policy while almost entirely avoiding economic policy. They brazenly attack the citizen's moral beliefs, but they timidly decline to touch his pocketbook. Of course, one can cite a number of cases in which courts have provoked intense public animosity by ordering the levying of taxes to pay for some pet project of social engineering; but such actions have been largely limited to lower courts and have therefore affected only local communities. In contrast, the illegitimate judicial legislation issued by the Supreme Court has touched the entire population, but also has been cautiously confined to issues—abortion, pornography, school prayer—that radically remake the average American's moral universe without disturbing his bank account.

Moreover, the people have also behaved as Tocqueville would have predicted. Since the Second World War, America has enjoyed a remarkable growth in material prosperity, and during that period her citizens have been largely content, in Robert Bork's words, "to watch democracy slip away." The American judiciary's breathtaking departures from the country's legal and moral traditions have excited no widespread and sustained outrage, provoking nothing more than fleeting public disapproval, followed by seemingly permanent acquiescence. The public mind is apparently preoccupied with something besides politics, and the only likely object of that preoccupation is physical comfort. After all, the alternative explanation of the public's political apathy, that Americans are engrossed in things higher than politics—say, philosophy and the fine arts—is simply too incredible to merit serious consideration. The average American, it seems, does not mind the radical remaking of his moral universe by judges—at least he can tolerate it without too much fuss—so long as he can enjoy economic prosperity.

THE NEED FOR SPIRITUAL STATESMANSHIP

For Tocqueville, preventing democracy's descent into despotism depends upon sufficiently restraining the people's materialism to keep them interested in politics. The means to this end he finds in religion, which alone, he believes, can turn democratic citizens away from the gratification of their selfish desires and toward the fulfillment of their public duties. Tocqueville remarks that, on Sunday in America, trade and industry cease and are replaced by a "deep repose, or rather solemn contemplation" of things spiritual. Turning to Holy Scripture, the American finds "sublime and touching accounts of the greatness and goodness of the Creator, of the infinite magnificence of the works of God, of the high destiny reserved for men, of their duties and of their claims to immortality." Religion appears to hinder despotism by explicitly attacking democracy's tendency toward materialism-induced indifference to politics, thus encouraging public-spiritedness. In church Americans are reminded of "the need to check" their "desires," "of the finer delights which go with virtue alone," and "of their duties."[30] That these obligations are specifically public in nature is suggested elsewhere, when Tocqueville observes that faith is especially useful among "egalitarian peoples" because "[e]very religion . . . imposes on each man some obligations toward mankind, to be performed in common with the rest of mankind," thus countering the democratic inclination of each man to think "only of himself."[31]

Because religion is so indispensable to the survival of freedom in conditions of equality, the fostering of faith is, according to Tocqueville, the essence of true democratic statesmanship. He speaks of "the lawgiver's art," the "essence" of which "is by anticipation to appreciate the natural bents of human societies in order to know where the citizens' efforts need support and where there is more need to hold them back." In an aristocracy, he contends, the "hereditary wealth of some and the irremediable poverty of others" work together to divert men from "the thought of bettering their lot" and holds them "in a state of torpor, fixed on the contemplation of another world." Therefore, the lawgiver's art as applied to aristocracy requires that statesmen counter its excessive indifference to material well being by finding ways to encourage the pursuit of prosperity. Tocqueville immediately adds, however, that "[l]egislators for democracies have other cares": "[I]t is ever the duty of lawgivers and of all upright educated men to raise up the souls of their fellow citizens and turn their attention toward heaven. There is a need for all who are interested in the future of democratic societies to get together and with one accord to make continual efforts to propagate throughout society a taste for the infinite, an appreciation of greatness, and a love of spiritual pleasures."[32]

This is to be accomplished, it seems, primarily by the good example of the statesman himself. Tocqueville, almost embarrassed to present his teaching, writes that "What I am going to say will certainly do me harm in the eyes of politicians. I think that the only effective means which governments can use to make the doctrine of the immortality of the soul respected is daily to act as if they believed it themselves. I think that it is only by conforming scrupulously to religious morality in great affairs that they can flatter themselves that they are teaching the citizens to understand it and to love and respect it in little matters."[33]

It is important to note, however, that this example is not to be set merely in their behavior as private citizens. It is, apparently, insufficient for democratic politicians merely to attend church and live personally as if the goods of the soul are as much to be desired as those of the body. Rather, this edifying example must be set in their behavior as statesmen; it must shine forth in their performance of their public duties. Thus Tocqueville insists that they must respect religious morality "in great affairs" and asserts that this duty belongs not just to citizens who happen to hold political authority but to "governments" themselves. In the laws they advocate and the policies they adopt, they must teach that the goods of the soul are important; they must not treat material prosperity as if it is the foremost public issue.

Tocqueville and the Symposium's Critics

In the light of this analysis of democracy's ills and their remedy, the despotic developments discussed in the *First Things* symposium appear all the more disturbing, for they are not only the bad effects of the people's materialism-induced indifference to politics. They tend also to delegitimize the spiritual statesmanship that is the only means to restrain that materialism and thus avert the consequent political apathy and loss of freedom. In other words, the courts' recent decisions are not only symptoms of the prime democratic disease, but also amount to an attack on the remedy. The tendency of contemporary constitutional jurisprudence, the editors of *First Things* point out, is to rule religion out of the "public square," to use Father Neuhaus's term. Law, as it is made by the courts today, has "declared its independence" from the "morality associated with religion," which "has been declared legally suspect and a threat to public order."[34] From Tocqueville's standpoint, America's judges have made themselves the enemies of democratic freedom by declaring war on the only thing that can prevent equality of social conditions from giving rise to political despotism, a robust role for religion in public life—even as a basis for public policy and law.

In addition to lending support to the *First Things* symposium's condemnation of the course currently pursued by the courts, Tocqueville's account suggests that certain criticims of the symposium strike wide of the mark because they are based upon a misunderstanding of democracy's nature and needs. On Tocqueville's analysis, what some critics regard as a threat to democracy is really no threat at all, while the understanding of politics they think most conducive to the preservation of democracy is actually a potent threat. Standing Tocqueville's argument on its head, they apparently view religion as democracy's bane and materialism as its salvation.

Certain critics of the symposium charge its participants with advocating theocracy. Jacob Heilbrunn styles the contributors to the symposium "theocons," conservative intellectuals who, he says, "are attempting to construct a Christian theory of politics that directly threatens the entire neoconservative philosophy" based upon the Declaration of Independence. The theocons believe that this country is founded not on the theory of "the rights of man" as articulated in the Declaration, but rather in the "ideal" of "Christianity." For them, "America is first and foremost a Christian nation," one that "accepts the idea of a transcendent divine law that carries universal obligations even for nonbelievers."[35]

Heilbrunn rejects what he takes to be the theocon position as contrary to the American spirit. Theoconservatism, according to him, is an "ideology to which only the faithful can subscribe," and hence incompatible with the rationally discernible and universally accessible principles of government upon which America is founded. On Heilbrunn's view, America's Constitution is "religiously neutral," and any attempt to impose "divine right" upon it is "un-American."[36]

A similar criticism also emerges from the right, specifically from Walter Berns, who holds that the "paleoconservative misunderstanding" that the Constitution is more Burkean than Lockean "has now been carried one step further by Father Richard John Neuhaus" and his "fellow essayists." These writers believe, according to Berns, that "the Constitution is essentially a religious document, embodying the moral law, and specifically. . . the natural law as espoused by Thomas Aquinas in the thirteenth century and enunciated in various papal encyclicals even today."[37]

Berns, like Heilbrunn, rejects the position he attributes to the symposium's participants as incompatible with the

American spirit, suggesting that the revolution was not based upon an appeal to traditional religious morality, but was rather undertaken in opposition to a king who was a representative of that very morality. He argues further that the Founders believed zealously-held religious opinions to be a danger to democracy, and that the Constitution they designed accordingly sought to minimize that danger by "consigning religion to the private sphere by separating church and state."[38]

Of course, the charge that the symposium's authors advocate theocracy is on its face absurd. Heilbrunn and Berns present no evidence that the authors seek a special constitutional status for Christianity or the morality associated with it—for the simple reason that there is no such evidence to be found. Nowhere in the symposium does any writer suggest that the Constitution is or should be considered a "religious document," that it should be infused with "divine right," or that it should be anything other than "religiously neutral." Nowhere in the symposium does any writer suggest that the Christian faith or the morality associated with it should have a constitutionally official or even privileged position in America. Rather, they merely object to the tendency of recent court decisions to disqualify Christian morality as a basis of public policy. They do not seek to enshrine Christian morality in our constitutional law, but only to resist those who misinterpret the Constitution to forbid that morality from being embodied in our statutory law and thereby arbitrarily deny Christianity the more robust public role it would otherwise naturally enjoy in a nation in which most citizens consider themselves Christians.

It is perplexing that such a patently false charge would

be brought by such apparently reasonable men. In order to avoid the implausible conclusion that they simply failed to understand the arguments advanced in the symposium, one is forced to surmise that, in the minds of Heilbrunn and Berns, the level constitutional playing field sought by the symposium's authors is so likely to lead to theocracy (or something very like it), that it is justifiable to label the advocacy of the former advocacy of the latter. In other words, behind Heilbrunn's and Berns's overheated rhetoric is perhaps the fear that the if the role of religon in our public life is not circumscribed by the courts, it will grow dangerously overbearing and amount eventually to a practical, if not constitutionally official, theocracy that threatens the liberty of non-believers. Such a fear seems to animate Berns, for example, when he expresses concern about what a "Christian commonwealth" would "do with" the Jews.[39] Such fears, moreover, are not altogether unreasonable. One can point to any number of sorry historical episodes in which the misplaced zeal of some believers has led to the political persecution of those who did not share the faith.

Tocqueville's account of democracy, however, suggests that any fear of the potential dangers of religion's public influence must be weighed against the potential dangers of its absence from public life. If it is true that an immoderate religious influence on politics is a threat to liberty, it is no less true that the lack of religious influence also threatens liberty. If religion's political role may lead to a faith-based tyranny of the majority, religion's absence from politics may, as we have seen, lead to a tyranny of the minority. Prudence, then, calls not for a dogmatic insistence upon religion's salutary political influence, on the one hand, or upon its political perniciousness, on the other, but rather for a careful estimation of whether in present circumstances religion is more likely to be helpful or dangerous. Put another way, we must judge which is more of a threat to democracy, religion or the materialism it restrains.

The argument of *Democracy in America* leaves little room for doubt that Tocqueville considers materialism the much greater threat of the two. As we have seen, he believes materialism is rooted in the very nature of democracy itself. It is necessarily the tendency of souls formed by the democratic social state. Religion, on the other hand, is rooted much more weakly in democracy. Indeed, Tocqueville suggests that religion is not rooted in democracy at all, that it is in fact alien to the spirit of democracy. Hence, he characterizes religion as a "heritage from aristocratic times."[40] Religious belief, it seems, is not natural to democracy: Faith does not emerge spontaneously under conditions of social equality.

The most obvious ground for Tocqueville's judgment on this score is the naturalness of materialism to the democratic temper itself. The ardent longing for physical comforts and the concomitant fixation of the imagination upon this world which arise so naturally from social equality clearly pose a serious obstacle to religious faith. There are, however, other aspects of equality that render the citizens of a democracy psychologically predisposed to reject religion, or at least to take it with minimal seriousness.

Democracy, Tocqueville argues, tends not to respect the wisdom of ancestors. Writing of the "Philosophical approach of the Americans," he observes that their belief in intellectual equality disinclines Americans to accept any intellectual authority. There is in America "a general distaste for accepting any man's word as proof of anything." Instead, they "seek by themselves and in themselves for the only reason for things."[41] This lack of trust, moreover, extends to tradition. And since religion, as we have seen, is not natural to democracy but rather exists there only as a "heritage from aristocratic times," that is, as a tradition, it seems unlikely to survive long as a vital force in men's minds.[42]

Moreover, Tocqueville suggests that democracy is by its nature hostile not only to traditional religious beliefs but to faith itself. As he continues his discussion of the American philosophic approach, he observes "other mental habits" that result from the intellectual independence typical of democracy. Impressed by their own ability to surmount without assistance the minor problems of daily life, Americans "are easily led to the conclusion that everything in the world can be explained and that nothing passes the limits of intelligence." Consequently, "they are ready to deny anything they cannot understand" and "have little faith in anything extraordinary and an almost invincible distaste for the supernatural."[43]

Such citizens as Tocqueville believes democracy inevitably tends to produce—obsessed with material comforts, distrustful of religion's traditional authority, and disinclined to believe in the existence of things unseen—are hardly the sort to be easily led into tyrannical enterprises rationalized on the basis of religion. Thus, from Tocqueville's standpoint, Berns's and Heilbrunn's fear of religion's political influence is misplaced, based on an insufficient knowledge of democracy. One can go much further than they realize in fostering the public role of religion without incurring any serious danger of theocratic tyranny—at least any danger of theocratic tyranny serious enough to compare with the danger of materialism.

Indeed, so mistaken are some of the symposium's critics that they actually seem to advocate a public life based only on materialistic concerns, and thus to strengthen the very tendency that Tocqueville believes is so deadly to liberty. Ramesh Ponnuru rightly notes the existence of a pronounced "Hobbesian streak among conservative critics of the symposium." This streak was most evident, according to Ponnuru, in *National Review's* criticism of the symposium. This criticism held that "Our general obligation to obey the laws rests upon the fact that the laws protect us (against our fellow man), not upon the ultimate justice of the government's founding, still less (fortunately) upon its general moral character." Here we find none of the concern with liberty or self-government that characterizes the thought of the symposiasts, Tocqueville, and, as Ponnuru rightly observes, America's founding generation.[44] Here instead we find an understanding of politics that appears purely materialistic: government's primary, and perhaps only, task is to protect citizens from bodily harm. Here we find a single-minded concern with physical well-being that not only excludes the spiritual statesmanship Tocqueville deems necessary to the preservation of liberty within democracy, but actually encourages the democratic materialism that so threatens liberty.

Berns argues that the founders sought to protect "republican (or limited) government" by constitutionally "confining the business of government to issues that did not give rise to zeal, anger, or moral indignation." He thus concludes that "Calvin Coolidge was not altogether

wrong when he said the nation's business was business."
After all, Berns continues, "James Madison said much the
same thing in *The Federalist*, Number 10. The government's business, he said, or at least its 'first object,' is the
protection of men's 'different and unequal faculties,' especially those 'from which the rights of property origi-
nate.' The result would be a variety of interests—landed,
manufacturing, mercantile, moneyed—and regulating these
various and interfering interests is 'the principal task of
modern legislation.'"[45]

Again we are confronted with a conservative view utterly devoid of expressed interest in the maintenance of
self-government. True, Berns does hold that the confine-
ment of politics to questions of commerce is undertaken
with a view to the protection of "republican" government;
but, as he makes clear, by republican government he means
merely "limited" government. Berns displays no interest
in the preservation of government that is republican in
the sense that it guarantees the people's ability to participate, however indirectly, in ruling themselves. Instead,
he offers a vision of public life which, because it is focused primarily on material well-being, leaves no room
for the spiritual statesmanship Tocqueville prescribes and
which in fact encourages the very liberty-destroying
materialism that Tocqueville hopes to remedy.

HOPE OR DESPAIR?

There is, among those who agree that judicial usurpation
is real and poses a serious threat to our democracy, disagreement over whether to be optimistic or pessimistic
about the possibility of reform. Or, to put it more accu-

rately, there is disagreement over the extent to which we should be pessimistic.

Such optimism as can be found among this group is concealed in the dire predictions of the symposium's editors. Their introduction suggests that judicial usurpation, if it continues, could prove "fatal" to "popular support for our present system of government."[46] "What is happening now," the editors argue, "is a growing alienation of millions of Americans from a government they do not recognize as theirs; what is happening now is an erosion of moral adherence to the political system." They ask us to consider "the consequences when many millions of children are told and come to believe that the government that rules them is morally illegitimate."[47] A concern similar to this one is raised by Charles Colson, who claims that contemporary judicial usurpation calls into question "whether millions of Americans are still part of the 'We the People' from which democratic authority is presumably derived."[48]

The possibility of such mass alienation is of course alarming in one sense: No one can say with certainty what would happen if the government came to be widely perceived as illegitimate. At the same time, this possibility is also comforting. After all, the prospect of a large-scale withdrawal of popular support could lead to significant reform, the rollback of judicial usurpation, the restoration of democracy.

Such optimism, however, is rejected unequivocally by James C. Dobson in his response to the symposium. He observes that "any institutional reforms will require a groundswell of public support" that he doubts will emerge. "On this matter," he says,

the editors are more optimistic than I . . . I doubt
very much that our culture, having established tol-
erance as the new absolute, has the moral rectitude
to insist that the government move in the direction
of traditional morality. The flaw in the design of
our system of government has been revealed not
merely because our courts (as well as our legislatures)
are creating law ex nihilo, but because our culture
is operating on the same philosophical premise, stated
in *Casey*, that we all have a fundamental right to
create and live by our own sense of reality.[49]

Our discussion suggests that Tocqueville would disagree with some of the particulars of Dobson's argument,
but would agree with his conclusion about the prospects
for a rollback of the moral tyranny of the contemporary
judiciary. Tocqueville would no doubt agree with Dobson that our culture lacks the "moral rectitude" necessary
for significant reform. Yet he would probably disagree
with Dobson's characterization of our moral failing. On
the Frenchman's account, the problem is not that the citizens of a democracy are inclined to accept a nihilistic
moral, political, and legal theory, but rather that they are
far too interested in the pursuit of physical comforts to
care about or even notice such theories and their public
consequences. The normal American would probably
reject, upon reflection, the democratized Nietzscheanism
expressed by Justices Kennedy, Souter, and O'Connor in
the *Casey* decision. The trouble is that it is extremely difficult to get the democratic citizen to reflect on or care about
such questions.

Indeed, Tocqueville insists that the materialism to
which democracy is susceptible is "decent" and not de-

praved. Democratic materialism is extreme not in the sense that it seeks or approves the sort of extravagant or bizarre sensuality that would seem to be permitted by the any-thing-goes philosophy of the *Casey* dictum. Rather, it is extreme in the sense that it is excessively interested in physical pleasures that are, in themselves, unobjection-able. Democratic materialism is characterized not by "sumptuous depravity and startling corruption"—which, on the contrary, are the part of decadent aristocrats—but by the almost complete abandonment of "the heart, imagi-nation, and life itself" to morally permissible physical pleasures.[50] Democratic man, unlike his aristocratic coun-terpart, has neither means nor imagination capacious enough to lead him into outlandishly evil indulgences. On the contrary, the precariousness of his economic circum-stances, his need to work to maintain the level of com-fort he desires, guarantees that he will not allow for himself, nor approve for others, physical pleasures incompatible with a certain orderliness of life.

On Tocqueville's account, then, in contrast to Dobson's, the problem is not so much that the people approve the moral innovations imposed on the country by the courts as that the people are not disposed to care very much even though they do disapprove. Nevertheless, Tocqueville's understanding of democracy also leads him to pessimism about democracy's prospects. Like Dobson, Tocqueville sees little reason to believe that millions of Americans will come to view the new regime as illegitimate. After all, the Frenchman would hold, judicial usurpation has already progressed so far not in spite of, but because of, the people, because of their indifference. The cause of the emerging despotism is not, Tocqueville teaches, the imperiousness of judges, so much as the slavishness of the people. Our difficulty is not that democracy has been snatched away from a public-spirited citizenry by an ambitious judiciary. Rather it is that rule has been ceded to an ambitious judiciary by a citizenry apparently more interested in widescreen televisions and backyard swimming pools than in maintaining its legitimate political authority. Moreover, materialism and the political apathy to which it gives rise are not accidents of time and place, but rooted in the nature of democracy itself. A popular preoccupation with physical comforts, Tocqueville teaches, is a necessary consequence of social equality, which, by allowing upward economic mobility, emancipates the desire for material well-being. And the natural consequence of materialism is political apathy, which opens the way to despotism.

Tocqueville's appreciation of the weakness of the only available remedy for democratic materialism also leads to pessimism. That remedy is, as we have seen, religious belief. In contrast to the concerns raised by certain critics of the symposium, Tocqueville's teaching suggests a confidence that democracy will not succumb to a religion-inspired tyranny of the majority. The basis of that confidence is his awareness of the natural weakness of religion's hold upon the democratic imagination. The natural corollary of this confidence in democracy's immunity to pernicious religious influence, however, is a fear of democracy's immunity to salutary religious influence. Tocqueville's account of democracy's spirituality-stunting materialism, its distrust of traditional religious beliefs, and its distaste for faith suggests the disquieting possibility that the spiritual statesmanship he advocates as necessary to democracy's salvation will have little effect.

Despite the sobriety of his judgement about the future of democracy, Tocqueville is no counselor of despair. His book, after all, has as its purpose the improvement of democracy. He offers his "new political science" in the hope that democratic leaders will learn from it how to restrain democracy's "blind instincts" and secure its "true interests" and thus turn equality "to the profit of mankind."[51] Hence he concludes his book by insisting that enlightened political action can render equality compatible with freedom.[52]

Perhaps, then, it is better to say that Tocqueville, while he is without question more inclined to Dobson's pessimism than to the implied optimism of the *First Things* editors, is nonetheless somewhat more optimistic than Dobson. Dobson is pessimistic because of his awareness of our culture's corruption. Tocqueville would probably agree with Dobson about the extent—though not, as we have seen, the character—of our culture's corruption. The basis of Tocqueville's slender hope, is his acknowledgement of something more fundamental than culture, human nature, which culture can greatly influence but never completely eradicate. Tocqueville teaches that the desire for spiritual pleasures is "natural to the human heart," and therefore physical comforts can never fully satisfy human beings.[53] There must remain, even in the soul of the democratic man, some glimmering of a natural dissatisfaction with the materialism that threatens to destroy democratic liberty and a natural receptivity to the spiritual statesmanship that can save it.

7

THE QUEST FOR EQUITY

Frederick Vaughan

> *The judicial Power shall extend to all Cases in*
> *Law and Equity arising under this Constitution,*
> *the Laws of the United States, and Treaties made,*
> *or which shall be made, under their authority.*

> Constitution of the United States,
> Article III, sec. 2

I F WE WERE TO ASK AMERICAN JUDGES to give an account of those judgments the *First Things* symposiasts found objectionable, they would not admit to "usurpation." Rather, they would be inclined to describe their work as that of finding a fair, or equitable, solution to contentious social or moral issues. They would say that they act as "judges in equity" in such cases. The equity power, derived from English common law and enshrined in the Constitution,[1] is most readily understood as the power of judges to "do the right thing" in a particular case where adherence to the letter of the law, intended by the law-makers to implement a certain idea of justice, would inadvertently produce in a specific instance an injustice. A standard example relates to contracts. In general, the common law assumes that valid contracts are binding and the courts will enforce them. But the equity power gives judges the authority to refuse to enforce formally valid contracts when to do so would result in substantive injustice. Equity is thus available to the judge to mitigate the severity of the law due to its generality.

Those who worry about the alarming pace, over the past few decades, of judicial intrusion into the legislative sphere find the judicial appeal to equity unsatisfactory. To many American and non-American observers, it seems that American judges lean towards a "lower law", that is, the imperatives of modern liberal culture which are grounded in the primacy of bodily pleasure and convenience. This new lower positivism favors and sponsors abortion, homosexual "lifestyles," and all publicly funded efforts to impose "progressive values," especially those "values" which are in explicit opposition to the traditional Judeo-Christian norms of public and private morality.

This peculiar form of judicial activism has been associated, until recently, almost exclusively with the United States Supreme Court. But it has begun to surface in other Anglo–Saxon-based democracies.[2] For example, a Canadian judge in early October, 1997, struck down Ontario legislation that denied recognition to "same-sex couples." The judge wrote that the law "simply carries forward and nurtures now abandoned stereotypical concepts that have no place in the fabric of our community." He went on to say that "the denial of equal benefit contained in the legislative provisions is deliberately based only on sexual orientation and runs against the preservation of human dignity and self-worth for part of our society." The issue of the intrusive activism of the judiciary is therefore important for more than American citizens.

The roots of judicial usurpation may be traced to the corruption of the long established Anglo-Saxon judicial quest for equity and the duty imposed on judges to seek the equitable in specific cases. More provocatively stated: Are not judges trained in the Anglo-Saxon tradition, who read substance into the law or the intention of the legislature, doing what they are supposed to do as judges in equity? In a certain sense the U. S. courts are doing what the legislators do not have the power or the audacity to do, that is, openly defy majority sentiment. The liberal legislator loves the liberal judge because he will dare to do what the legislator would not dare to do.

I begin with ancient sources on equity and then review the leading modern authorities on the British constitution, especially Francis Bacon, Lord Coke, Thomas Hobbes, Baron Montesquieu, and William Blackstone. In the concluding pages I turn to nineteenth-century authorities and uncover a new teaching on equity that emerged at this time in John Austin's *The Province of Jurisprudence Determined.*

EQUITY IN THE ANCIENT WORLD

The modern teachings on equity have much in common with the teachings of the ancient political philosophers. For both Aristotle and Hobbes, for example, the judge in equity was duty-bound to apply the imperfect expression of the law—imperfect due to its universality—to specific cases, keeping in mind always the intention of the legislator or sovereign. Aristotle, in his *Poetics*, states that ". . . equity is that idea of justice which contravenes the written law. And this contradiction happens partly indeed against the will, and partly with the will of the legislator: it then happens against the will, when the question may have escaped his notice; but, with his will, whenever he has it not in his power accurately to make distinction, but it is necessary that he pronounce universally, though the case be not so absolutely without exceptions, but generally only."[3] In the same work, Aristotle observes that "Equity also is the having a sympathy for human failings; and the having an eye, not to the law but to the lawgiver; and not to the language, but to the intention of the lawgiver. And not to the conduct, but to the principles of the agent; not to his conduct in one particular, but to its whole tenor."[4]

In the *Nichomachean Ethics*, in his most explicit treatment of equity, Aristotle explains the relation of justice and equity in the following manner:

> The same thing then is just and equitable, and while both are good the equitable is superior. What creates the problem is that the equitable is just, not however the legally just, but a corrective of legal justice. This is because all law is universal, whereas there are some things about which it is not possible to make a universal statement that shall be correct. In those cases, therefore, in which it is necessary to speak universally, but impossible to do so correctly, the law takes the usual case though not unmindful of the possibility of error. And it is none the less

right in doing so; for the error is neither in the law nor in the legislator, but in the nature of the thing, since the material of practical affairs is of this kind from the start.[5]

Before a contemporary judge rushes to embrace this comment in justification of his activism, he would be well-advised to ponder Aristotle's conclusions on this matter: "And so when the law speaks universally, and a case arises which does not fall within the terms of that universal statement, then it is right, where the legislator fails us and *has erred by an excess of simplicity,* to correct his omission by saying what he himself would have said if he had been present and would have included in the law if he had foreseen such a case."[6] The implications are clear from what Aristotle says: The judge is obliged to follow the will of the legislator.

Aristotle concludes his treatment of equity with the remark that since all law is defective by virtue of its universality, the search for the equitable necessarily follows. "It is for this reason," he concludes, "why all things are not determined by law. There are some things for which it is impossible to frame a law, and recourse must be to an executive decree."

COURTS OF CONSCIENCE?

The early modern period was dominated by the thought of Thomas Hobbes. And anyone even remotely familiar with his work knows that Hobbes would never countenance a role for judges which would permit them to usurp the prerogatives of the sovereign, be it of one man or an assembly of men. Indeed, Hobbes's entire life's work was given over to establishing the supreme sovereignty of the civil power. As Joseph Cropsey has put it, Hobbes's enterprise could be summed up in the attempt at the "resumption of the supreme clerical power into the civil sovereign." All his efforts were directed towards "the resumption of the supreme judicial power into the civil authority . . . [where the] private priests of (legal) reason must be checked as the private priests of revelation needed to be checked."[7]

For Hobbes there could be no separation of power, let alone a judiciary armed with the ability to correct the legislative authority. The "right of judicature," that is to say, "of hearing and deciding all controversies, which may arise concerning law, either civil or natural; or concerning fact," must reside in the sovereign.[8] There could be no doubt that the "judgment of what is reasonable, and of what is to be abolished, belongeth to him that maketh the law, which is the sovereign assembly or monarch."[9] As for equity, Hobbes defines it as "the equal distribution to each man of that which in reason belongeth to him."[10] And Hobbes makes it abundantly clear that it is not private reason of individuals that judges what is reasonable: "It is not meant of any private reason; for then there would be as much contradiction in the laws, as there is in the Schools."[11] And everyone knows what Hobbes thought of the discord sown by "the Schools."

Nor is the reason to be found in the musings of Sir Edward Coke, for Hobbes explicitly says "nor yet, as Sir Edward Coke makes it; an *artificial perfection of reason, gotten by long study,* observation *and experience,* as his was."[12] And lest anyone remain in doubt, Hobbes concludes "it is not *that juris prudentia,* or wisdom of subordinate judges;

but the reason of this our artificial man the commonwealth, and his command, that maketh law."[13] As for anything remotely resembling judicial review, Hobbes says "In all courts of justice, the sovereign, which is the person of the commonwealth, is he that judgeth: the subordinate judge, ought to have regard to the reason, which moved his sovereign to make such law, that his sentence may be according thereunto; which then is his sovereign's sentence; otherwise it is his own, and an unjust one."[14]

One of the most celebrated early modern statements on the role or function of judges was penned by Lord Chancellor Bacon. In his famous essay "Of Judicature," Bacon begins with the assertion that "Judges ought to remember that their office is *jus dicere*, and not *'jus dare'*— to interpret law, and not to make law, or give law."[15] And he warns that "judges must beware of hard constructions and strained inferences, for there is no worse torture than the torture of laws." The closest Bacon comes to discussing equity in this essay is when he says that "In causes of life and death, judges ought (as far as the law permitteth) in justice to remember mercy, and to cast a severe eye upon the example, but a merciful eye upon the person."[16] But one notes that even here Bacon restricts the judge's mercy by the constraint "as far as the law permitteth." There was, in short, no room for the free roaming of judges; they were to be, wrote Bacon, "lions, but yet lions under the throne; being circumspect, that they do not check or oppose any points of sovereignty."[17]

These sentiments embroiled Bacon in a long and heated controversy with Lord Coke, the great champion of the common laws of England. On its face, the common law, that is, judge-made law, so strong a part of English domestic law, would tend to give legitimacy to judicial activism. And this was one thing both Bacon and Hobbes attempted to prevent. Yet as early as 1690, equity in England had virtually ceased to evolve as a corrective to the common law. "The evolution of the doctrine of binding precedent must be blamed for this," according to R. J. Walker and M. G. Walker, "though the conservatism of the judges doubtless played a part."[18] And by 1878 the Master of the Rolls, Sir George Jessel, made the pronouncement that "This Court is not, as I have often said, a Court of Conscience, but a Court of Law."[19] But equity, however much refined and restricted to procedural matters, remained a solid part of the English law. As George Burton Adams has noted,

> There is no escape from the conclusion that institutionally the modern system of equity has come down to us in a continuous and unbroken growth from the system which was started upon a new development by the reforms of Henry II. There is no point between 1066 and the twentieth century where there occurs such a break that we cannot easily see the passage of the institutions which were administering equity through and beyond it. In fact there is no break at all. The institutional history of equity is as continuous as the history of the English language from the same date.[20]

THE SPIRIT OF THE LAWS

Writing on the English constitution in the middle of the eighteenth century, Montesquieu, in *The Spirit of the Laws*, went beyond recommending the institutional separation of the judicial power from the other two powers. There is a very clear sense that Montesquieu believed the judicial branch of government more likely to establish tyranny than either the legislative or the executive branches. Montesquieu's aim in writing about the judiciary was not simply to call attention to the need for the separation of this third branch of government from the other two, he was concerned to show that it must become invisible:

> The judiciary power ought not to be given to a standing senate; it should be exercised by persons taken from the body of the people at certain times of the year, and consistently with a form and manner prescribed by law, in order to erect a tribunal that should last only so long as necessity requires. By this method the judicial power, so terrible to mankind, not being annexed to any particular state or profession, becomes, as it were, invisible. People have not then the judges continually present to their view; they fear the office, but not the magistrate."[21]

The members of this judiciary are to be taken from the body of the people, whereas the representatives who constitute the legislative body ought not to be chosen "from the general body of the nation." "The judges ought likewise to be of the same rank as the accused, or, in other words, his peers; to the end that he may not imagine he is fallen into the hands of persons inclined to treat him with rigor."[22] Not surprising, there is no room in Montesquieu's theory for anything resembling equity. Indeed, Montesquieu appears determined to leave little room for equity when he says that though the courts "ought not to be fixed, the judgments ought; and to such a degree as to be ever conformable to the letter of the law. Were they to be the private opinion of the judge, people would then live in society, without exactly knowing the nature of their obligations."[23]

Later in the eighteenth century William Blackstone, the first Vinerian professor of Law at Oxford argued in his famous commentaries that the courts could and must serve as a corrective to bad legislation. Indeed, he wrote in 1753, "almost all the perplexed questions, almost all the niceties, intricacies and delays (which have sometimes disgraced the English, as well as other courts of justice) owe their original not to the common law itself, but to innovations that have been made in it by acts of parliament."[24] Nevertheless, he made it clear that judges were there to enforce the will of the legislature: "[T]he fairest and most rational method to interpret the will of the legislator, is by exploring his intentions at the time when the law was made, by signs the most natural and probable. And these signs are either the words, the context, the subject matter, the effects and consequences, or the spirit or reason of the law."

As for equity, that depends "essentially upon the particular circumstances of each individual case, there can be no established rules and fixed precepts of equity laid down without destroying its very essence and reducing it to a positive law."[25] Be that as it may, Blackstone was adamant that "the liberty of considering all cases in an equitable light must not be indulged too far, lest thereby we destroy all law, and leave the decision of every question entirely in the breast of the judge." He concluded his reflections on this aspect of the English law with the warning that "law without equity, though hard and disagreeable, is much more desirable for the public good, than equity without law: which would make every judge a legislator, and introduce most infinite confusion; as there would then be almost as many different rules of action laid down in our courts, as there are differences of capacity and sentiment in the human mind."[26]

The Assault on Equity

The formal assault on the English practice of equity which had been in place for so many centuries came in the nineteenth century from the pen of John Austin. In a sharp rebuke to Bentham, by and large his mentor, Austin wrote in *The Province of Jurisprudence Determined*: "I cannot understand how any person who has considered the subject can suppose that society could possibly have gone on if judges had not legislated, or that there is any danger whatever in allowing them that power which they have in fact exercised, to make up for the negligence or the incapacity of the avowed legislator. That part of the law of every country which was made by judges has been far better made than that part which consists of statutes enacted by the legislative."[27]

As for Bentham, Austin concludes: "I cannot but think that, instead of blaming judges for having legislated, he should blame them for the timid, narrow, and piecemeal manner in which they have legislated, and for legislating under cover of vague and indeterminate phrases." Austin would have no cause for accusing the justices of the Supreme Court of the United States for being "timid" or "piecemeal" given their creative reading of the Constitution.

In his important study of equity and the Constitution, Gary L. McDowell identifies *Brown v. Board of Education* (1955) as the turning point in recent American constitutional jurisprudence.   According to McDowell,

> In the Brown (II) opinion, the Chief Justice planted the seed of the new sociological understanding of equity, which took as its primary concern the social class or group instead of the individual.   In subsequent opinions this new idea would be brought to fruition in the form of relieving against both *de jure* and *de facto* segregation and granting relief to those groups suffering the effects of "past discrimination".   And in each opinion based on the Brown equity principle, the Court would become more and more embroiled in the "sensitive areas of social policy".[28]

McDowell shows how the Supreme Court moved away from equity as a remedy in concrete cases, to hypothetical injuries that might at some future time emerge. Commenting on Chief Justice Earl Warren's dismissal of tangible evidence in the *Brown* case, McDowell observed that

> Warren then moved into the realm of the intangible. Applauding the social-science *obiter dicta* of the lower court in the Kansas case (in spite of which the lower court had denied relief), he boldly proclaimed that to separate children "solely because of their race generated a *feeling* of inferiority as to their status in the community that *may* affect their hearts and minds in a way *unlikely* ever to be undone" (at 494). Thus, in the realm of the intangible factors of segregation, it appears that the injury to the complainants was in no way clear, nor was it certain that the injury was irreparable.   But historically, both clarity and

irreparable injury were essential for determining whether a court of equity could exert its "extraordinary powers."[29]

There can be little doubt that McDowell has got it exactly right: The Warren decision in *Brown* opened the floodgates for a new judicial activism that has clearly usurped the legislative authority of Congress and the state legislatures. But what influenced the judiciary to take this new direction? What forces were at work, behind the scenes, as it were, that moved the Courts in this new direction?

I believe that there are two answers to these questions. First, the swell of popular opinion that arose following World War II calling for a closer scrutiny of human rights issues prodded the legal profession and the courts to re-examine their roles in protecting human rights. Americans who viewed the Nuremburg trials on television or in theatres understood that the judicial process has a peculiar role to play in ensuring the rights of citizens against the abuse of government power. If one peruses the debates in the legal literature following World War II, one finds a clear concern with "human rights" and the need for judicially enforceable constitutional provisions. This determination was reinforced by the adoption of "The Universal Declaration of Rights" by the United Nations. A strong conviction emerged throughout the Western nations following the Nuremburg trials that the judiciary must be formally engaged in the mission to ensure that Naziism would never again rise in democratic countries of the West.

Second, education in the laws schools began to undergo transformation following World War II. Immediately following the War, American law schools became alive with controversy over legal realism and over the much touted Harvard Law School "case method" of instruction. Since the case method, by definition, concentrated on how and why judges reached their decisions, the important role played by judges became a paramount concern.[30] It was left for Harvard Law professor Lon L. Fuller to identify the subtle if not pervasive influence of John Austin's views of the superiority of judge-made laws in these matters.[31] Fuller had been vigilant for years in drawing attention to Austin's influence on American legal reasoning by identifying Hans Kelsen and his "legal realists" as the principle conduit for Austin's teaching on the superiority of judge-made law.[32]

In addition to this trend in post-War legal education, there was a definite campaign by the leading law schools of the country to bring allied social science disciplines into the formal study of law. Erwin N. Griswold, Dean of Law at Harvard Law School, explicitly called for the introduction of such "extra-legal materials . . . [as] history, sociology, economics, psychology, philosophy, ethics and anthropology."[33] It is easy to understand that with this new focus the so-called "Brandeis brief"—which formally invites the court to take into account psychological, ethical, and sociological considerations previously thought to be within the province of the legislature only— becomes of greater importance. Clearly the *Brown* Court made greater use of the Brandeis brief than any previous court in American history.

It is important to keep in mind that the debate over the role of the judiciary in constitutional government necessarily involves the problem of "judicial review" it-self. As Paul Eidelberg has written, "[t]o inquire into the intended role of the Supreme Court is to enquire into the doctrine of 'judicial review'."[34] The ability of judges to strike down as unconstitutional acts of legislative bodies was foreign to common law countries until very recently. One of the greatest exports to the world at large (not simply Western nations) has been the American under-standing and practice of "judicial review." It is safe to say that no instrument of government has spread so widely throughout the world since World War II than has the power of judicial review. As Edward McWhinney has noted, "The major influence, indeed inspiration, in the present day practice of juridical review, in the Common-wealth countries, has been the Supreme Court of the United States."[35] And, one might add, where judicial review appears it is only a matter of time before judicial activism takes on a form of judicial usurpation.

It would appear that when judges adopt Austin's view of the judicial function and are armed with a constitu-tional bill or charter of rights that calls for "equal pro-tection of the laws" or "equal benefit of the law" (as in the the Canadian Charter of Rights and Freedoms), the temptation to overreach the strict intention of the legis-lature becomes virtually irresistible. In the United States, and to a lesser extent in Canada, many federal judges have succumbed to this powerful temptation. Constitutional instruments such as bills and charters of rights inevita-bly invite vested-interest litigation which, in turn, dis-torts the law by awarding in the courts what such interests could never hope to win in the legislature or at the polls. In the Canadian province of Alberta, a trial judge who had ruled that the provincial Individual's Rights Protec-tion Act (IRPA) must be interpreted to include "sexual orientation." The judge ruled that, by omitting sexual orientation, the IRPA violated the Canadian Charter of Rights and Freedoms. The trial judge dismissed the Alberta Legislature's explicit unwillingness, or two occa-sions, to include "sexual orientation" in its IRPA. The gov-ernment of Alberta appealed the decision and it was overturned by the provincial Court of Appeal. The case was appealed to the Supreme Court of Canada and that court rendered judgment on April 2, 1998. The appel-lant, Delwin Vriend, had been a laboratory instructor at a private Christian college in Alberta. The college had a policy that excluded practicing homosexuals from em-ployment. Mr. Vriend openly admitted he was a prac-ticing homosexual and was, accordingly, terminated.

The Supreme Court of Canada, in a majority judg-ment written jointly by Mr. Justice Peter Cory and Mr. Justice Frank Iacobucci, ruled that the trial judge was correct in ruling that the Alberta Individual's Rights Pro-tection Act violated the Canadian Charter of Rights and Freedoms by excluding "sexual orientation." As with the Warren Court in *Brown*, the Canadian court left the realm of particulars and based its judgment on generalities: "The exclusion of the ground of sexual orientation, considered in the context of social reality of discrimination against gays and lesbians, clearly has a disproportionate impact on them as opposed to heterosexuals. The IRPA, in its underinclusive state, therefore denies substantive equal-ity to the former group."[36] The majority concluded that "the exclusion from the IRPA's protection sends a mes-sage to all Albertans that it is permissible, and perhaps even acceptable, to discriminate against individuals on the basis of their sexual orientation."[37]

It should be noted further that the *Canadian Charter of Rights and Freedoms* excluded "sexual orientation" from its terms after extensive debate in the Parliament of Canada. The Supreme Court of Canada read "sexual orientation" into the equality provisions of the *Charter* just three years after its adoption in 1982. So, after reading "sexual orientation" into the *Charter* in 1985, the Supreme Court has now read "sexual orientation" into the Alberta statute. Neither the members of the Parliament of Canada nor the members of the Legislature of Alberta wanted this in the *Charter* or the IRPA. No matter: The Supreme Court of Canada in its wisdom has overruled the explicit and formally announced intentions of the two legislative bodies.

In the lone dissent, Mr. Justice John Major, addressed the issue of judicial usurpation and concluded that the "words 'sexual orientation' should not be read into the act . . .While reading in may be appropriate where it can be safely assumed that the legislature itself would have remedied the under-inclusiveness by extending the benefit or protection to the previously excluded group, that assumption cannot be made in the appeal." Major's partial dissent is consistent with respect for the legislative process: "[T]here are numerous ways in which the legislation could be amended to address the under-inclusiveness. As an alternative, given the legislature's persistent refusal to protect against discrimination on the basis of sexual orientation, it may be that it would choose to override the Charter breach by invoking the notwithstanding clause in Section 33 of the Charter. In any event, it should lie with the elected legislature to determine this issue."

And if anyone remains in doubt as to extent of the influence of American judicial activism on the Supreme Court of Canada they would be well to read Madam Justice L'Heureux-Dubé's extrajudicial article entitled "Making a Difference: The pursuit of a Compassionate Justice."[38] L'Heureux-Dubé makes it quite clear that her role as a justice of the Supreme Court she has a mission: "Our concern must not stop at forming a representative bench. Rather, we must extend our efforts to transform the approach to judging taken by all the members of the judiciary." L'Heureux-Dubé makes it clear here and in several of her court decisions that women judges should recognize that they have a special obligation to champion the cause of modern feminism: "I have continuously emphasized the necessity of incorporating [women's diverse experiences] in our judicial decisions. I also believe it is crucial to have more women in positions of power, whether they be judges, legislators, politicians or other important decision makers."[39]

CONCLUSION

In view of the deep entrenchment of judicial activism throughout common law countries and of the willingness of judges to enter into the preserve formerly thought to belong to democratic legislatures, the situation would appear to be hopeless. McDowell recommends that Congress and the state legislatures begin to recognize the seriousness of the problem and give consideration to restricting the equity role of the courts. He also recommends a two-fold recovery: "first, the older understanding of the problematic nature of equity in a nation based on a written constitution and dedicated to the rule of law; second, a stricter procedural distinction between law and equity."[40] But would it be possible for Congress and the States to do these things without having their efforts reviewed by the Supreme Court? And is there any likelihood that the Court would validate such efforts? The challenge, if not the solution, would appear to have judges return to the older and wiser view of equity. But is that likely when our future judges currently in the law schools are being indoctrinated with the doctrines of American liberalism so steeped in the Austin's contempt for the democratic process? Are we truly left no other option than the refusal to comply with court decisions as recommended by the *First Things* symposium?

PART III

EXTRAORDINARY POLITICS?

8

The Inauguration
of Extraordinary Politics

Scott H. Moore

W HO WOULD HAVE THOUGHT we would have arrived at an age in which disagreements between
Gertrude Himmelfarb and Richard John Neuhaus would be so grievous as to produce prolonged public debate, but that Daniel Berrigan and Ralph McInerny
would make common cause? During the fall and winter
seasons of 1996 and 1997, two events demonstrated that
the currency of the stereotypes of "liberal" and "conservative" with respect to religion and politics is now bank-
rupt. The two events in question have both been described
in the national media as "confusing" the very categories
used to make sense of our national conversation on religion and public life. "Confusing" is an understatement.
In truth, while observers of the delicate church-state
balance in this country have long recognized that "liberal" and "conservative" are at best stipulative labels, the
terms of the debate can now be recognized to be radically, if perhaps reluctantly, recast. There is much more

at stake than merely our convenient stereotypes: At issue is the continued viability of our contemporary political and religious discourse.

The events in question were the symposium (and its response) on the judicial usurpation of politics in *First Things* and the controversial hiring of a young priest at the University of Notre Dame. Critics of both lodged strong protests on both procedural and substantial grounds. On this much, at least, most agree: The church-state issues raised by the two controversies strike at the heart of questions about how Christians (and serious religious believers of all faiths) should relate to government, particularly the present government of the United States.

The cast of characters and the issues underlying these events overlap in numerous ways and place in clear relief an inadequacy of the traditional labels of "left" and "right" with respect to religion and politics. These traditional labels now seem unsatisfactory because the larger context of Enlightenment Liberalism, for which these labels were designed and within which they made sense, can no longer be taken for granted.

THE END OF DEMOCRACY?

Since its initial publication in March 1990, *First Things* has become one of the most visible national magazines on religion and perhaps the most widely read publication on religion and politics. Though it presents a wide range of opinions in its feature articles, by most standards *First Things* is a decidedly "conservative" publication. Its editorials, opinion essays, and reviews echo conservative themes, and editor in chief Richard John Neuhaus's

monthly column, "The Public Square," is an often ram-
bunctious, satirical commentary on current publications
and happenings and on what he takes to be liberalism's
self-delusory seriousness.

Neuhaus is the heart and soul of *First Things*. Described by *U.S. News and World Report* as one of the thirty-
two most significant American intellectuals, Neuhaus is
a vocal opponent of abortion rights and a principal player
in the "culture wars." Neuhaus converted to Catholicism
from his Lutheran faith in 1990. As a Lutheran pastor
in the 1960s, he had been a proponent of civil rights and
has noted that he "was proud to have been sent to jail
with Dr. King." In recent years, though his activism has
certainly not diminished, he has become far more identified
with traditionally conservative causes.

In the November 1996 issue of *First Things*, a symposium appeared, entitled "The End of Democracy? The
Judicial Usurpation of Politics."[1] The symposium included
articles by Russell Hittinger, Robert Bork, Hadley Arkes,
Charles Colson, and Robert George, and an introductory
editorial authored by Neuhaus. The symposium investi-
gated the question of whether the consent of the governed
is compromised, or even forfeited, by a judiciary which
has "in effect declared that the most important questions
about how we ought to order our life together are outside the purview of 'the things of [the citizenry's] knowledge.'" The symposiasts asked whether the judicial
usurpation of politics (i.e., the judiciary's repeated foreclosing on the process of legislative debate and decision
through the creation of previously unrecognized constitutional rights) perhaps constituted the end of the American experiment in democracy.

In the introduction to the symposium, Neuhaus notes that it is an "extension" of a May 1996 *First Things* editorial, "The Ninth Circuit's Fatal Overreach." The "overreach" in question was the Ninth Circuit's decision to overturn a Washington State law banning physician-assisted suicide on the grounds that the Constitution guarantees a "liberty right" to assisted suicide. The May editorial suggested that if "the Supreme Court upholds the Ninth Circuit, the battle over abortion would likely be transformed into near unconditional warfare against the arrogance of the courts that short-circuit democratic deliberation by the imposition of their moral (or grossly immoral) dictates."[2]

In the November symposium, the contributors do find such dictates to be immoral. Invoking the principle shared by Dr. Martin Luther King Jr. and a multitude of others that "Among the most elementary principles of Western Civilization is the truth that laws which violate the moral law are null and void and must in conscience be disobeyed," the symposiasts explored the question of "whether we have reached or are reaching the point where conscientious citizens can no longer give moral assent to the existing regime."

The symposium did not (*pace* its critics) condone or even offer an analysis of the range of responses ("from noncompliance to resistance to civil disobedience to morally justified revolution") which conscientious citizens might employ when confronted with legal obligations which they find to be morally suspect. Indeed, in an editorial entitled "To Reclaim our Democratic Heritage," accompanying a collection of follow-up essays in the January 1997 issue of *First Things*, the editors were at pains to state explicitly their purposes and to guard their ideas from being misappropriated by the ever-expanding, anti-government militia culture in the United States. Reiterating that none of the November essays asserted that the present government of the United States is in fact illegitimate, the editors emphasized that the recognition of "the displacement of a constitutional order by a regime that does not have, will not obtain, and cannot command the consent of the people" is an important step in inaugurating a national conversation designed to reclaim our democratic heritage. Near the end of the essay, the editors affirm

> the delusions of weekend revolutionaries should not set the boundaries of political discussion. Indeed, acquiescence in judicial usurpation, far from warding off extremism, would likely increase the number of Americans who believe there is no alternative to violent change. We therefore call for the vigorous pursuit of every peaceful and constitutional means to return our country to its democratic heritage, and to encourage its people to take up again what Professor Glendon calls the hard work of citizens rather than subjects.[3]

Response to the *First Things* Symposium

The response to the symposium was not long in coming. Gertrude Himmelfarb and Peter Berger resigned from the *First Things* Editorial Board, and Walter Berns resigned from the Editorial Advisory Board. Though *National Review* offered an editorial[4] on and the *Weekly Standard* devoted an entire article[5] to the symposium immediately after it was published, it was Jacob Heilbrunn's cover article in the *New Republic* ("Neocon v. Theocon") which focused national attention on the symposium and delivered to us the new abbreviations of the hour. Heilbrunn examined not just the symposium but also Himmelfarb's, Berger's, and Berns's resignations.[6] To Heilbrunn, the brouhaha at *First Things* was indicative of "the widening schism on the intellectual right."

Heilbrunn tells the story of the symposium and the subsequent resignations with an eye toward demonstrating how the Catholic, theologically-oriented conservatives (the "Theocons") at *First Things* edged out the largely Jewish, economically-oriented neoconservatives (the "Neocons") because the former (in concert with the Religious Right) have aspirations for a "Christian nation" which the latter can neither stomach nor understand. In truth, Heilbrunn's essay is embarrassingly inaccurate. Most of his gaffes are enumerated in a published exchange between Robert George, Michael Novak, and Heilbrunn in the February 3, 1997 issue of the *New Republic*.[7]

In January 1997, *First Things* attempted to clarify matters and continue the discussion by offering a response to some of the early criticism. January and February also saw a spate of articles from the *Washington Post*, *Lingua Franca*, the *Chronicle of Higher Education*, the *American Spectator*, *National Review* (again), the *New Republic* (also again), and *Crisis*, among others. *Commentary* devoted most of its February issue to a symposium of its own, entitled "On the Future of Conservatism."[8] Most of the *Commentary* contributors repudiated the "incendiary" rhetoric of the original *First Things* symposium and lamenting the damage done to national conservative causes and politics. I will return to this objection because it is an important one, but which I believe suffers from a fundamental misunderstanding of the aims and purposes of the *First Things* symposium.

MICHAEL BAXTER AND NOTRE DAME

The University of Notre Dame was founded by the Priests of the Congregation of Holy Cross (csc) in 1842. Though the order no longer exercises primary control of the institution, the csc maintains a prominent, if less visible, presence on campus. There are certain provisions in Notre Dame's by-laws which guarantee the university's connection to the order. Among other things, the by-laws require that the President of Notre Dame shall be a priest of the csc (of the Indiana Province) and that, with regard to faculty hiring, the csc shall constitute an affirmative action category at Notre Dame. (To hire a csc priest, an academic department is given an additional faculty line, but the person must meet expected qualifications.)

Michael Baxter, in his early forties, is a priest of the Congregation of Holy Cross. A past graduate of the Notre Dame theology department, Baxter received his doctorate in theological ethics at Duke University. While at Duke he received several awards, including the prestigious Charlotte W. Newcombe Doctoral Dissertation Fellowship. Before coming to Notre Dame, Baxter received a Visiting Research Fellowship at the Center for the Study of American Religion at Princeton University. He has spoken at numerous conferences and published in theological and jurisprudence journals. He serves on the editorial board of the American Journal of Jurisprudence.

A pacifist, Baxter is also a proponent of the Catholic Worker Movement begun by Dorothy Day and exemplified by Catholics seeking to curb the exploitative consequences of market-driven capitalism. In the 1980s, Baxter served as co-founder and later director of the Andre House of Hospitality for the homeless and poor and the St. Joseph the Worker Job Service, both in Phoenix, Arizona. During his years at Notre Dame, he had established the Center for Draft and Military Counseling. In Germany, during the Gulf War, he counseled conscientious objectors in the United States military.

If the *First Things* symposiasts explored the question of "whether we have reached or are reaching the point where conscientious citizens can no longer give moral assent to the existing regime," Baxter has already given his answer. In 1983, he was arrested and later convicted in a federal court for an anti-nuclear arms protest at the Davis Monthan Air Force Base near Tucson, Arizona. The conviction, which Baxter refers to as "one of our nation's highest honors," brought a sentence of two years probation and two hundred hours of community service. Requiring a priest whose calling includes serving the homeless to perform community service might also be seen as one of our nation's most astute sentences.

In the spring of 1996, Baxter applied for a position in the Notre Dame theology department and was rejected by the appointments committee. University President Edward A. Malloy, csc, subsequently appointed Baxter to a visiting three-year position in the department over the wishes of the appointments committee.

During the fall academic term, the theology department's rejection of Baxter and his subsequent appointment by Malloy were all the rage on the Notre Dame campus. The rationale behind both actions was far from clear, however. While some members of the theology department expressed dismay over Baxter's rejection, others defended the appointments committee's action on the substantial grounds that Baxter was not a qualified candidate. Malloy clearly believed otherwise.

In a letter written July 24, 1996, to theology department chair Lawrence Cunningham, Malloy emphasized that he intended Baxter's *visiting* appointment as a "compromise." Malloy gave the following reasons for his decision to give Baxter this appointment: (1) The president is entrusted with the responsibility of ensuring that university statutes and by-laws are faithfully discharged. These statutes include "mak[ing] full use of the unique skills and dedication of the members of the Priests of Holy Cross" and "eagerly and openly" pursuing qualified c s c priest-scholars. Malloy felt that Michael Baxter was not eagerly pursued. (2) Recognizing that Baxter's dissertation director at Duke, Stanley Hauerwas, was not only a former member of the Notre Dame theology department but also a participant in "some of the more controversial discussions" within that department, Malloy felt that Baxter "was unfortunately connected, if only unconsciously, with certain disputes in the Department's history." (3) On the basis of a professional judgment about Baxter's "scholarly and teaching credentials in [Malloy's] own subfield of theological ethics," Malloy felt that Baxter's qualifications warranted the appointment.

During the fall term, members of the theology department brought this situation to the attention of the Notre Dame community at large. Critics of Malloy's action

voiced first substantial and later procedural objections to
Baxter's appointment. It was, of course, exclusively a matter
between the administration, the department, and the candidate, but it quickly became a matter of campus-wide
controversy. As Alfred Freddoso of the philosophy department would later say, "certain members of the [the-
ology] department have vociferously urged the rest of us
on the faculty to treat *their* business as *our* business," and
such certainly seems to have been the case. In the year's
first issue of the left-of-center independent newspaper
Common Sense, Joseph Blenkinsopp, John A. O'Brien Professor of Theology, lamented Malloy's tendency to make
major policy decisions during the summer when many faculty "resist the temptation to enjoy the summer in the heart
of rural Indiana." Without mentioning Baxter by name,
Blenkinsopp reported how a csc priest with a ph.d from
Duke University had applied for a position, been rejected
by the department, and "unilaterally appointed" to a visiting position. Noting that the Notre Dame department
ranked twelfth nationally, Blenkinsopp asserted that "It
is therefore hardly one of those depressing cases of a me-
diocre department rejecting an outstanding candidate."[9]

The case had already become a depressing one for most
of those involved. On September 11, Faculty Senate vice
chair (and member of the theology department) Jean Porter
reported to the Senate and presented a resolution from
the Executive Committee which expressed "grave concern"
over the manner in which the appointment was made. By
way of background, Porter affirmed (in summary) that the
theology department "did not consider him qualified for
an appointment and turned down the application."[10] The
Senate appointed its Academic Affairs Committee to

investigate the matter in order to see if there had been any improprieties of governance with respect to Baxter's appointment over the wishes of the theology appointments committee and report its findings to the Senate. The Senate did not question Malloy's prerogative to overrule or his ultimate responsibility in matters of faculty appointments.

In its November 7 meeting, the Academic Affairs Committee presented its report along with a minority report authored by G. Robert Blakey, O'Neil Professor of Law, Notre Dame Law School. Blakey alleged that there were grievous procedural violations in that the Academic Affairs Committee did not conduct a full and fair investigation. It neither heard testimony nor gathered evidence beyond assembling various correspondence. Blakey argued that it was improper for the Senate to speak on matters about which it had not gathered adequate evidence.

For its part, the Senate accepted both the majority report and Blakey's dissenting views and (*contra* Blakey) found "no evidence that the Theology Department failed to observe its responsibility to give 'special consideration' to a csc candidate" and "no justification either for President Malloy's unilateral decision to appoint or for the manner in which he appointed a csc candidate to a faculty position." Noting that the President's action "harms the Theology Department and the University as a whole by undermining the well-established and beneficial model of rational collaboration that exists between a departmental faculty and the university's administration with regard to hiring decisions," the Senate expressed "its strong disapproval of President Malloy's handling of the 'special relationship' and its strong disapproval of his decision to appoint a Visiting Professor." On December 3, 1996, the Senate passed a resolution which affirmed that President Malloy's decision "seriously erodes the confidence that a faculty ought to have in a President." The resolution passed twenty-nine to five, with three abstentions.[11]

RESPONSE TO THE BAXTER CONTROVERSY

The *Chronicle of Higher Education* described the controversy in its "Faculty Notes" section of the December 13, 1996 issue. It asserted, erroneously, that Baxter's appointment had come against the unanimous recommendation of the department. The event was also the subject of an article in the *National Catholic Reporter* (NCR). Pamela Schaeffer described how the priest had been "imposed on the faculty," and "[f]ollowing months of controversy, the university's Faculty Senate denounced the president's administrative style in a formal resolution."[12] Schaeffer did note that it was the five-member theology appointments committee, and not the entire theology department, which had unanimously opposed Baxter's hiring.

Baxter was not, however, without his supporters. Fifteen scholars from six prestigious universities who knew Baxter and his work responded with a letter to the *Chronicle of Higher Education* correcting its assertion that departmental opposition to Baxter's appointment was unanimous and affirming that they were "highly impressed" with his scholarly work. The fifteen signatories were Scott Appleby, John Garvey, Philip Gleason, George Marsden, Marvin O'Connell, and David Solomon from Notre Dame; Alasdair MacIntyre, Frank Lentricchia, and Kenneth Surin

from Duke; Robert George, Leigh Schmidt, and Rob-
ert Wuthnow from Princeton; Thomas Hibbs from Boston
College, Beth Wenger from Pennsylvania, and Ruth Marie
Griffith from Northwestern.[13]

Other Notre Dame colleagues David Burrell, c s c,
Hesburgh Professor of Philosophy and Theology, and
Alfred Freddoso, professor of Philosophy, both responded
to n c r. In Burrell's letter of December 11, he expressed
confusion over the entire incident. Why should such an
extraordinarily well- qualified candidate be rejected? Not
because of any bias against c s c priests since "discrimination against the Congregation of Holy Cross would
hardly characterize the department of Theology." Burrell
believed the answer lay in the fact that "many extraneous factors impeded a clear appreciation of [Baxter's]
intellectual prowess as well as of his potential to carry
forward theological discussion with those willing to engage in a thoroughgoing inquiry."[14]

What are the extraneous factors? Apparently one of
the dominant factors was Baxter's dissertation director,
Stanley Hauerwas, to whom Malloy alluded. Burrell noted
that this connection was problematic for Baxter; Freddoso
cut to the chase: "an ongoing and nasty feud between
[Baxter's] dissertation director, a former Notre Dame
theologian, and several senior members of the theology
department." Richard McBrien, Crowley-O'Brien-Walter
Professor of Theology, denied that such was the case,
though Malloy, Burrell, Freddoso, and others thought otherwise. Their opinion seemed confirmed by Cunningham's
assessment of Baxter's dissertation: "He [Baxter] also shows
traces of his mentor's habits of pugnaciousness and bombast
but in conversation pulls back when challenged."[15]

Feuds, rumors of feuds, and rampant pugnaciousness are neither new nor uncommon to the academy. On the contrary, the old joke about why academic politics is so dirty (because the stakes are so small) seems confirmed on every campus in the country, from the most obscure community college to the most visible research university. Thus, in many respects, the Baxter controversy is unremarkable, however much grief, pain, and mistrust it may have bred in South Bend. Why did the appointment of a clearly radical priest, supported by Berrigan and lauded in the pages the *Houston Catholic Worker*,[16] generate such animosity at a bulwark of the Catholic and religious left as the Notre Dame theology department? And to understand this we have to turn to Schaeffer's second NCR article.[17]

The *National Catholic Reporter* describes itself as "The Independent, Lay-edited Catholic Newsweekly." It is a veritable mainstay of the liberal Catholic establishment in the United States. Its pages regularly report the institutional silencing of dissident priests and the progress of liberationist and base community movements in Latin America and elsewhere; its editorials frequently call for the Catholic Church to embrace more "democratic" procedures for the establishment of accepted doctrine and practice. The NCR has long valued the unique contributions of leftist Catholic scholars, priests, and activists; indeed, Richard McBrien has a regular column which appears in its pages. It is for this reason that the NCR's positive assessment of Baxter is so interesting and so profound.

In this second article, Schaeffer recognized that the controversy at Notre Dame focused on a "question critical to American Catholicism—the right relationship of Catholicism to culture, of religion to politics." Though on the surface the question appeared to be why a bright and accomplished priest failed to gain the support of the department, "under the surface lurks a youthful challenge to American Catholicism's old guard." Baxter represented a shift, according to Schaeffer, "in the way Catholicism is defined and practiced in the United States. Baxter's allies say he blows apart the usual liberal-conservative categories that have often been used to describe Catholics since the Second Vatican Council in the 1960s." And indeed he does. I will return to Schaeffer's assessment of Baxter.

Much Ado About Nothing?

Some might question both the significance of and the connection between these events. The Baxter affair might be just another squabble between university administrators and faculty, not unlike the sorts of disputes that erupt every year on every campus in the land. Furthermore, could the *First Things* symposium possibly be just a tempest in a teapot? Francis Fukuyama is correct: It is hard to imagine "Richard John Neuhaus holed up in a farmhouse shooting it out with ATF officers anytime soon."[18] Even if it is granted that Catholic ethicists and natural law theorists might find something provocative in these two events, it is not immediately obvious why Protestants, secularists, non-residents of South Bend, and others should take an interest in these matters.

Yet these events are not only connected, but significant for the larger conversation on the relation between church and state, or more precisely, between the exercise of Christian faith and democracy. Just as Neuhaus and the *First Things* symposium have wreaked havoc with traditional sensibilities about religion and politics on the right, so has Baxter rendered problematic the traditional sensibilities about religion and politics on the left. Viewed together, these events offer a window through which to view the incoherence of Enlightenment Liberalism's status quo.

How are these events connected? There are a number of individuals whose projects and associations are intertwined with both the Baxter and *First Things* controversies. Some of these individuals have been major contributors toward the emerging critique of Enlightenment Liberalism. Alasdair MacIntyre certainly stands at the top of any such list. Through his volumes, *After Virtue, Whose Justice? Which Rationality?*, and *Three Rival Versions of Moral Enquiry*, he has done as much as anyone to call into question the hegemony of Enlightenment Liberalism. George Marsden and Robert Wuthnow have played similar roles: Marsden with respect to history and the role of religion in higher education and Wuthnow with respect to the sociology of the American religious experience. Robert George, one of the original *First Things* symposiasts, was also one of the fifteen signatories to the letter of support for Baxter which appeared in the *Chronicle of Higher Education* and the *Observer*.

The most obvious individual relevant to both controversies, of course, is Stanley Hauerwas, Baxter's dissertation director and member of the *First Things* Editorial Board. Described by *Lingua Franca*'s David Glenn as "impossible-to-pigeonhole," Hauerwas has expressed support for the *First Things* symposium: "I think it shows that the magazine has great integrity." Hauerwas asserts that "The problem isn't with the courts. The problem is the American people! The conservatives don't want to admit that this is what the American people want! They *want* assisted suicide! They believe in autonomy!"[19] These allegedly "autonomous Americans" are the embodiment of Enlightenment Liberalism.

Charles Colson refers to Hauerwas in his contribution to the *First Things* symposium. Colson agrees with David Smolin's conclusion that in an increasingly hostile environment, religious believers will be forced either "to abandon their religious beliefs and accommodate themselves to an amoral, libertarian regime" or abandon "their political interests, becoming what the theologian Stanley Hauerwas has called 'resident aliens' in America—no longer concerned about the fortunes or misfortunes of a flawed republic, no longer considering this land their country."[20] (David Brooks cites this passage as evidence of the "anti-American temptation".) Colson's presentation of Hauerwas's position is misleading. While Hauerwas and William Willimon have popularized the notion of "resident aliens," it is inaccurate to suggest that Hauerwas is "no longer concerned about the fortunes or misfortunes of a flawed republic."

And yet it is this inaccurate rendering of Hauerwas which is at the heart of the theology department's rejection of Baxter. Hauerwas is often regarded as affirming a "sectarian" stance concerning the engagement of religion and politics. The *HarperCollins Encyclopedia of Catholicism*, edited by McBrien, defines "sectarian" as "one who defines the church as the exclusive locus of God's activity, and the mission of the church as limited to a countercultural, otherworldly salvation."[21] Schaeffer noted that McBrien "alluded to his concerns about Hauerwas and his Catholic students in his encyclopedia, where he wrote, 'Although sectarianism is diametrically opposed to Catholicism, a certain sectarian orientation has emerged in recent years in portions of the Catholic peace movement and in some younger Catholic moral theologians influenced by Protestant sectarian ethicists.'"[22]

Alasdair MacIntyre in his *Three Rival Versions of Moral Enquiry* described the "Encyclopaedia" approach as one of the three dominant attempts to classify and define moral enquiry.[23] The Encyclopedist assumes an ahistorical posture and attempts to present a clear distinction between "facts" and "values." The "facts" can be labeled and defined in such a way so that one may simply "look up" a definition in order to know what a thing might be. This is the essence of the encyclopedia. The Enlightenment is in many ways exemplified by this quest for "definitive" representations. However, if the definition in question turns out to be a contested one (as most definitions of interesting terms are), the "definitive" nature of the encyclopedia is undermined. In the modern context, the classic Enlightenment Liberal move is to offer definitions in such a way as to determine the terms (and consequences) of the debate. This phenomenon is clearly illustrated in the polemical definition of "sectarianism" that appears in McBrien's *Encyclopedia of Catholicism*.

The entry describes sectarians as "appealing to the individualistic aspects of Christianity,"[24] but that hardly seems the best way to describe Hauerwas. Rather than "sectarian," Hauerwas's approach, and that of Baxter, is better described as affirming confessionally particularist approaches to morality, politics, and faith. Hauerwas is a Methodist; Baxter, a Holy Cross priest. The sources of their moral engagement with politics differ, but they concur in their affirmation that one must employ confessionally particular resources; there are no religiously generic resources. It is safe to say that one of the dreams of Enlightenment Liberalism was the desire to remove the "scandal of particularity" from the engagement of religion and politics. It is for this reason that Liberalism eventually insists upon the privatization of religion: Historical religions cannot be divorced from their particularities. Baxter and Hauerwas recognize that the scandal of particularity cannot be removed without compromising authentically Christian convictions.

Now while Neuhaus cannot be described as "sectarian," he also recognizes the tension between the confessionally particular and the religiously generic and the role this tension plays in the debate over the place of religion in the public square. Indeed, the dispute between the generically religious and the particularly Christian is at the heart of the conflict between Himmelfarb and Neuhaus. This tension is exemplified by Neuhaus's increasing recognition of the inadequacy of purely procedural commitments for ensuring the legitimacy of government. The strong commitment to "procedure" is typical of the Enlightenment and is clearly seen in Himmelfarb's assertion that the legitimacy of government should not be discussed under the rubric of religious commitments and that the question of the very nature of government is not open to discussion.

Neuhaus and Baxter (and Hauerwas) share a dissatisfaction with Himmelfarb on this point. But a clarification

is in order. Neuhaus, Baxter, and Hauerwas are not suggesting alternative forms of government, and contrary to
popular opinion, Hauerwas does not advocate the modern retreat to Walden Pond (or Ruby Ridge), which might
be inferred from Colson's comment. But Neuhaus, Baxter,
and Hauerwas are suggesting (Neuhaus more reluctantly
than the others) that it is not inconceivable that "the
American experiment in democracy" should fail in its ability either to define an acceptable relationship between religion and the state or to protect religious expression
therein defined.

This observation leads to one of the most obvious
similarities between Baxter and the *First Things* symposiasts
which is also one of the most odd. Both have been labeled "anti-American." To be specific, Heilbrunn described
the Thomism of *First Things* symposium as "not so much
anti-American as un-American,"[25] and David Brooks's
entire essay is entitled "The Right's Anti-American Temptation."[26] These are curious charges to be leveled against
"conservatives"—especially conservatives like Neuhaus who
are allegedly the brains of the "God and country" Religious Right.

As for Baxter, he has consistently articulated a critique of the "Americanist" impulse in Catholic thought
(the notion, exemplified by John Courtney Murray and
others, that the guiding principles of American polity fit
neatly with Catholic doctrine and social teachings), so the
charge of "anti-Americanism" might come as no surprise.
What is curious, however, is who has made the charge.
Law-rence Cunningham had written in his analysis of
Baxter's dissertation that "The supreme irony, of course,
is that Baxter wants an appointment in an institution that

is the embodiment of the Americanist tradition. How does Baxter hope to be a member of a community which holds up as its ideal: God, Country, and Notre Dame?"[27] In his letter to the NCR, Freddoso responded "As far as I know, other departments in the University do not use nationalism as a criterion for appointment."[28] Cunningham later reported to Pamela Schaeffer that his comment (though included in his official evaluation of Baxter's dissertation) was made in jest.

The irony of Cunningham's accusation (jest or no) extends far beyond Freddoso's jab. Academic departments at major American universities are one of the last places one would expect to find inordinate nationalism. These departments are largely populated with what Richard Rorty has described as contestants in "the America sucks sweepstakes."[29] One would think that Baxter's critique would be appealing to most traditionally liberal departments of theology, but such is not the case. Furthermore, the presence of an alternative vision like Baxter's seems compatible with the current academic preoccupation with multiculturalism, diversity, and pluralism. But again, such turns out to be not the case.

When Schaeffer asked McBrien if the unpopular nature of Baxter's views about the Americanist tradition was the reason for his rejection, McBrien replied, "I'm saying [the countercultural approach] is not representative of the Catholic tradition. It's like a dissenting opinion. Should it be represented? Of course. Should it be over represented? I hope not." Schaeffer noted that McBrien believed that Baxter's view was adequately represented in the theology department by John Howard Yoder, a Mennonite.[30] Of course, Baxter is not a Mennonite, and whatever similar commitments Baxter and Yoder may share about "counterculturalism," Baxter represents a challenge to Catholicism. And this, of course, is the heart of the matter. Baxter's work poses a challenge to what he calls the "Catholics to the rescue" mentality embodied in the Americanist tradition. It is obvious that an Americanist Catholic who might be intrigued by Yoder might reject Baxter, precisely because Yoder's work does not pose an internal challenge to Catholic sensibilities in the way that Baxter's does. Neither Schaeffer nor McBrien commented on whether there was a *Catholic* theologian in the department who affirmed Baxter's position.

This commitment to "superficial or cosmetic" diversity usually amounts to a commitment to what Stanley Fish has called "boutique multiculturalism." According to Fish, "boutique multiculturalists will always stop short of approving other cultures at a point where some value at their center generates an act that offends against the canons of civilized decency."[31] In the end, the differing vision cannot be tolerated because it calls into question the core commitments of the establishment vision. In this case, both Neuhaus (reluctantly) and Baxter (emphatically) reject the notion that it is always possible to be both faithful Christians and "good Americans." Neuhaus writes that "'God and country' is a motto that has in the past come easily, some would say too easily, to almost all Americans. What are the cultural and political consequences when many more Americans, perhaps even a majority, come to the conclusion the question is 'God *or* country'"?[32]

When the very different Michael Baxter and Richard Neuhaus agree and the extraordinarily different neocons and Notre Dame liberals find the substance of the Baxter-

Neuhaus agreement appalling, we can recognize that we have indeed reached the end of our convenient stereotypes.

The Inauguration of "Extraordinary Politics"

One of the difficulties in writing an essay such as this one is that I must employ the very terminology which my thesis calls into question. To these ends, a word of clarification is in order. As is common, when I speak of (capital "L") Liberalism (or "Enlightenment Liberalism"), I am referring to the grand Western Liberal tradition which professes to affirm "value neutrality" and regards the autonomy of the individual as not only an intrinsic good that democratic government can guarantee, but also as a foundational good which trumps all other values. It is this grand tradition, always affirming that it is not a "tradition" strictly speaking, which has secured religious liberty but which is increasingly accused of privatizing (and trivializing) religion in the process. When I speak of (lower case "l") liberalism, I am referring to the recent tradition which values comprehensive government in the modern welfare state. Likewise, the term "conservative" refers to the corresponding tradition of minimalist government. (In this essay I do not treat the grand and complex Western Conservative tradition.) Both liberals and conservatives participate in the larger Enlightenment Liberal culture.

These traditional labels of "left" and "right" now seem unsatisfactory precisely because the larger context of Enlightenment Liberalism, which defines the spectrum on which the traditional labels fall, can no longer be taken for granted. To say that the tradition "can no longer be taken for granted" is not to say that it has passed from the scene, has been replaced, or is even challenged by a viable alternative; rather, the tradition's giveness is simply now problematic. One can draw an analogy to Thomas Kuhn's analysis of how scientific revolutions proceed.[33]

According to Kuhn, during periods of "normal science" within which there is a single dominant paradigm, scientific activity takes the form of "puzzle solving." There are always problems in science which cannot be solved, but as long as these problems are at the margins of inquiry or are dwarfed by more pressing concerns, the dominant paradigm remains unchallenged. Making the analogy to politics, Liberalism has been the dominant "puzzle solving" paradigm of the West for the last three hundred years.[34] In the twentieth century, Enlightenment Liberalism has reached its apex and, as many have speculated, begun its decline.

There is an interesting historical question toward which I can only gesture and for which I will not argue at this time. It seems obvious that while there were always difficulties with Enlightenment Liberalism (enumerated, for instance, in the work of Friedrich Nietzsche or Max Horkheimer), Liberalism has looked utterly compelling in the face of the twentieth century options of Nazism, Stalinism, and Communism. (Jacques Maritain seems to be making a point similar to this one in *Integral Humanism*.) A Constantinian Christianity of the day (though quite different from what Maritain had in mind) could even make common cause with this Enlightenment Liberalism in order "to make the world safe for democracy."

Notice, however, how even this common catch phrase ("to make the world safe for democracy") betrays the conviction that the guiding teleology was not one of religion but of a certain sort of politics. (Some readers may even be thinking, "Yes, of course, that was the point.") But why was that the point? Because the culture of Enlightenment Liberalism condoned the exportation of our Western political morality even while it rejected the exportation of our Western religious morality. Indeed, Christianity is seen here as a precursor and ground clearer for the development of a more essential state that is to come, namely, that of secular democracy in places where it does not yet exist. In common parlance, "It would be nice if those folks were Christian, but it is a necessity that they become Democratic."

The question remains, however, once the world has been made safe for democracy, what need does it have of Christianity? Very little. Hence, we see the increasing privatization and the trivialization of religion in the public square. Eliminating religious discourse from public life becomes, as Wendy Kaminer suggests, "the last taboo."[35] Indeed, Christianity becomes more and more to be viewed through Enlightenment Liberalism's "neutral" eyes as not only unnecessary but as dangerous in its "unregulated" forms. This is Richard Cohen's argument in his *Washington Post* editorial, "When Morality Begets Violence." Responding to the *First Things* symposium, Cohen suggests that "the prospect of 'a showdown between church and state' [Colson's phrase] is downright chilling," and he asserts that those who frame debate in "moralistic terms have to understand that, inadvertently or not, they are providing a justification for violence."[36] Jean Bethke Elshtain responds to Cohen by noting that to label debate which appeals to morality *chilling* "is to desire political speech itself to be chilled, so long as those put in the deep freeze are not those whose views one shares."[37]

Liberalism's internal tensions become obvious in an exchange such as this one. What starts out as a defense of neutral procedure against an intolerant viewpoint becomes a defense of an opposing, equally intolerant viewpoint which must suspend procedure in response to newfound dangers. It is another version of Fish's boutique multiculturalism and is further evidence of his more general claim that "Liberalism doesn't exist."[38]

My suspicion is that once the Cold War began to wind down and the external challenges to Liberalism receded into the shadows, its internal problems, which had been at the margins, came to the forefront. We begin to see just how thin and brittle Enlightenment Liberalism really is.

For Kuhn, rival paradigms emerge because the "puzzle solving" resources are no longer adequate to meet the challenges of the new day. The emergence of rival paradigms during a period of "normal science" inaugurates a period of "extraordinary science." Periods of "extraordinary science" are often chaotic not only because fundamental assumptions have been called into question but also because any appeal to the "facts" will be inconclusive precisely because the interlocutors cannot agree on what the "facts" are, since to do so would require agreement on interpretative, foundational assumptions. As Fish has noted in another context, "Disagreements are not settled by the facts, but are the means by which the facts are settled."[39]

So too is it the case with regard to our contemporary discourse on religion and public life. The *First Things*

and Baxter affairs have inaugurated a period of "extraordinary politics" with respect to discourse on church and
state. In terms of the two cases before us, the commitments of the principal figures will only look incoherent
or confused if one assumes that they are seeking to articulate one of the traditional agendas within American
politics. Within the traditional agendas, it might seem
incoherent for one to offer a vocal protest against both
the pervasive abortion-rights culture and the pervasive
military culture in our country. But that merely demonstrates how distorted the traditional agendas are. Both
movements protest the ease with which our country con-
dones institutions which are predicated upon the violent
destruction of life. In this sense, both of these institutions contribute to what Pope John Paul II has called "a
culture of death."

If, however, Baxter and Neuhaus have an altogether
different objective (including different objectives—as we
all know to be the case), it is quite possible that there is
nothing incoherent about their thought at all. Moreover,
it might be that their thought is *more* coherent when
viewed apart from the distorting traditional labels and
agendas of our "politics as usual." If such is the case, it
is quite obviously beside the point that one or the other
has "damaged" national conservative or liberal religious
politics. I will return to this point.

Make no mistake: Baxter and Neuhaus disagree on
many things. They differ with regard to national economic
policy as well as national military policy. This latter
difference is exemplified by their contrasting opinions on
the Gulf War.[40] They perhaps differ with regard to how
moral convictions inform theology (and *vice versa*). This

alleged difference has been recently articulated by Neuhaus. In the April 1997 issue of *First Things*, Neuhaus offered a critique of what he took to be Baxter's use of pacifism as the lens through which Christian theology should be viewed. Even though Neuhaus acknowledges that Baxter is "philosophically and theologically light years removed from Kant," he described Baxter's approach as an instance of Kantian "religion within the limits of morality"—an interpretation which Baxter would no doubt dispute.

And yet, even in his negative assessment, Neuhaus expressed sympathy with much of Baxter's larger critique. Indeed, in a parenthetical note, Neuhaus noted Baxter's Notre Dame woes and asserted, "the above criticisms notwithstanding, I'm on his side."[41] In the May 1997 issue of *First Things*, Neuhaus followed this comment with an expanded statement on Baxter's "furious dispute" at Notre Dame. And yet, as this statement also makes amply clear, their profound differences notwithstanding, both are un-wavering in their fidelity to the Christian Gospel over and against a political agenda which, though it may affirm common elements, requires the person of faith and con-science to violate both in the name of procedural ratio-nality and democratic process. While Neuhaus cannot bring himself to emulate Baxter's embrace of Hauerwasian (for lack of a better word) "particularism," he has become a reluctant belligerent in the clash with an Enlightenment Liberalism of which his own cultural and political con-servatism is part and parcel.

As a devout Christian, Neuhaus recognizes that he can have no personal *religious* agendas. And since Neuhaus agrees with Aristotle that politics is free persons delib-erating the question "how ought we order our lives to-

gether," Neuhaus's political program is not ultimately about
propping up conservatism in general or the Religious Right
in particular, though he seems pleased when he can. For
Neuhaus, the question is one of conscience and Christian faith—but not about the creation of a mythical "Christian nation." He has reluctantly found himself in his
present role, but it is a role he has not shirked.

One is reminded of that marvelous scene in the film
Chariots of Fire. The young Scottish Christian Eric Liddel
has refused, on grounds of principle, to race on Sunday
during the 1924 Paris Olympics. Sitting in the stands on
the day of race immediately prior to its running, Liddel's
coach turns to the Olympian and asks, "Any regrets?"
Liddel responds, "Regrets? Yes. But no doubts." This
is the situation into which both the Supreme Court and
the larger Liberal culture have placed a reluctant Richard John Neuhaus.

These observations about Neuhaus's "reluctant sectarianism" may be mistaken: His May 1997 article "The Liberalism of John Paul II"[42] demonstrates the depth of the
passion of his tortured soul on these questions. This article
is critical not only of current defenses, which Neuhaus
calls "distortions," of Liberalism (like that of Rawls and
Dworkin) but also of current critiques of Liberalism (like
that of Hauerwas and MacIntyre). Neuhaus is clearly
calling for the Church to engage in an extraordinary
politics of a sort, though he mistakenly thinks it can be
achieved through the attempt to "reappropriate and re-
build the liberal tradition." Neuhaus understands this
endeavor as "contending for the soul of the liberal tradition." However, to understand oneself as "contending for
the soul of the liberal tradition" is already to have placed

oneself against and outside of Liberalism. This "tradition," so-called, is one which denies the very idea of soul and which has lived and died on the assumption that it is *not* the embodiment of a tradition but rather of those neutral, self-evident realities the recognition of which is necessary to sustain a rather truncated version of human freedom in society. Neuhaus certainly recognizes this difficulty even if he thinks it might be accomplished through a reinvigorated Liberalism.

Be that as it may, there is evidence that Neuhaus and Baxter are compelled by a different agenda from that of our dominant, secular Liberal culture, which has traditionally manifested itself in the Religious Right and the Religious Left. Two "conversations", one prior to both the *First Things* symposium and the Baxter controversy and one following them, set the disagreements between the principals (and those closely associated with them) and the Enlightenment Liberal culture in bold relief.

The End of Neutrality

While tensions between the supposed "Theocons" and "Neocons" have run deep for some time, the distinctions between them (as well as their connection to the Baxter affair) were obvious on at least one occasion some fourteen months before the "End of Democracy?" symposium. Himmelfarb and Neuhaus, together with James William McClendon of Fuller Theological Seminary and David Solomon (who supported Baxter) of Notre Dame appeared on stage together at an academic symposium in Waco, Texas at the inauguration of Robert B. Sloan, the twelfth president of Baylor University.

It is not inappropriate to suggest that McClendon, a noted "baptist" theologian, represents a perspective which Baxter shares. Baxter has spoken of his great respect for McClendon, "especially McClendon's understanding of the proclamation of the Word as shaping how we see the world. Much of my work has been an attempt to expand on that point by means of a liturgical understanding of proclaiming and reading scripture." McClendon and Baxter's now (in)famous dissertation director Hauerwas are close friends. In a festschrift for McClendon which he co-edited, Hauerwas described McClendon as "a master craftsman" who has taught us that "in a world without foundations, all we have is the church. That such is the case is no deficiency since that is all we have ever had or could ever want."[43]

The subject of the Baylor symposium was "University, Church, and Society: Traditions in Tension," and Solomon was the moderator. Though the question of what relation the Christian should have to the University is a very different question from that of what relation the Christian should have to the government,[44] both questions address the complex issue of faith and institutional identity. Moreover, both questions are (inadequately) framed by the procedural and substantial assumptions of Enlightenment Liberalism.

McClendon spoke first on "The Baptist Idea of a University."[45] Arguing that the university has an unpaid moral debt to the church from whence it has come, McClendon suggested that this debt can only be satisfied if the university gives to society what it has been given by the church. Noting that "moral thinking attends to *practices*," McClendon defined "practices" as "complex traditional human endeavors, carried on by those engaging in them with a view to moral ends whose achievement justifies the practices and fulfills the lives of those so engaged." Agreeing with Jonathan Edwards that morality can express itself better in terms of "beauty" than with the metaphor of "debt," McClendon argued that by "fitly nurturing its own proper practices," the university not only discovers and progressively repays its moral debt but also answers to and corresponds with the beauty which is "the holiness of redemption, the wholeness of creation, God's holy wholeness."[46]

Himmelfarb offered an essay under the title "The Christian University: A Call to Counterrevolution." The counterrevolution, according to Himmelfarb, is the conservative attempt "to restore and revitalize the traditional academic dogma" against the postmodern dangers which threaten the university. Himmelfarb cited approvingly Matthew Arnold's definition of culture as "the best which has been thought and said in the world." This understanding of culture betrays her commitment to a supposed neutrality based on the presupposition that the "best" ideas are always the exemplification of a culture's heritage. (The best team always wins the knowledge olympics.) This notion has become problematic given the increasingly marginalized status of the Enlightenment perspective. If Enlightenment ideals are supplanted by "post-Enlightenment" (or "postmodern") ones, were they really superior? Of course, even to speak in these terms assumes that there is a standard by which one can evaluate (and rank) ideas. Enlightenment proponents (like Himmelfarb) will contend that the postmodernists have not "played by the rules;"

they have cheated, so to speak, hence one cannot right-
fully speak of their "winning" anything.

The issue which is most important for our purposes
is Himmelfarb's use of Robert Nisbet's *The Degradation
of the Academic Dogma.* Himmelfarb explicitly points to
Nisbet's use of religious terminology to describe the revolution which occurred in universities during the 1960s.
Himmelfarb notes that "Nisbet reminded them of the
'dogma,' as he called it, that had sustained the university
for centuries: the 'faith' (again, this was his word) in reason and knowledge, in the rational, dispassionate search
for truth, and in the dissemination of knowledge for the
sake of knowledge."[47] Himmelfarb uses this religious terminology throughout her presentation. In speaking of
the commitment of the university, she affirms, "throughout the centuries, the essential dogma—the commitment
to truth, knowledge, and objectivity—remained intact."
Later, Himmelfarb juxtaposes the new postmodern "un-
holy Trinity of race, class, and gender" with the traditional
"dogma" of "truth, objectivity, and knowledge."

It is not mere coincidence that Himmelfarb should
speak of the academic "dogmas" in this way. Himmelfarb's
"faith" in the Enlightenment ideal is profoundly religious.
In truth, the Enlightenment commitment to "the rational, dispassionate search for truth, and "the dissemination of knowledge for the sake of knowledge" is a kind
of religion. More important, it is a fundamental religion
which requires an absolute faithfulness since it alone
possesses the capacity to adjudicate between the irrational excesses of traditional religions. As stated above, Enlightenment doctrine is not plagued by the "scandal of

particularity" which consumes every historical religion. It
is accessible to all and in every place. This rational religion need not necessarily deprecate traditional faiths since
it is "neutral" and "dispassionate" with regard to the traditional faiths. Neuhaus, of course, practices a different
religion.

The third presentation was made by Neuhaus, and the
deep tensions between Neuhaus and Himmelfarb could
not have been more striking, even if on the surface they
identified common enemies and celebrated common causes.
Neuhaus offered "Eleven Theses"[48] on the idea of the
Christian University. The former Lutheran pastor quipped
that the audience "will no doubt be grateful that there
are not ninety-five theses." The first thesis set Himmelfarb's faith in Enlightenment neutrality in bold relief:
"There is no such thing as a university pure and simple."
Unequivocally denying the neutrality thesis, Neuhaus continued: "A secular university is not a university pure and
simple; it is a secular university. Secular is not a synonym
for neutral."

Neuhaus's eighth thesis was "In a Christian university there is no 'role' for religion. Rather, it is within religion—more accurately, it is within the Christian
understanding of reality—that everything finds its role."
Neuhaus's clarifying clause ("more accurately, it is within
the Christian understanding of reality") is important for
two reasons. On the one hand, he is rejecting the generic account of religion in favor of a particular (i.e., a
Christian) one. On the other hand, he (like McClendon
here) is recognizing the comprehensive nature of the
Christian commitment. Himmelfarb fails to recognize
either distinction. In her presentation, she had spoken

of religious universities as "respectful of religion and of the moral virtues derived from religion." Neuhaus's point is the opposite. Within a Christian university, "religion" does not occupy a respected "role" precisely because it is from within that commitment that all else finds its role.

Similarly, the Christian operating in the public square does not "respect" religion in a way in which the secularist does not. Rather, the Christian is simply a Christian. Whether he or she will be able to consent will ultimately have a material rather than a formal explanation. Himmelfarb assumes that these matters can be decided upon formal grounds; indeed, to do otherwise would violate the Enlightenment commitment to neutrality which is the formal guarantee. To place religious commitment outside of the province of the endeavor itself (whether in a respected or depreciated position) is still to domesticate religion. Himmelfarb mistakenly assumes that "being respectful of religion" will be enough. But this move already entails the privatization and trivialization of specific religious commitments.

However, for Neuhaus, McClendon, and Baxter, where the Enlightenment dogmas hold sway, there is always the possibility that the Christian will not be able to consent. In point of fact, when Enlightenment dogma is taken as the arbiter of "acceptable" religious convictions, there can never be a real "separation of church and state" because the principle itself is predicated upon the prior establishment of a particular faith, a conflicting dogma.

Robert George made this point to the *Chronicle of Higher Education* about the *First Things* symposium. George remarked that "Our objection is to the idea that liberalism itself is a kind of neutral playing field, as opposed to a substantive theory about human nature, destiny, and dignity. We dispute the idea that liberalism itself is a neutral view that doesn't compete with others. It certainly has the right to compete in the public square with other philosophies, but it is certainly not given any privileged position by the Constitution."[49]

Baxter and Hauerwas make a similar point about Liberalism (though not about the Constitution) in their essay "The Kingship of Christ," and it is the point which, it seems to me, Neuhaus has reluctantly come to articulate. The difference, of course, is that while Baxter and Hauerwas seem to imply that such could never be otherwise, Neuhaus wishes that such were not the case; indeed, he longs to hold the two sides in respectful tension. This is not to suggest that Neuhaus desires an equilibrium, but rather that he thinks that if the state respects the natural law, the areas where Christians will find a conflict of conscience will be limited. This is the hope of traditional natural law theory, especially as it has been articulated by Thomists like Maritain and Ralph McInerny.

BEYOND LIBERALISM AND CONSERVATISM

If the seeds of discontent were obvious at the Baylor gathering, it is possible to see the flowering of these disagreements in the ways in which the principals have responded to the juxtaposition of Christian faith with Enlightenment Liberalism.

Time, space, and prudence do not allow for engagements and summaries of all of the many responses to and critiques of the *First Things* symposium. In light of her comments at Baylor, however, Gertrude Himmelfarb's response to the *First Things* symposium is particularly illuminating and bears a closer look. To my knowledge, she has responded in print to the *First Things* symposium three times: her letter of resignation to *First Things*, a letter to the *American Spectator*, and her contribution to the *Commentary* symposium. In her letter of resignation she expressed her agreement with the symposium's participants that the courts had overstepped their bounds, but she strongly disagreed with the notion that such a conclusion warrants questioning the legitimacy of the government. She found that it was "absurd and irresponsible" to suggest an analogy between the "revolutionary" situations of 1776 and the present day. She objected to the use of the word "regime" for such "suggests that it is not the legitimacy of a particular institution or branch of government that is at stake but the very nature of our government." For Himmelfarb, this is not "a proper mode of political discourse." In effect, Himmelfarb is arguing not only that the legitimacy of government should not be discussed under the rubric of religious commitments and morality but also that the question of the very nature of government is not up for discussion.

Himmelfarb amplified these comments in her longer contribution to *Commentary*'s February symposium. Here she also begins by contrasting the "Gingrich revolution" with the specter of revolution behind the *First Things* symposium but quickly notes that talk about "revolution" is not "a proper mode of conservative discourse or politics."[50]

In Himmelfarb's opinion, it is when the *First Things* editors cite the "authority of Western civilization and two papal encyclicals" that "laws which violate the moral law are null and void and must in conscience be disobeyed" that their argument becomes confused. She is quite frankly shocked and dismayed at this line of reasoning. It is understandable that Himmelfarb would be confused at this point because she is using the converse of the hermeneutical principle employed by the *First Things* editors. For some of them, "Western civilization" is interpreted in the light of the encyclicals; for Himmelfarb, it has to be the other way around.

But Himmelfarb misunderstands the confusion. She takes the "real issue" to be "abortion and euthanasia."[51] Himmelfarb goes on to speculate how the *First Things* editors would respond if the legalization of abortion had come through the legislature instead of the judiciary: "if it betokened not the 'end of democracy' but the very exercise of democracy."

Essential to the Enlightenment Liberal culture is an advocacy of a procedural "come what may." Himmelfarb makes precisely this point. She writes, "If conservatives do take democracy and the Constitution seriously, if we are truly exercised by the usurpation of judicial power, we must also be prepared for the possibility that *vox populi* might differ from many of us on the subject of abortion."[52] Whereas Neuhaus interprets the "legal" in light of the "moral," Himmelfarb does the opposite. According to Himmelfarb, those who disagree with the properly procedural implications of democracy, "have neither the moral nor the legal right, in the name of democracy, to impose their view upon the polity, any more than the judiciary today has that right."

Surely Himmelfarb has missed the point. Neuhaus and company were arguing that until recently, the consent of the governed was not in question. Recent judicial actions have called that consent into question. Nowhere does Neuhaus (or by extension, Baxter) suggest that his view should be imposed upon the polity. His view is that the repeated violation of conscience makes the question of consent problematic.

The point of Himmelfarb's article is to demonstrate that the *First Things* symposium places the delicate alliance of "economic conservatives and social conservatives, evangelicals and secularists, federalists, pro-lifers, flat-taxers, and a variety of one-issue partisans" in peril. Surely Neuhaus regrets such a consequence, but it is equally the case that such is obviously beside the point. The theocons and Baxter have taken the positions they have on the basis of principle—not on the basis of procedural politics. Thus all the *Commentary* authors' complaints about how the *First Things* symposium hurts national conservative politics is both true and trivial. In my opinion, the symposium was never about sustaining or affirming a national conservative agenda; had it been so, it would have been the contradiction in terms which its critics lamented. More to the point, if the *First Things* symposium was merely about affirming a traditional conservative political agenda, it would never have been written.

The case is even more stark with regard to Baxter. As Freddoso noted, "Baxter has forcefully articulated the position that there is an inherent tension between the demands of Christian witness and the founding principles of the American polity, with the result that Christian witness in the American context will inevitably be counter-cultural." It is precisely the founding principles of this polity which Himmelfarb refuses to subject to scrutiny.

According to Himmelfarb and the neocons in general, the founding principles of the American polity are immune from scrutiny because they assume that the political and economic realms can be separated from the spiritual realm. While such a separation is entirely consistent with the culture of Enlightenment Liberalism, it is not acceptable from a Christian position, as recent papal encyclicals have demonstrated.

Pope John Paul II has been more than willing to subject these principles of Enlightenment Liberalism to scrutiny. John Paul II's *Centesimus Annus* (1991) celebrates the hundredth anniversary and follows the tradition of Leo XIII's *Rerum Novarum*. (It is worth remembering that it was Leo XIII and *Aeterni Patris* to whom Alasdair MacIntyre turned for an example of Tradition-constituted moral inquiry over and against Enlightenment "Encyclopedia" and Counter-Enlightenment "Genealogy" models.) *Rerum Novarum* challenged the Liberal notion that economics is determined exclusively by its own laws and processes. Hauerwas, in an essay entitled "In Praise of *Centesimus Annus*," notes that *Rerum Novarum* sought to undermine this alleged independence of economics by making a worker's just wage "*the* criterion for good economic relations. For the 'just wage' is determined by calculating what is required for the sustaining of families and children, not by the exigencies of the autonomous market."[53]

Centesimus Annus focuses on the extraordinary changes which occurred in the world in 1989, not the least of which was the collapse of the communist states and their collectivist economies. While *Centesimus Annus* celebrates the progress and the potential of democracy over totalitarian regimes it also explicitly rejects the neocons' assumption that economics can be separated from the spiritual realm. Noting that the "modern business economy has positive aspects," John Paul II asserts that economic activity "includes the right of freedom as well as the duty of making responsible use of freedom."[54] And later, "economic freedom is only one element of human freedom."[55] This responsible use of freedom includes a recognition of the moral character of work: "It is becoming clearer how a person's work is naturally interrelated with the work of others. More than ever, work is work with others and work for others: It is a matter of doing something for someone else."[56] There is, of course, a tension between a capitalist and a communitarian orientation here, and the capitalists have often downplayed the fact that life and work in a capitalist economy does indeed have a communally recognized spiritual dimension. John Paul II leaves no doubt where the Christian tradition stands on this matter: "Even prior to the logic of a fair exchange of goods and the forms of justice appropriate to it, there exists *something which is due to the person because he is a person,* by reason of his lofty dignity. Inseparable from that required 'something' is the possibility to survive and, at the same time, to make an active contribution to the common good of humanity."[57] In *Evangelium Vitae* (1995), John Paul II's endorsement of democracy has become even more qualified. As such, the Pope has amplified his comments by affirming that there is more to the moral life than talk about democratic and economic rights. For John Paul II, a democracy worthy of the name must recognize the value of human life: "Democracy cannot be idolized to the point of making it a substitute for morality or a panacea for immorality. Fundamentally, democracy is a 'system' and as such is a means and not an end. Its 'moral' value is not automatic, but depends on conformity to the moral law."[58]

Both Baxter and Neuhaus are responding in accordance with John Paul II's insight that Enlightenment Liberalism's regulation of difference through mere procedural rationality is not sufficient. Democracy is "a mere mechanism for regulating different and opposing interests" not a moral justification. According to John Paul II, "peace which is not built upon the values of the dignity of every individual and of solidarity between all people frequently proves to be illusory. Even in participatory systems of government, the regulation of interests often occurs to the advantage of the most powerful, since they are the ones most capable of maneuvering not only the levers of power but also of shaping the formation of consensus. In such a situation, democracy easily becomes an empty word."[59]

Gertrude Himmelfarb could never affirm this language or the ideas it expresses because it allows discussion on "the very nature of our government." Democracy could never become an empty word. And here is the final irony: An Enlightenment Liberalism which professes to be committed only to formal procedure and never material substance in the end affirms a particular substance over any and all procedural challenges. Of course, as ironies go, this one is not all that surprising.

CONCLUSION

What follows from these observations? The notion that the traditional labels of "left" and "right" with respect to religion and politics are now clearly inadequate seems pretty tame and rather inconsequential itself. "Okay, so the labels don't work. We'll invent new ones." But this conclusion is more problematic than it might first appear. First, what would the new labels look like? What label will we employ which adequately identifies two Catholic priests, who, though they have more in common than in difference, move in almost exactly opposite directions with respect to economic theory or the possible use of violence? Obviously, any such acceptable labels will require a new set of grounding assumptions about what kinds of agreement are essential and what kinds of disagreement are marginal. Our period of extraordinary politics demonstrates that we probably have only the barest of outlines of those assumptions at the moment.

Second, what will our political and religious discourse look like without our favorite *ad hominems*? Can we even imagine a state of affairs in which we abandon recourse to the convenient stereotypes of "fundamentalist" or "liberal"? (Our contemporary political discourse encourages the inevitable and speedy extension of extremist labels. Here, "right of me" quickly becomes "fundamentalist". The situation is equally grievous with regard to the left. Here, even the traditional label "liberal" is disparaged.) Depending on one's community or context, to establish that my opponent is a "fundamentalist" or a "liberal" produces the *de facto* conclusion that his or her opinions need not be considered. In the case of this new "f-word," it is such a mainstay of mainstream politics in this country that its mere presence as an accusation is the definitive conversation stopper and ultimate put-down. It is another whopping irony that we so-called intellectuals take so much undeserved comfort in this petty fallacy. Real fundamen-

talists produce plenty of genuine evidence of the challenge they pose; if we fear or reject their politics and
ideology, we have ample resources without stooping to self-
satisfying (and increasingly, unpersuasive) accusations.

Of course, many will be unimpressed with this assessment. To some, where one stands on the issue of abortion is ultimately all that matters in determining political
identity. For these observers, because Baxter and Neuhaus
both vocally oppose abortion, they are necessarily "right-
wing fundamentalists," and that's all there is to it. But
this is wrong-headed on several counts. First, it is now
common knowledge among reflective observers that the
abortion controversy pulled off the great switcheroo on
politics as usual in this country. If coherence and consistency mattered to any of the principals, then the free-
dom-loving, "keep the government out of my affairs"
conservatives should have been the proponents of abortion rights and the pro-environment, "government has the
obligation to protect what can't protect itself (especially
from the money-grubbing technological-industrial complex)" liberals should have been defending the rights of
the fetus. Does it make sense that the spotted owl de-
serves the government's protection more than a human
fetus? The answer may not be obvious to all, but it is
certainly curious why these vulnerable groups have different
defenders.

Second, and perhaps more important, the inadequacy
(and inaccuracy) of the single-issue identity determinant
(particularly the issue of abortion) is more obvious now
than ever. More and more pro-life Democrats and feminists are emerging precisely as an ever-more vocal minority
of the Republican party seeks to eliminate the abortion

plank from its platform. Could the hobgoblin of little minds be re-entering American politics? No, this is simply more evidence of the insufficiency of the traditional labels of "left" and "right."

The problem here, of course, is not just that the current labels are no longer satisfactory. The problem is that, without our labels, we increasingly recognize that we do not know how to think and talk about what it means to be a Christian in the public square. Perhaps we do not know what it means to be a Christian in the public square because we harbor such conflicting understandings about what it means to be a Christian at all. Perhaps we do not know how to speak as Christians in the public square because we know so few public languages which have not been formed by Enlightenment Liberalism. We Christians must move beyond Liberalism's convenient stereotypes. We Christians must craft a new literacy if we want to remain Christians at all. A new way of thinking and speaking will not dissolve old disagreements, but it may offer us new (and old) resources for addressing the new circumstances in which we encounter those disagreements.

It is far from clear what will come from a new way of thinking and speaking about religion and politics. Even (especially?) among Christians there will continue to be tensions over many questions—from economics to national defense. Hopefully, there will be few disagreements over whether the Christian will contribute to a culture of life (in all its many and varied forms) rather than be used by a culture of death (in all its many and varied forms). Perhaps there will be more honesty, less self-delusion, better Fourth-of-July church services and sermons. There most certainly will not be a "Christian nation," a "Christian political party," or some other such nonsense; there will most assuredly be much miscommunication and failure (at least as far as our society reckons success). But perhaps there will be more integrity, less willingness to co-opt and to be co-opted by groups who do not share the Christian confession of faith. As stated above, a new model of politics will require a new set of grounding assumptions about what kinds of agreement are essential and what kinds of disagreement are marginal. The end of our convenient stereotypes does not necessarily mean the "end of democracy," but it does mean the beginning of extraordinary politics.

9

THE PHILADELPHIA CONSTITUTION: DEAD OR ALIVE?

George W. Carey

THE CONCERNS I DEAL WITH HERE arise from a course I have taught for the past few years entitled "Theories of Constitutional Interpretation." The course deals with the ways in which the Constitution has been interpreted over the course of our history, as well as with the dominant schools of thought which have emerged in roughly the last fifty years that set forth rules and prescriptions for interpreting the Constitution. These modern theories, I think it is safe to say, range from originalism, which holds that the justices are bound to interpret the Constitution according to the intentions of the Framers and ratifiers, to what is called non-interpretivism—or what I think is more appropriately called activism—which maintains that the justices should, when possible, advance the basic values embodied in the spirit of the Constitution. The course, I should add, also deals with other schools of thought that claim to fit in somewhere between these two extremes.[1]

My concern here, I hasten to add, is not with these theories as such, but with the questions they raise about the current status of our constitutional order. Specifically, that there should be differences of such magnitude over how to interpret the Constitution can only be a sign of far deeper troubles in our republic. To begin with, these differences mean that we are not agreed on the terms or language of the basic document that establishes our political order, at least in those quarters where it counts. In turn, this means that the Constitution takes on a totally different role, purpose, and character for individuals, depending upon what school of interpretive thought they happen to subscribe to. Equally alarming, what might seem to one school of thought to be a legitimate exercise of the power of judicial review by the Supreme Court might not seem so legitimate to another. What is more, as we think about the implications of the positions of these modern schools of thought, the entire question of how power or authority is allocated in the Constitution comes into play. Controversy, as we shall see, not only arises over the legitimacy of a particular judicial decision, but also arises over whether the judiciary is the proper constitutional forum for the resolution of the matter at issue. Thus, controversy arises over the legitimate scope of the powers and functions of the branches of government, a concern vital to the primary and basic ends of constitutionalism, particularly the rule of law.

These concerns are far from academic. Clearly the most important question that eventually arises from a critical examination of the different schools of constitutional interpretation concerns the proper role of the Supreme Court in our system of government. To be sure, from almost the beginning of our constitutional republic, the Supreme Court has been recognized as having a special role, namely, imposing constitutional limitations on the other branches of government. But this role derived from the logic of the Constitution itself. How, for instance, could limitations on congressional power be enforced save through judicial review? The Court's role in that capacity, though, is a narrow one, providing no justification for the positive role urged on it by modern activists who maintain that the Court is empowered to advance the "spirit" of the Constitution, to spell out concretely, whenever possible, what its "vision" of "human dignity" means in the modern world.[2] The originalists, who, by and large, support the traditional and limited judicial review, view this activism as a usurpation of the legislative function.

But the differences go even further. Many originalists argue that activists have devised a theory of interpretation—that is, the advancement of the underlying values or "spirit" of the Constitution—as a "cover" to advance political ends that could not otherwise gain enactment through the political processes. Those holding this view maintain that non-interpretivism is result oriented, that it is intentionally designed and used to lend justification for the Court's role in advancing what can fairly be regarded as a liberal political agenda. If this charge is substantially true, then what we have is the subordination of the Constitution and the rules it provides for decision making to the political ends of a minority. This subordination, of course, by itself constitutes a very serious state of affairs.

Even if we assume that the Supreme Court is "neutral" in the sense that it lacks an institutional inclination to advance an ideological agenda, we still confront inter-related questions concerning what role the Court ought have in our system and what constitutes a legitimate method of constitutional interpretation. This is to say, our initial and basic concern remains: If one accepts as a rule of interpretation that the Court is entitled to look beyond the text of the Constitution to its spirit and to its inherent, unarticulated values, then one must also make an additional and even grander assumption about the character of the constitutional system; namely, that our Constitution was designed to allow the Court to advance the ideals implicit in the Constitution that at the very least, such a judicial power is not incompatible with the original design of the Constitution. Otherwise activism would rest on an unconstitutional usurpation of powers.

In what follows, I want to explore this and related matters in greater detail by way of addressing the central question concerning the status of our Constitution.

JUDICIAL TYRANNY?

Now, in dealing with the controversy surrounding the Court and its role in our system, I am fully aware that throughout our history there have been disputes between the branches, as well as between the state and national governments over the extent of their authority. As my remarks indicate, what I am referring to is more funda-mental. We now encounter disagreement about the na-ture of the regime—for instance, to what extent the Constitution was designed to allow for popular self-gov-ernment through our representative institutions—and to what extent the judiciary is authorized to guide the legislative branch and the states, to impose upon them policies presumably mandated by its interpretation of the Constitution's animating values. Most prior disputes, on the other hand, could be settled well within the parameters of the traditional regime by the use of powers and authority found in the Constitution. This one, however, centers on the very meaning and nature of the Constitution itself.

The role that the modern Court has assumed is questionable, quite apart from its incompatibility with republicanism. We can see this by turning to the separation of powers, clearly one of the fundamental principles embodied in our Constitution. The major reason for this separation, infrequently remarked upon today, was the Framers' fear that tyranny would result from a union of the legislative, executive, and judicial powers. Indeed, as we see from both *The Federalist* and the Massachusetts Constitution of 1780, the union of any two branches was sufficient to produce a state of tyranny.[3] The tyranny which they feared consisted of arbitrary and capricious rule, marked by the absence of the rule of law. They believed that a constitutional concentration of powers by itself would constitute tyranny because it would establish a relationship between the rulers and ruled not unlike that between a master and slave. The essential point here is not what the rulers might do, but the permanent establishment of this relationship in the basic law. A master, for instance, might treat his slaves with utmost kindness. Yet, the master-slave relationship would still exist along with the legitimate apprehensions among the slaves generated by the potential power of the master. From the viewpoint of traditionalists, therefore, judicial activism amounts to judicial tyranny because the Court has taken on the legislative function, at least in its efforts to advance the implicit values and aspirations buried in the Constitution. Moreover, as critics of the Court are wont to point out, modern presidents have felt it their constitutional duty to enforce the decisions of the Court, so that what we have in practice is a concentration of all three powers, not just two, in the hands of the judiciary.

Modern courts, by all evidences, have not been reluctant to use their powers. As Lino A. Graglia, an outspoken critic of the Court, puts it,

> in the years since *Brown* [*Brown v. Board of Education,* 1954], nearly every fundamental change in domestic national policy has been brought about not by the decentralized democratic (or more accurately, republican) process contemplated by the Constitution, but simply by the Court's decree. The Court has decided, on a national basis and often in opposition to the wishes of a majority of the American people, issues literally of life and death, as in its decisions invalidating virtually all restrictions on abortion and severely restricting the use of capital punishment. It has decided issues of public security and order, as in its decisions greatly expanding the protection of the criminally accused and limiting state power to control street demonstrations and vagrancy, and issues of public morality, as in the decisions disallowing most state controls of pornography, obscenity, and nudity.

"The Court," Graglia continues, "has both prohibited the states from making provision for prayer in the schools and disallowed most forms of aid, state or federal, to religious schools. It has required that children be excluded from their neighborhood public schools and bused to more distant schools in order to increase school racial integration." It has also, he observes, "invalidated most of the law of libel and slander." And, he concludes, "in terms of the issues that determine the nature and quality of life in a society, the Supreme Court has become our most important institution of government."[4] It has become, as many critics have noted, the primary engine for social change.

But there are matters that Graglia doesn't mention that also point to rule by the judiciary. Shortly after the *Brown* decision in the mid-1950s which called for the desegregation of the public schools, a majority of the Court declared for the first time that the Constitution means what the Court says it means and that its decisions are constitutionally binding on the other branches. This declaration was something new under the constitutional sun; it sought to overturn the traditional morality which held that each branch was entitled to interpret the Constitution according to its best lights and then act accordingly. The older morality was that embodied in the statement reputedly made by President Jackson after Marshall's decision in the Cherokee Indian Case: "Justice Marshall has made his decision, now let's see him enforce it." The import of the Court's assertion is to say that branches are equal and coordinate, but one branch— that is, the judiciary—is more equal than the others.

Lest you think that this new morality has not taken hold in the judiciary, consider the decision of District Court Judge Russell Clark, who ordered Kansas City, at the cost of seven hundred million dollars, to build new schools to draw whites back into the inner city schools. The centerpiece of this new system was the high school which, at the order of the judge, included a planetarium, a vivarium, greenhouses, a model United Nations wired for language translation, radio and television studios, movie editing and screening rooms, olympic size swimming pools, a zoo, a farm, a wild-land area, and a temperature controlled art gallery. His decree also specified aesthetically pleasing carpets and fifteen computers per classroom.[5]

When the citizens of Kansas City refused to raise the tax levy to finance this project—a levy that exceeded the limitation specified in the Missouri Constitution—Judge Clark declared the Missouri constitutional limitation unconstitutional and levied a property tax on the citizens to cover the costs of his school plan. The Supreme Court, in a five to four vote, upheld Judge Clark. In protest of his decision, some citizens of Kansas City took up the chant of our forbearers, "no taxation without representation" and actually dumped tea bags on the steps of the federal court building.

THE CONSTITUTION: A DEAD LETTER?

My purpose in pointing to the character of the pronouncements and orders of the modern courts is that they give us reason to question whether activism conforms in any sense with the original constitutional mission assigned the courts. Indeed, as my remarks to this point intimate, the controversies surrounding the courts on important decisions point convincingly to judicial supremacy, if not tyranny, and lead me to ask whether the Constitution is now, in fact, a dead letter. I ask this in a very special sense. I do not mean to say that we no longer have a House of Representatives, a Senate, a Supreme Court, and a president. What I do mean is that there is no longer a consensus, an understanding, or agreement among the people concerning fundamental constitutional questions of the relationships between the branches, the locus of power, the intended restraints on government and the people, or even the proper relationship between the national and state governments. Put another way, our system operates as if we lack basic agreement as a people about the character of the Constitution, the dynamics and operations of the constitutional institutions and processes. This being the case, the Constitution and the processes it provides for are of no use in answering the basic questions surrounding our political order.

Let me briefly point out the gulf that separates the traditionalists from the activists that would tend to support the proposition that the Constitution is dead in the sense I have indicated above.

Those who contend that the Court is acting *ultra vires*—that is, acting unconstitutionally, beyond its legitimate powers—certainly have a strong case. There is no way, in my estimation, that the debates in either the Philadelphia Convention or the ratifying conventions can be read to support the role of the modern Court. Hamilton in *The Federalist* described the Court as the weakest of the three branches—incapable of taking any active resolution, as it depended on the executive and Congress for the enforcement of its decisions. He quoted from Montesquieu to the effect that the judiciary is next to nothing; so weak in fact that life tenure was needed to protect the judges from bowing to the will of the other branches. What is more, Hamilton set forth a morality, the key elements of which were repeated by Marshall when he first exercised the power of judicial review in *Marbury v. Madison*. This morality held that the Court should exercise "judgment," not "will"; it should only use its power of judicial review to invalidate laws that were manifestly contrary to the Constitution and, in this connection, he offered the prohibitions against *ex post facto* laws and bills of attainder as examples—easily defined constitutional prohibitions on congressional action that the Court should uphold, if the Congress should ever waver. He believed that the Court should only use its power to nullify laws when there was an "irreconcilable variance" between the law and the Constitution.[6] In any case, Hamilton and Marshall asserted and defended the doctrine of judicial review on originalist grounds: that the Court should uphold the constituent will—the will of those who ratified the Constitution—over the political will of those operating through the institutions created by the Constitution. The Court's power was to be a negative one—and no one at the time of founding suggested otherwise; no one, this is to say, set forth the proposition that the court possessed a positive power to actually make laws in the course of deciding cases.

This constitutional morality, with its insistence on the limited and deferential role of the judiciary in the exercise of judicial review, prevailed until well into the twentieth century. In a classic article, which appeared in 1893, summarizing the origin, scope, and nature of judicial review, James B. Thayer termed the reluctance of the courts to use their power of judicial review a "rule" because it was articulated over and over again up to that point in our history by judges at the state and national levels. These courts, he maintained, would only use their power of judicial review when they were convinced that those responsible for making the laws "have not merely made a mistake, but have made a very clear one,—so clear that it is not open to rational question." This constitutional morality or "rule" embraced beliefs that invited such restraint. It recognized, as Thayer put it, "that having regard to the great, complex, ever-unfolding exigencies of government, much which will seem unconstitutional to one man, or body of men, may reasonably not seem so to another; that the constitution often admits of different interpretations; that there is often a choice and judgment; that in such cases the constitution does not impose upon the legislature any one specific opinion, but leaves open this range of choice; and that whatever choice is rational is constitutional." Thayer cites Judge Cooley to the effect that a legislator might vote against a bill on the grounds of its being unconstitutional, but if that bill became law, and subsequently that same legislator sat on the bench and had to rule on its constitutionality, he might well find it constitutional. Such was the nature of the "rule"; judges were bound to look beyond "their own judgment" in passing on the "constitutionality" of a law.[8]

But clearly we are now in a constitutional universe quite different from that in which Thayer wrote. Indeed, it would seem that we have, in effect, two constitutional universes, so to speak, that of the Framers, which is coherent, fully developed, and allows only a limited and negative role for the judiciary, and that of the activists, which, though not fully articulated, clearly centers a powerful judiciary authorized to set down the goals and guidelines for the more politically responsive departments of government. The standards and morality of one are not suitable or relevant for the other; the two stand apart, there being no common or accepted standards to judge the "validity" of one over the other. The activists, to put this into the context of our previous remarks, would dismiss Thayer's "rule" as inhibiting the judiciary to a degree that renders the Constitution lifeless, inert, incapable of meeting the demands of the modern world and of adjusting to new and refined moral standards. Thayer's rule, they would continue, in the most profound sense violates the intentions of the Framers who realized that new meanings would have to be read into the Constitution for it to endure.

THE QUESTION OF LEGITIMACY

Sooner or later any inquiry into the disputes arising from these different views of the Constitution and, in particular, the role of the Supreme Court (which serves as a convenient focal point to indicate their essential differences), the question of legitimacy must arise. Let us then begin our inquiry into this matter by first briefly examining the standard of legitimacy that originalists use. As we have already intimated, originalists are quite at home with the traditionalist view of our Constitution. Indeed, as we have seen, the two go hand in hand; the originalists want the courts to uphold the "constituent will" of the people, that "will" embodied in the Constitution at the time of ratification. The argument for judicial review as presented by both Hamilton and Marshall hinges on the proposition that this constituent will, found in the Constitution, is superior to the "political" will of the people that is expressed through the institutions of government created by the constituent will. Hamilton addresses this matter directly in *The Federalist*, Number 78 by maintaining that in preferring "the constitution" to a "statute" does not mean that the judiciary is superior to the legislature, but rather that "the power of the people is superior to both." In this vein, he continues, the will of the people "declared in the constitution" is superior to the "will of the legislature" or even to the will of popular majorities that seek measures "incompatible with provisions of the existing constitution." The Constitution is "fundamental" law that takes precedence over laws that "are not fundamental," that is, legislative acts.[9]

From this traditionalist perspective, then, judicial activism is not constitutionally legitimate, nor are the decisions of activist courts which reach beyond the "constituent will." We can identify at least two dimensions of this illegitimacy or departure from traditional constitutional morality. The first relates to the courts' invalidating legislation or other expressions of the popular will. On this issue, we should note, the traditionalist position outlined above gives a wide berth for the people to enact their will and this for reasons spelled out by Thayer.[10] In Hamilton's original formulation the only limitation on the popular will is that it not violate the express provisions of the Constitution. Consequently, when the courts invalidate policies of long standing, such as state financed military schools for men only, or "overturn" referenda such as the one in California on affirmative action or in Colorado that denied homosexuals special minority status, they only fuel the traditionalists' charge that the judiciary is removing from "democratic control" the "most important moral, political, and cultural decisions affecting our lives."[11] Or, as another critic put it, the Supreme Court in recent decades has undermined popular self-government "in the political sense of the term. It excludes from the political process the objects of mutual deliberation that make political order desirable. indeed even possible."[12]

A second, and perhaps more controversial dimension of illegitimacy, from the traditionalist perspective, involves positive policy pronouncements from the Court, normally anchored in a creative interpretation of a general capacious constitutional provision. This "positive" dimension emerged first in the desegregation decisions of the 1950s,[13] decisions which elevated the Court to a "new plateau" of judicial power. Prior to these decisions the Court had been criticized for abusing its powers in nullifying legislation on "substantive due process" grounds, whereby the judges merely substituted their will or ideas of the common good for those of the legislators. Yet in these instances, the Court merely restored the status quo ante; it invalidated the legislation, but did not attempt to dictate policies that the elected branches were constitutionally bound to enforce. The segregation decisions, however, were profoundly different. In the words of one careful student of the judiciary, Charles S. Hyneman, these decisions "had a social consequence of a vastly different order. They called for a rewriting of state and federal legislation relating to public education." "The Supreme Court," Hyneman continues, "did not order Alabama and Mississippi and South Carolina to forget about an innovation in public policy and continue as they had lived it before the promulgation of that innovation; the Court ordered people in those states to fashion legislation of a kind they had never had on their statute books and to institute some social relationships that had never prevailed in those places."[14]

The desegregation decisions escaped critical scrutiny at the time, largely because their goal, to advance the cause of racial equality, was considered morally right. But such was not the case with the Court's decision legalizing abortion.[15] Again, in effect the Court legislated, this time to advance the "right of privacy"—a right not to be found in the Constitution. This, for originalists, exemplified creative constitutional interpretation well beyond the constitutionally prescribed judicial function.

For all of this, however, the activists are not without answers. In the first place, their stance rejects the notion that Court's function is to discern and enforce the "constituent will" in the sense that Hamilton describes it. Activists simply reject the standards of the traditionalists because they view the Constitution as a "living" document, its values constantly undergoing refinement with the passage of time and new circumstances. What is more, they would point out that the political institutions—the president and the Congress—could take steps to curtail the Court's authority; that the process of appointment and confirmation of judges could be used to effectuate a change in the direction of the judiciary; and that the people through amendments to the Constitution could overturn Court decisions not to their liking.[16] But none of this, they point out, has occurred.

Russell Hittinger, an outspoken critic of the modern Court, puts the difficulty associated with the legitimacy of the activist position quite well. It might be argued, he points out, that the "commands" of the Court are "not legitimate" on the basis of the principle that the "rule of law prohibits reallocation of share of authority without the consent of the governed" and "obedience should not be given to an act that violates the foundation of the rule of law." But, Hittinger goes on, whether this principle applies to an activist Court is "ambiguous and admits no clear answer." "There is no doubt," he observes, "but we live today under an altered constitutional regime, where the rules are no longer supplied by a written document but by federal courts defining the powers of government *ad hoc*, through their own case law." Now this state of affairs, he acknowledges, really constitutes a "new regime" that has not been "ratified by amendment or constitutional convention." Moreover, he writes, it has come about in a manner "often hidden by political and judicial rhetoric that gives honor to and even cites the written Constitution." Yet, he maintains, "this profound and confusing change does not necessarily make the new constitutional order illegitimate." "It is plausible to argue," he points out, "that this new regime evolved over time with the tacit consent of the government"; that "every sector of government has acquiesced in the Court's understanding of its own powers"; and that "the elected representatives," though they "may complain about particular judicial rulings" and attempt "to influence those rulings through judicial appointments and party platforms," have not "challenged the authority of the ruling principle itself."[17]

With Hittinger's observations we end up back where we started. The question of legitimacy cannot be answered by applying the standards of one school of thought to the other. These schools, as I noted above, represent independent universes of thought with virtually no common ground, certainly none that would suffice to provide for any accommodation between them. The traditionalist school upholds the Constitution as the authoritative guide for providing the rules and standards for the regime. The activists offer a new regime wherein "judicial interpretation rules the text, according to the Court's perception of the common good and the changing needs of the polity."[18]

Legitimacy and the "New Regime"

Perhaps the paramount question in American politics today is whether the "new regime," signified by the judicial activism we have surveyed, is legitimate. Clearly the basic values and principles of the older regime that characterize the traditional understanding of our constitutional order, have been ignored and in some instances transgressed. But are these transgressions only the outgrowth of a legitimate displacement of the older, traditional understanding by the values, goals, and principles of a new regime? Does the tacit consent to the decisions of the activist judiciary amount to a bestowal of legitimacy on the new regime?

In my view, this question must be answered in the negative for the following reasons. Let us for the sake of argument stipulate that, at a minimum, legitimacy depends on popular acceptance of or consent to the principles, goals, and operations of a regime. This presumes, of course, a knowledge of these principles, goals, and operations. Now, whereas one could argue that the broad outlines of the older, traditional regime are laid out in, say, *The Federalist* and in countless civics books that have been written over the decades, the new regime offers up scarcely anything in the way of primary sources for understanding its values and goals, unless we look to the likes of Ronald Dworkin's *Taking Rights Seriously* or John Rawls's *A Theory of Justice*, both tedious, arcane, and perplexing works. Moreover, neither work will serve to define the proper role of the judiciary, much less the structures and operations of other institutions within the new regime. The fact is, to speak more generally, the proponents of judicial supremacy have been so busy defending it as something akin to the conscience of the American soul that they have paid scant attention to the place, functions, or powers of other institutions and what their relationship to it ought to be. Even with respect to the judiciary itself there are no clear limits set forth regarding its powers.

To put this in terms we spoke of before, the traditional understanding of the Court and its role in our system is supported by a constitutional cosmos wherein the order of the whole and the relationship of the parts are explained. The activists, on the other hand, clearly reject the traditional constitutional cosmos and act as if there is another that can replace it. But my point is that, as yet, they have not outlined such a cosmos. Rather, they have merely carved out a new and revolutionary role for the Court.

Perhaps more important, the literature supporting judicial activism, which is presumably advancing a new regime, offers little by way of justification, that is, answering critical questions by telling us why, on what grounds or for what reason, the Supreme Court should be the locus of power in a new regime. What are the strengths and weaknesses of the judiciary relative to, say, representative institutions in identifying problems and providing workable solutions? Are the judges better equipped to secure a consensus over major policy concerns than elected representatives? If so, why? What is it in their education, perspective, or temperament that better equips them for this task?

I do not believe it is necessary to belabor what seems obvious, namely, the new regime, to which Hittinger among others refers, is really not a regime in the ordinary sense of that word. Looking to the writings of those who defend judicial activism we find a narrowness of focus, a fuzziness or unconcern about the institutions and operations other than the judiciary, a silence about the most salient questions relating to justification, even with regard to the scope of judicial power. This points to the fact that what many have taken to be a new regime is in reality a narrow "movement" that has managed to distort and severely damage a vital component of the old regime. It can be likened to a torpedo that hits a particularly vulnerable portion of a large ship, causing the ship to sink ever so slowly. In these terms, then, we may say that the Constitution is not dead, but it clearly is dying. The advocates and defenders of judicial activism only appear to be advancing a new regime largely because judicial activism ignores, undercuts, and even abrogates the values, beliefs, and practices that characterized and undergirded the old.

In my view, the tacit consent that judicial activism seems to enjoy derives in large measure from the moral capital the judiciary has accumulated over the decades through its place, function, and morally elevated position in the old regime; an inherited reverence derived from, we might say, the homage paid to it over many decades. I must immediately add to this, by way of explaining this seeming tacit consent, the abysmal ignorance of the American people about their Constitution and how it was designed to operate. If, for instance, the American people could be made aware of what judicial activism entails, how it impacts on other institutions and the values of the older regime, then I venture to say that Court, as an institution, would scarcely enjoy any more popular support than, say, recent Congresses. It might even enjoy less.

The question then becomes, why can't this be done? There is no one answer to this question. But certainly a major one is that judicial activists possess a political agenda that they seek to advance. Thus, the issue of legitimacy, of even whether judicial activism is compatible with the principles of the old regime, are soon converted into political issues by the proponents of activism. When this happens a confusing and seemingly endless array of interrelated charges and counter-charges ensue (for example, the Court's behavior would not shock the Framers; originalism as an alternative poses even greater difficulties; there is no difference between what the Court does today and what it has done on occasion in the past; or critics of the Court are just sore losers). In short order, the basic issues and charges are obfuscated at least in the public arena. The average American, lacking a knowledge of the Constitution and politically apathetic to begin with, soon comes to regard the debate as just another partisan wrangle.

William Gangi offers an interesting alternative explanation that is not completely at odds with the foregoing. He uses Plato's cave metaphor to describe in operational terms how it comes to pass that the integrity of the old regime can be subverted. He pictures the Supreme Court justices "casting shadows on the front wall" of the cave. Behind the justices arc to be found, in order, "constitutional scholars," "members of the intelligentsia (other lawyers, political scientists, and educators)," "elected officials," media representatives," and, in the back rows, the "common citizens." In his view, the common citizens receive interpretations of the shadows (that is, the Court's decisions) from those seated in from of them. And these interpretations, as he points out, are usually couched in terms of "greater personal liberty and social justice," with nary a word about how the Court's power is undermining the traditional order. Thus, the common man associates the Court with "God" words—"social justice," "rights," and "liberty."

But what of Congress, our Senators and Representatives? Surely, one might well believe, they know better. Yet this is not necessarily the case. They fall into one of four categories. One group, like the common man, is really unaware of what is going on; its members view the Court's activities as largely beneficent. A second group understands what is going on, the extent to which the older regime is being subverted, but its members are result-oriented and like the decisions made by the activist Courts. A third knows what is going on, does not like it, but is aware of the adverse political consequences that might flow from an attack on the Court. The members of the fourth group, small in number, see the implications of the Court's behavior and say so. But they are usually drowned out.

Our dilemma today, we must repeat, is almost totally attributable to the public's ignorance of the principles and morality of the older regime. In our view, a better informed public would see beyond the partisan bickering and the sophistry of the intelligentsia and media elite, groups favorably disposed to judicial activism because it advances an ideological agenda to which they stand committed.

Given all of these factors, we may, by way of concluding, put the status of the Constitution in the following terms: The old regime, that which corresponded with the principles, values, and goals of the original Constitution, is dying. It has been mortally wounded by an opportunistic attack at a vital point that totally distorts its allocation of powers and authority. Conversely, the attacking forces have provided none of the rationale and justification for a new regime; they are seemingly content to operate within the shell of the older regime, pretending as if they are its true heirs. Finally, there seems to be no way to repel the attack and reestablish the older regime in the immediate future.

What this means is that down the road a significant number of people, those who are becoming increasingly aware of the gravity of the situation, are going to challenge the legitimacy of the Court's behavior, perhaps even through disobedience when possible. The question of legitimacy that is rearing its head with greater frequency with each passing year indicates the depth or intensity of the resistance to kritarchy. At some point, the activists will be called upon to give an honest accounting, to spell out the implications of their stance in the broader setting of republican government. They will have to justify their positions to a wider audience, one that promises to be more skeptical than law school deans. There is hope that we ought eventually see an affirmation of the older regime, once this process has taken place. What seems apparent is that sooner or later we are going to have to "regularize" matters, that is, come to some kind of coherent and consistent understanding of the rules, principles, and goals that should guide our decision-making processes.

For now, however, we are in a state of "limbo" wherein the most basic questions about the placement of authority cannot be answered, not even by reference to the Constitution itself.

NOTES

INTRODUCTION

1. Gertrude Himmelfarb: "In these few years, we have begun to think the unthinkable. . . . We have even begun to do the undoable." Mitchell S. Muncy, ed., *The End of Democracy? The Judicial Usurpation of Politics* (Dallas: Spence Publishing Company, 1997), 88. Hereafter, this first *End of Democracy?* volume will be referred to as EOD.

2. William Kristol: "Creating . . . a majority is the radical task before us. The problem with the *First Things* symposium is that its 'radicalizing mood' distracts from this truly radical task." EOD, 94.

3. Peter L. Berger: "The conservative mandate on the 'values' issue is to spell out an authentically conservative position without falling into a radicalizing mood that proposes nonnegotiable absolutes." EOD, 73.

4. William J. Bennett: "My concern with declaring the American 'regime' illegitimate is that it assumes that because of the actions of an out-of-control Court, America has become (or is about to become) a nation that is irredeemably antidemocratic, that we have exhausted all our options, that we are powerless to rein in the Court. That is simply not so." EOD, 69.

5. Midge Decter: "What we are dealing with is, in short, a cultural, rather than primarily a judicial, problem." EOD, 79.

6. Norman Podhoretz: "I am appalled . . . by the seditious measures you contemplate and all but advocate; and by the aid and comfort you for all practical purposes offer to the bomb-throwers among us." EOD, 101-02, quoting from a letter from Podhoretz to Richard John Neuhaus.

7. Midge Decter: "Could you not see, in the twentieth of all centuries, how profoundly offensive it is to speak this way when even the truly morally justified revolutions of our time—against Hitler, Stalin, Mao, and their acolytes and imitators—never, alas, took place?" EOD, 79.

8. Peter L. Berger: "It is only with great difficulty that I can entertain the idea that abortion is an 'icon of absolute evil' to be placed alongside the Holocaust. Indeed, that idea, even if taken as a theoretical exercise, strikes me as, precisely, a 'moral enormity'." EOD, 73.

9. Peter L. Berger: "A key concern of *First Things* is a usurpation of power by the courts. . . . But is this enough reason to cast doubt on the legitimacy of the system? The American separation of powers has always been a creaky affair." EOD, 72.

10. Peter L. Berger: "Imagine that abortion in the United States had achieved its present legal status through an act of Congress [and] the Supreme Court had then ruled this act to be unconstitutional. I doubt very much that most of the *First Things* contributors would have viewed the latter action as a serious usurpation of power, let alone a reason to question the legitimacy of the American polity." Compare Gertrude Himmelfarb: "But what if the legalization of abortion were the product not of the judiciary but of the legislature—if it betokened not the 'end of democracy' but the very exercise of democracy? This is, in fact, the case in most Western countries. . . . Does this mean that all these regimes . . . are also in violation of the moral law and hence illegitimate?" EOD, 73, 90.

11. Though Stanley Hauerwas remains more ally than critic, his comment illustrates the point: "The problem isn't the courts. The problem is the American people! The conservatives don't want to admit that this is what the American people want! They *want* assisted suicide! They believe in autonomy!" EOD, 213.

12. Gertrude Himmelfarb: "If conservatives do take democracy and the Constitution seriously, if we are truly exercised by the usurpation of judicial power, we must also be prepared for the possibility that *vox populi* might differ from many of us on the subject of abortion." EOD, 90.

13. The editors of *National Review*: "[D]emocracy provides legal avenues of protest and reform which remove the justification for resistance to specific unjust laws—or at least shrink it to the level of conscientious objection and modest civil disobedience (which, to be sure, is all that Professor Hittinger *et al.* are claiming). . . . because a democracy never finally makes up its mind but allows infinite debate, it cannot be said to have embraced a crime or entrenched a sin." EOD, 97.

14. Samuel Francis: "[N]o one is commanded to have or perform an abortion or to suffer or perform euthanasia. The laws to which the symposiasts object are permissive, not compulsive, and how one might 'resist' such permissive laws is never clear." EOD, 136.

15. Walter Berns: "It is the Constitution, the product of [the American] Revolution, and not a recondite 'moral law,' that the President swears to 'protect and defend,' the members of Congress to 'support,' and the judges to 'support and defend'.... [T]he Constitution . . . consign[s] religion to the private sphere." EOD, 77.

16. Perhaps this is what Gertrude Himmelfarb meant: "This is not, it seems to me, a proper mode of political discourse, still less of conservative political discourse. Indeed it discredits, or at the very least makes suspect, any attempt by conservatives to introduce moral and religious considerations into 'the public square'—as if morality and religion necessarily lead to such apocalyptic political conclusions." EOD, 113.

17. In justified war theory, these correspond to the criteria of Last Resort and Legitimate Public Authority.

18. For further discussion see Milton R. Konvitz, "Conscience and Civil Disobedience in the Jewish Tradition," in Milton R. Konvitz, ed., *Judaism and Human Rights* (New York: W.W. Norton; © 1972 by B'nai B'rith Commission on Adult Jewish Education).

19. The latter suggestion is from Michael W. McConnell's thoughtful essay "Bending the Law, Breaking the Law," *First Things* 74 (June/July 1997): 13-15.

20. This is why it was such an important event when abortion advocate Naomi Wolf admitted in 1995 that she and her fellow feminists have known all along what abortion really is. See her article "Our Bodies, Our Souls," *New Republic*, October 16, 1995.

21. "The Public Square," *First Things* 84 (June/July 1998): 61-65.

22. "They are independent of the people, of the legislature, and of every power under heaven. Men placed in this situation will generally soon feel themselves independent of heaven itself." Brutus, Essay No. 15.

23. "The measures of popular legislatures naturally settle down in time, and gradually approach a mild and just equilibrium; while the rigid systems of the law courts naturally become more severe and arbitrary, if not carefully tempered and guarded"; moreover, "we are more in danger of sowing the seeds of arbitrary government in this department than in any other." The Federal Farmer, Letter No. 15.

24. "Every extension of the power of the general legislature, as well as of the judicial powers, will increase the powers of the courts; and the dignity and importance of the judges, will be in proportion to

the extent and magnitude of the powers they exercise." Brutus, Essay No. 11.

25. "In determining [Constitutional] questions, the [Supreme] court must and will assume certain principles, from which they will reason, in forming their decisions. These principles, whatever they may be, when they become fixed, by a course of decisions, will be adopted by the legislature, and will be the rule by which they explain their own powers .... For as on the one hand, they will not readily pass laws which they know the courts will not execute, so on the other, we may be sure they will not scruple to pass such as they know they will give effect, as often as they may judge it proper." Brutus, Essay No. 12.

26. The Anti-Federalists were transfixed by the manner in which the English court of exchequer expanded its jurisdiction. Intended by Parliament only for suits by debtors of the king against third parties whose actions had injured their ability to repay, it was opened to everyone by the simple expedient of allowing anyone to call himself a debtor of the king. Compare the way in which our own courts have manipulated the rules of standing.

27. Its most widely quoted instance is the following remark of the editors of *National Review:* "Our general obligation to obey the laws rests upon the fact that the laws protect us (against our fellow man), not upon the ultimate justice of the government's founding, still less (fortunately) upon its general moral character." EOD, 97, 160.

28. For his part, Neuhaus concedes the tension but demurs from the idea that his "tortured soul" has been "reluctantly" forced to confront it. "The Public Square," *First Things* 84 (June 1998): 61-65. Other reflections by Neuhaus about Baxter can be found in *First Things* 72 (April 1997): 59-61, and 73 (May 1997): 61-62, as well as EOD, 214-216.

29. EOD, 264.

1 Rebuilding the Civil Public Square

1. EOD, 3-62.
2. EOD, 175-267.
3. EOD, 8-9.
4. EOD, 175.
5. EOD, 8.
6. EOD, 175-267.
7. "We Hold These Truths: A Statement of Christian Conscience and Citizenship," *First Things* 76 (Oct. 1997): 51.
8. *Planned Parenthood v. Casey,* 505 U.S. 833 (1992).
9. *Roe v. Wade,* 410 U.S. 113 (1973).
10. *Planned Parenthood v. Casey,* 868.

11. "These Truths," 53.
12. *Everson v. Board of Education*, 330 U.S. 1 (1947).
13. See Richard J. Neuhaus, *The Naked Public Square* (1984).
14. See U. S. Constitution, amend. 1.
15. *Lee v. Weisman*, 505 U.S. 577 (1992).
16. *Lee v. Weisman*, 589.
17. *Romer v. Evans*, 517 U.S. 620 (1996).
18. *Planned Parenthood v. Casey*, 851.
19. The Declaration of Independence (U.S. 1776), para. 1.
20. Pope John Paul II, *Centesimus Annus* (1 May 1991), 88–89.
21. Ibid.
22. Ibid., 89.
23. Ibid.
24. *Brown v. Board of Education*, 347 U. S. 483 (1954).
25. *Engel v. Vitale*, 370 U.S. 421 (1962).
26. *Roe v. Wade*, 113; *Doe v. Bolton*, 410 U.S. 179 (1973).
27. *Planned Parenthood v. Casey*, 833.
28. "These Truths," 52–53.
29. Ibid., 53.
30. *Washington v. Glucksberg*, 117 Sup. Ct. 2258 (1997).
31. *Washington v. Glucksberg.*
32. *City of Boerne v. Flores*, 117 Sup. Ct. 2157 (1997).
33. George Washington, "First Inaugural Address," in *Documents of American History*, ed. Henry S. Commage and Milton Canto, 10th ed. (1988), 1:152.
34. George Washington, "Farewell Address," in *Documents of American History*, ed. Henry S. Commage and Milton Canto, 10th ed. (1988), 1: 169, 173.
35. U.S. Constitution, amend. 1.
36. Richard J. Neuhaus, "A New Order of Religious Freedom," *George Washington Law Review* 60 (1992): 627.
37. Pope John Paul II, *Centesimus Annus*, 89.
38. The Declaration of Independence, para. 1.

2   GOVERNMENT BY THE "THOUGHTFUL PART"

1. *Dred Scott v. Sandford*, 60 U.S. 393 (1856), superseded by U.S. Constitution, amend. 13 and 14.
2. Abraham Lincoln, "Speech at Columbus, Ohio (Sep. 16, 1859)," in *Lincoln Speeches and Writings 1859–65* (Library of America, 1989), 53.
3. Ibid.
4. EOD, 131.

5. EOD, 131.

6. EOD, 131.

7. EOD, 131.

8. EOD, 88.

9. EOD, 89.

10. "On the Future of Conservatism: A Symposium," *Commentary* 103 Feb. 1997): 14.

11. EOD, 78.

12. "Conservatism," 14.

13. EOD, 72.

14. EOD, 72.

15. *Planned Parenthood v. Casey*, 505 U.S. 833 (1992).

16. Gerard V. Bradley, "The New Constitutional Covenant," *The World & I* (Mar. 1994): 375.

17. For example, *Cooper v. Aaron*, 358 U.S. 1 (1958); *Dred Scott v. Sanford*; *Marbury v. Madison*, 5 U.S. 137 (1803).

18. *Olmstead v. United States*, 277 U.S. 438, 478 (1928) (Brandeis J., dissenting).

19. In *Washington v. Glucksberg*, 117 Sup. Ct. 2258 (1997), Chief Justice Rehnquist refused to extend the *Casey* dictum about liberty to the issue of physician-assisted suicide. See *Planned Parenthood v. Casey*, 851 ("At the heart of liberty is the right to define one's own concept of existence, of meaning, of the universe, and of the mystery of human life. Beliefs about these matters could not define the attributes of personhood were they formed under compulsion of the State.") With respect to the *Casey* dictum, Rehnquist stated that "Casey described, . . . in light of our prior cases, those personal activities and decisions that this Court has identified as so deeply rooted in our history and traditions, or so fundamental to our concept of constitutionally ordered liberty, that they are protected by the Fourteenth Amendment." He concluded that "many of the rights and liberties protected by the Due Process Clause sound in personal autonomy does not warrant the sweeping conclusion that any and all important, intimate, and personal decisions are so protected." *Washington v. Glucksberg*, 2271. Yet this is not a repudiation of the *Casey* dictum; it only puts the breaks on its application to physician-assisted suicide. And it leaves completely untouched the *Casey* dicta about the social contract.

20. Here, I rely upon the useful discussion of this matter in Paul A Rahe, *Republics Ancient & Modern: Classical Republicanism and the American Revolution* (1992), 8–13.

21. *Planned Parenthood v. Casey*, 853.

22. *Planned Parenthood v. Casey*, 853.

23. *Roe v. Wade*, 410 U.S. 113 (1973).
24. *Planned Parenthood v. Casey*, 865 (emphasis added).
25. *Planned Parenthood v. Casey*, 845-46.
26. *Griswold v. Connecticut*, 381 U.S. 479 (1986).
27. *Roe v. Wade*, 113.
28. *Planned Parenthood v. Casey*, 847.
29. *Planned Parenthood v. Casey*, 851.
30. *Planned Parenthood v. Casey*, 851.
31. As the authors of the joint opinion wrote: "It will be recognized, of course, that *Roe* stands at an intersection of two lines of decisions, but in whichever doctrinal category one reads the case, the result for present purposes will be the same. *Roe*, however, may be seen not only as an exemplar of *Griswold* liberty but as a rule (whether or not mistaken) of personal autonomy and bodily integrity, with doctrinal affinity to cases recognizing limits on governmental power to mandate medical treatment or to bar its rejection. If so, our cases since *Roe* accord with *Roe*'s view that a State's interest in the protection of life falls short of justifying any plenary override of individual liberty claims." *Planned Parenthood v. Casey*, 857.
32. *Plessy v. Ferguson*, 163 U.S. 537 (1896).
33. *Brown v. Board of Education*, 347 U.S. 483 (1954).
34. *Lochner v. New York*, 198 U.S. 45 (1905).
35. *West Coast Hotel Co. v. Parrish*, 300 U.S. 379 (1937).
36. *Planned Parenthood v. Casey*, 856. As the joint opinion noted: "Abortion is customarily chosen as an unplanned response to the consequence of unplanned activity or to the failure of conventional birth control, and except on the assumption that no intercourse would have occurred but for *Roe*'s holding, such behavior may appear to justify no reliance claim. . . . To eliminate the issue of reliance that easily, however, one would need to limit cognizable reliance to specific instances of sexual activity. But to do this would be simply to refuse to face that fact that for two decades of economic and social developments, people have organized intimate relationships and made choices that define their views of themselves and their places in society, in reliance on the availability of abortion in the event that contraception should fail. The ability of women to participate equally in the economic and social life of the Nation has been facilitated by their ability to control their reproductive lives." *Planned Parenthood v. Casey*, 856.
37. *Planned Parenthood v. Casey*, 856.
38. *Planned Parenthood v. Casey*, 856.
39. I freely borrow the term from John Rawls, who explains that the Supreme Court is "the exemplar of public reason." John Rawls,

Political Liberalism (1993), 236. My use of the term emphasizes the implicitly despotic character of exemplarism. Its ideological and historical precedents are Continental (Rousseauian). I make no argument here that exemplarism (in the sense I shall give to the term) comports with Rawl's position.

40. *Planned Parenthood v. Casey*, 866-67; emphasis added.

41. *Planned Parenthood v. Casey*, 865.

42. Bradley, 374.

43. *Marbury v. Madison*, 137.

44. *Cooper v. Aaron*, 358 U.S. 1 (1958).

45. *Marbury v. Madison*, 137.

46. *Cooper v. Aaron*, 1.

47. *Marbury v. Madison*, 177-78.

48. Abraham Lincoln, "First Inaugural Address (Mar. 4, 1861)", in *Speeches and Writings*, 220-21; emphasis added.

49. *Cooper v. Aaron*, 18.

50. *Cooper v. Aaron*, 23.

51. *Planned Parenthood v. Casey*, 868 (emphasis added).

52. *Planned Parenthood v. Casey*, 833. Rawls maintains that "[t]he constitution is not what the Court says it is. Rather, it is what the people acting constitutionally through the other branches eventually allow the Court to say it is." On its face, this seems very close to the *Casey* doctrine. He goes on to suggest that the people, acting through Article V, could not amend the First Amendment, without revolution. Rawls, *Political Liberalism*, 237, 238-239. Would the same be true if the people amended the Constitution to remediate a judicial mistake?

53. *Planned Parenthood v. Casey*, 864. "In constitutional adjudication as elsewhere in life, changed circumstances may impose new obligations, and the thoughtful part of the Nation could accept each decision to overrule a prior case as a response to the Court's constitutional duty." *Planned Parenthood v. Casey*, 864.

54. *Boerne v. Flores*, 117 Sup. Ct. 2157 (1997).

55. Religious Freedom Restoration Act, 42 U.S.C. (1994) H.R. 2000(b).

56. *Boerne v. Flores*, 117 Sup. Ct. 2157 (1997).

57. *Employment Division v. Smith*, 494 U.S. 872 (1990).

58. *Employment Division v. Smith*, 877-82.

59. See *Boerne v. Flores*, 2158.

60. *Boerne v. Flores*, 2172.

61. EOD, 26.

62. See EOD, 26.

63. *Planned Parenthood v. Casey*, 864.

3 PRUDENT WARNINGS AND IMPRUDENT REACTIONS

1. Edmund Burke, "Thoughts on the Cause of the Present Discontents [1770] in Burke, *Selected Writings and Speeches*, ed. Peter J. Stanlis (Anchor Books, 1963), 123.

2. See the Speech at Springfield, Illinois (June 16, 1858), in *The Collected Works of Abraham Lincoln*, ed. Roy P. Basler (New Brunswick, N.J.: Rutgers University Press, 1953), 2:461-69.

3. Mary Ann Glendon, Comment in Antonin Scalia, *A Matter of Interpretation: Federal Courts and the Law* (Princeton: Princeton University Press, 1997), 113-114.

4. See *Bowers v. Hardwick*, 478 U.S. 186 (1986).

5. 410 U.S. 113 (1973).

6. See 28 U.S.C. Sec. 1738 (c) (West Supp. 1997).

7. EOD, 30-40.

8. 134 L Ed 2d 855 (1996).

9. See Leo Strauss, *Natural Right and History* (Chicago: University of Chicago Press, 1953), 135-36.

10. For my own treatment of this problem, See my book, *First Things* (Princeton: Princeton University Press, 1986), 224-27.

11. Letter to Joshua Speed (August 24, 1855), in *Collected Works*, ed. Basler, 2:320: "It is hardly fair for you to assume, that I have no interest in a thing which has, and continually exercises, the power of making me miserable. You ought rather to appreciate how much the great body of the Northern people do crucify their feelings, in order to maintain their loyalty to the constitution and the Union."

12. See Lincoln, Speech at Cooper Union (February 27, 1860), in Ibid., 3:547-48.

13. See Ibid., 3:301-302 (debate with Stephen Douglas at Alton, Illinois, October 15, 1858).

14. Quoted in Richard Wade, *Slavery in the Cities* (New York: Oxford University Press, 1964), 98.

15. Harry V. Jaffa, *Crisis of the House Divided* (Chicago: University of Chicago Press, 1982); originally published, 1959.

16. *Collected Works*, 3:256-57.

17. Debate at Charleston (September 18, 1858), in ibid., 181.

18. Jaffa, 336.

19. Ibid., 334.

20. Quoted in ibid., 281.

21. *Collected Works*, 2:222-23.

22. Clay, cited in Jaffa, 337.

23. For an interesting argument converging with this one, see Richard Neuhaus, "Can Atheists Be Good Citizens?," *First Things* (August/September 1991): 17-21.

24. See Russell Hittinger, "When the Court Should Not Be Obeyed," *First Things* (October 1993): 12-18, esp. 16.

25. See *Bowen v. American Hospital Association* 476 U.S. 610 (1986).

26. See, e.g., Marshall's comments during the oral argument in the *Bowen* case, U.S. Supreme Court, Oral Arguments, Vol. 8, Cases Nos. 84-1573-84-1560; October Term 1985, 16, 23.

27. Without pronouncing a judgment on the matter, the Supreme Court took note of these kinds of arguments in in *Planned Parenthood v. Aschcroft* (1983). Justice Powell noted the testimony of a Dr. Robert Christ, "that "the abortion patient has a right not only to be rid of the growth, called a fetus in her body, but also has a right to a dead fetus." Justice Powell pronounced this argument to be "remarkable in its candor." But to describe the argument as "remarkable" is not exactly to pronounce it "wrong," and still less is it to supply the reasons that make it a wrongful construction of the doctrines put forth by the Court. See 76 L Ed 2d 733, at 740, n. 7. We may remind ourselves that, without exactly saying so, Judge Haynesworth had been willing to install, in effect, the same understanding—of a right to an effective abortion— in his opinion in *Floyd v. Anders*, 440 F. Supp. 535 (1977).

28. For an account of the so-called partial birth abortions, see Arkes, "The Politics of 'D & X': A First Step?," *Crisis* (July–August 1995): 8-9.

29. See her testimony in opposition to the bill on partial-birth abortions in "Partial-Birth Abortion: The Truth," Joint Hearing before the Senate Committee on the Judiciary and the Subcommittee on the Constitution of the House Committee on the Judiciary; 105th Cong., 1st Sess., March 11, 1997, 19-21. And see also the testimony from the representatives from other groups that have been engaged in the defense and promotion of abortion: the Planned Parenthood Federation, and the National Abortion Federation, 23-26, 31-35.

30. See, as a notable case in point, the opinion by Judge Stephen Reinhardt, in *Compassion in Dying v. Washington* 49 F. 3d 790 (1996), the opinion that was overruled by the Supreme Court in *Washington v. Glucksberg*, 138 L Ed 2d 772 (1997).

31. See *In re [Nancy] Jobes* 529 A. 2d 434 (1987).

32. See, for example, *In re Guardianship of [Barbara] Grant*, 747 P. 2d 445, 452 (Wash. 1987) (en banc), modified, 757 P.2d 534 (Wash. 1988), and *Bouvia v. Superior Court ex rel. Glenchur*, 225 Cal. Rptr. 297, 304 (Ct. App. 1986).

33. See *In re Jobes* and *Bouvia v. Superior Court ex rel. Glenchur.*

34. See Michael Uhlmann, *Last Rights* (Grand Rapids, Mi., Eerdmans, 1997).

35. See, for example, Frankfurter in *Screws v. United States*, 325 U.S. 91, at 160 (dissenting opinion) [1945], and see Frankfurter writing for the majority in *U.S. v. Williams*, 341 U.S. 70 (1951), and *Monroe v. Pape*, 365 U.S. 167 (1960). And of course, there was his resistance to the Court entering into the political thicket of reapportionment in *Baker v. Carr*, 369 U.S. 186 (1962). Cf. his opinion for the Court, in resisting intervention in "political questions," in *Colegrove v. Green*, 328 U.S. 549 (1946).

36. See "Abortion and Moral Beliefs: A Survey of American Opinion," The Gallup Organization (Princeton, N.J.), 925058 Abortion Study (1992), pp. 20, 21, 29. Respondents were asked, among other things, "At what point in a pregnancy do you personally feel that the uborn child's right to be born outweighs the woman's right to choose whether she wants to have a child?" Fifty per cent marked that point as "the moment of conception." Seventy-six percent thought abortions would not be justified for the sake of avoiding the interruption that a baby might cause in a professional career. And 64.9 percent supported legislation that would bar abortions late in pregnancy, say, after five months. But the surveys show, at the same time, strands that cannot quite be reconciled. Around 60 percent of the people in this survey by Gallup thought that the "law" or the "government," at any level, had the weakest claim to influence the decision on abortion. For some reason, there seems to be a disconnection between the notion of "government," to be avoided, and that disinterested force, called the "law," that people seem willing to invoke to restrain abortions they regard as wrongful.

37. See my pieces, "Anti-Abortion, But Politically Smart," *Wall Street Journal* (March 28, 1995), editorial page, and the original statement of this position, "How to Roll Back *Roe*," *National Review* (October 28, 1988): 30ff.

38. See *Marbury v. Madison*, 1 Cranch 137, at 177, 178 (1803).

39. See Bork, *Slouching Toward Gomorrah* (New York: Regan Books, 1996), 96-119, esp. 117.

40. See Lincoln, First Inaugural Address, in *Collected Works*, 4:268.

41. Ibid., 2:255 (debate with Stephen Douglas at Quincy, Illinois, October 13, 1858).

42. See *The Federalist* (New York: Random House), Number 78, 504.

43. For a review of these cases, see my book *First Things*, 418-22.

44. This is a point that the Justice has made recurringly, and made

again then, quite recently, in his lectures at Princeton, published under the title, *A Matter of Interpretation: Federal Courts and the La.w* (Princeton: Princeton University Press, 1997).

4 JUSTICE, LEGITIMACY, AND ALLEGIANCE

1. EOD, 53-62
2. Pope John Paul II, *Evangelium Vitae* (25 March 1995), 2.
3. Ibid., 73.
4. Ibid., 56. This language seems clearly to exclude the possibility of a purely retributive justification for the death penalty. In the sentence immediately following it, the encyclical also seems to rule out as a matter of moral principle, and not merely on the basis of sociological considerations, a justification based on the belief that punishing some criminals with death deters others: "Today however, as a result of steady improvements in the organization of the penal system, such cases [i.e., cases in which the execution of a wrongdoer is absolutely necessary for the protection of society] are very rare, if not practically non-existent." Ibid.
5. See "The Authoritative Catechism, and . . .," *Catholic World Report* (Oct. 1997): 6-7.
6. See Pope John Paul II, *Evangelium Vitae*, 68-74.
7. Ibid., 70.
8. On these critics, see Richard John Neuhaus, "The Liberalism of John Paul II," *First Things* (May 1997): 16.
9. See Pope John Paul II, *Centesimus Annus* (1 May 1991), 46.
10. Ibid.
11. Pope John Paul II, *Evangelium Vitae*, 70.
12. Ibid.
13. Ibid.
14. See John M. Finnis, "Law as Co-ordination," *Ratio Juris* 2 (1989) (citations omitted).
15. Ibid.
16. See Augustine, *The Problem of Free Choice: De Libero Arbitrio* (trans. Dom. Mark Pontifex, Newman Press, 1955), 1.5.11 (stating that an unjust law seems not to be law).
17. See Thomas Aquinas *Summa Theologiae* (trans. Fathers of the English Dominican Province, Benziger Bros., 1947), I-II, q. 95, a. 2 (stating that an unjust law is not a law but a corruption of law); ibid., I-II, q. 96, a. 4 (stating that unjust laws are not so much laws as they are acts of violence).
18. Plato, *The Laws*, trans. A. E. Taylor (Aidine Press, 1966), 4.715.
19. See Aristotle *The Politics* (trans. Ernest Barker, Oxford Uni-

versity Press, 1995), 3.6.1279a8.

20. See Cicero *Laws: De Legibus* (trans. Clinton Walker Keyes, Harvard University Press, 1996), 2, v. 11-13.

21. See Pope John Paul II, *Evangelium Vitae*, 72.

22. Ibid.

23. Ibid., 72. John Paul II goes on to argue that such laws call for disobedience and even "conscientious objection." Ibid., 73. On the necessarily indirect nature of the disobedience and conscientious objection demanded by unjust laws which are permissive in nature, see EOD, 58.

24. Pope John Paul II, *Evangelium Vitae*, 71.

25. EOD, 72. A similar point is made by Gertrude Himmelfarb in her contribution to the same symposium, EOD, 87-92.

26. EOD, 72.

27. See Robert H. Bork, *Slouching Towards Gomorrah: Modern Liberalism and American Decline* (Regan Books, 1996), 173-85.

28. See Justice Antonin Scalia, "Of Democracy, Morality, and the Majority," *Origins* 26 (1996): 81.

29. *Roe v. Wade*, 410 U.S. 113 (1973).

30. *Planned Parenthood v. Casey*, 505 U. S. 997-1000 (1992) (Scalia, J., concurring in part and dissenting in part); *Webster v. Reproductive Health Services*, 492 U.S. 490, 532-37 (1989) (Scalia, J., concurring).

31. See Scalia, "Of Democracy," 87.

32. See *Webster v. Reproductive Health Services*, 532-37.

33. See Scalia, "Of Democracy," 87.

34. See Robert P. George, "Natural Law and Positive Law," in *The Autonomy of Law: Essays on Legal Positivism*, ed. Robert P. George (1996), 330-332.

35. U.S. Constitution, amend. 14, para. 1.

36. *Roe v. Wade*, 113.

37. *Roe v. Wade*, 113.

38. *Roe v. Wade*, 156-57.

39. U.S. Constitution, art. 2, § 1, cl. 5; *Roe v. Wade*, 157.

40. *Roe v. Wade*, 157.

41. *Roe v. Wade*, 159.

42. See Dianene N. Irving, "Scientific and Philosophical Expertise; An Evaluation of the Arguments on 'Personhood,'" *Linacre Q.* (Feb. 1993): 18.

43. *Roe v. Wade*, 222.

44. ee *Planned Parenthood v. Casey*, 979.

45. See Germain Grisez, "When Do People Begin?" *Proc. Of the Amer. Cath. Phil Assoc.* 63 (1989): 31.

46. See Patrick Lee, *Abortion and Unborn Human Life* (1996).

47. See John Rawls, *Political Liberalism* (1993), 243 n. 32.

48. John Finnis, "Abortion, Natural Law, and Public Reason" (paper presented at the panel on Natural Law, Liberalism and Public Reason sponsored by the American Public Philosophy Institute at the American Political Science Association 1997 Annual Convention, Washington, D.C. Aug. 30, 1997, on file with author).

49. For a valuable account of such reasons, see generally Cass R. Sunstein, *Legal Reasoning and Political Conflict* (1996).

50. EOD, 86.

51. *Dred Scott v. Sandford*, 60 U.S. 393 (1856).

52. It was to secure fully this protection that the Fourteenth Amendment, after the abolition of slavery throughout the nation by the Thirteenth Amendment, introduced into the Constitution a guarantee of equal protection to be enforced by Congress against the states. U.S. Constitution, amend. 14.

53. *Dred Scott v. Sandford*, 393.

54. *Dred Scott v. Sandford*, 400-03.

55. See Robert H. Bork, *The Tempting of America: The Political Seduction of the Law* (1990), 28-34 (discussing the political climate surrounding the *Dred Scott* decision).

56. *Roe v. Wade*, 113.

57. Archibald H. Grimke, *William Lloyd Garrison: The Abolitionist* (1891), 310.

58. See Abraham Lincoln, "First Inaugural Address," in *Speeches and Letter of Abraham Lincoln*, ed. Merwin Roe (1912), 165.

59. Ibid., 171-72.

60. *Planned Parenthood v. Casey*, 867.

61. This familiar phrase, which was inserted into the Pledge of Allegiance in the 1950s, derives from President Abraham Lincoln's Gettysburg Address. See Abraham Lincoln, "Gettysburg Address," in *Speeches and Letters of Abraham Lincoln*, ed. Merwin Roe (1912), 214.

5 THE VENERABLE ARGUMENT AGAINST JUDICIAL USURPATION

1. *Cooper v. Aaron* 358 U.S. 18 (1958).

2. See note 14, *infra*.

3. *Dred Scott v., Sandford* 19 Howard 616, citing Justice Paterson for the Court in *Stuart v. Laird* (1803), Justice Story for the Court in *Martin v. Hunter's Lessee* (1816), Justice Marshall for the Court in *Cohens v. Virginia* (1821), Justice Story for the Court in *Prigg v. Pennsylvania* (1842), and Justice Curtis himself for the Court in *Cooley v. Port War-*

dens (1851).

4. *Dred Scott v., Sandford* 19 Howard 619.

5. *Dred Scott v., Sandford* 19 Howard 616.

6. *Dred Scott v., Sandford* 19 Howard 621.

7. "'The questions which arise exclusively under the Constitution and laws of the United States, this court . . . has the rightful authority finally to decide"(at 603, emphasis added). In the same paragraph where he says that the Court's overturning of fixed rules of interpretation means "we no longer have a Constitution" he says we have instead "a government which is merely an exponent of the will of Congress; or... an exponent of the individual political opinions of the members of this court" (at 621).

8. Alexander Hamilton in Jacob Cooke ed., *The Federalist* (Cleveland: World Publishing Co., 1965), 525. These papers, which were originally published in New York newspapers, have always been universally recognized as the official statements of those "founders" who developed the Constitution and secured its ratification. Hamilton's "irreconcilable variance" argument is the only argument any founder made which explains the consistency between democracy as government by the people and the right of the court to refuse to enforce an act of the peoples representatives. There was no disagreement among the founders on this matter. More than that, it is the only argument anyone has ever made which reconciles the judicial power with democracy.

9. *The Federalist*, 522. One reason for the furor among the dominant intellectual class over the *First Things* symposiasts' challenge to the legitimacy of certain Supreme Court decisions is the "legal realism" which dominates this class' thinking. This "realism" holds that the Constitution is whatever the justices say it is. This relativism makes it impossible to distinguish between legitimate use and illegitimate *abuse* of judicial power. Legal realism is simply a version of relativism. As such, it resonates with ordinary citizens whose own less sophisticated relativism inclines them to regard such distinctions as just "a matter of opinion," i.e., not a matter of the truth. It will clarify what the symposiasts are up against to consider that popular relativism may be as much an obstacle to persuading the people of the existence and harm of judicial usurpation as is intellectual class affection for the judiciary. Might not that popular relativism make the distinction between legitimate use and illegitimate abuse too subtle for even intelligent and thoughtful citizens to understand?

10. *The Federalist*, 60-61: "To secure the public good, and private rights, against the danger of such a faction [of a majority of the people] is then the great object to which our enquiries are directed."

11. "Judicial review" is the name now given to this power. However, that name appears only in the twentieth century, apparently in a law review article by the great constitutional scholar Edward S. Corwin. See Robert Lowery Clinton, *Marbury v. Madison and Judicial Review* (University Press of Kansas, 1989), 7. This is important to the symposiasts argument because "judicial review" suggests a general supervisory judicial power over, and thus judicial supremacy as against, Congress and the president. Such a power was not advocated by anyone at the founding and hence could not have been consented to by the people in 1789. On the contrary, the Constitution was publicly sold to the American people as one in which the three branches of government were co-equal, neither having supremacy over the others. See *The Federalist*, 523, where the branches are described as "coordinate," i.e. equal in rank, as opposed to "subordinate."

12. *The Federalist*, 525.

13. Theodore Roosevelt, "The Heirs of Abraham Lincoln" (February 2, 1913), in *Social Justice and Popular Rule: Essays, Addresses, and Public Statements Relating to the Progressive Movement (1910-1916)* (New York: Charles Scribner's Sons, 1926), 17: 359-60.

14. Ibid., 370. While there are very great limits to the propriety of connecting Lincoln to the Progressives on this matter, still there is a clear connection between them. One would still have to consider whether Lincoln's position did not aim to preserve and improve democracy according to the original constitutional design, whereas the Progressives aimed to free democracy from that design.

15. Ibid., 377. Roosevelt repeated this proposal in a speech at Philadelphia, April 10, 1912, "The Recall of Judicial Decisions": "If, in any case the legislature has passed a law under the police power for the purpose of promoting social and industrial justice and the courts declare it in conflict with the fundamental law of the State, the constitution as laid down by the people, then I propose that after due deliberation—for a period which could not be for less than two years after the passage of the original law—the people shall themselves have the right to declare whether or not the proposed law is to be treated as constitutional."

16. Lincoln's Speech at Cincinnati, September 15 or 16, 1859, quoted in *The Public Papers and Addresses of Franklin D. Roosevelt: The Court Disapproves* (1935), 10:14. The complete speech is in Basler, ed., *Collected Works*, 3:435.

17. Ibid., 13.

18. Robert Jackson, *The Struggle for Judicial Supremacy: A Study of a Crisis in American Power Politics* (New York: Random House, 1941). The same year, Roosevelt appointed Jackson to the Supreme Court.

19. Ibid., viii, ix, and x-xi.

20. Ibid., xii-xiii.

21. Ibid., xiv.

22. The suspicious quotation marks remind us that this so-called "constitutional law" cannot be distinguished from "unconstitutional law." People of common sense might wonder whether a subject matter that cannot be distinguished from its opposite is coherent to anyone except Humpty Dumpty. See note 28, *infra.*

23. Jackson, xiv.

24. Quoted in Richard G. Stevens, "The Prospects for Constitutional Law," *The Political Science Reviewer* 26 (1997): 270.

25. Rexford G. Tugwell, *The Compromising of the Constitution* (Notre Dame, In.: University of Notre Dame Press, 1976), 107-08.

26. Jefferson to Madison, 6 September 1789 in Robert Rutland et al., eds., *The Papers of James Madison* (Charlottesville, Va.: University Press of Virginia, 1979), 12:385. In adopting Jefferson's sovereignty of the present generation, however, progressivism omits an important part of it. See note 32, *infra*, and text.

27. This twentieth-century jurisprudence was famously described by an eighteenth-century philosopher: "'When I use a word,' Humpty Dumpty said, in rather a scornful tone, 'it means just what I choose it to mean—neither more nor less.' 'The question is,' said Alice, 'whether you *can* make words mean so many different things.' 'The question is,' said Humpty Dumpty, 'which is to be master—that's all.'" Lewis Carroll, *Through the Looking Glass* (New York: Clarkson N. Potter, Inc., 1960), chapter 6.

28. William Brennan, "Construing the Constitution," *U.C. Davis Law Review* 19 (1985): 7.

29. Ibid, 4.

30. I would like to thank Mr. Jamie Gold, currently a graduate student at Pennsylvania State University, for calling this to my attention.

31. This conclusion is based on more than inference, for Brennan concurred in the Court's opinion in *Cooper v. Aaron.* See note 1, *supra*, and text.

32. In the same paragraph of the letter to Madison cited in note 26, Jefferson argues that the power to repeal a law or constitution is not (for practical reasons) democratically equivalent to the power to establish one in the first place. Thus, Brennan's progressivism rejects an integral part of Jefferson's sovereignty of the present generation.

33. See the reflective and accessible presentation of Wilson's thought by Kent A. Kirwan, "Historicism and Statesmanship in the Reform Argument of Woodrow Wilson," *Interpretation* 9, nos. 2 and 3

(1981):339-351.

34. A recent careful and thoughtful study of Brennan's thought is David E. Marion, *The Jurisprudence of Justice William J. Brennan, Jr.: The Law and Politics of "Libertarian Dignity"* (Lanham, Md.: Rowman and Littlefield, 1997).

35. 74 U.S. 506.

36. Matthew Franck, testimony in hearing on "Congress, the Court, and the Constitution," subcommittee on the Constitution, Committee on the Judiciary, U.S. House of Representatives, 29 January 1998.

37. For example, in rights of accused criminals and in church-state matters.

38. For example, on obscenity and pornography, the rights of accused criminals, reapportionment, and religion.

39. Robert Bolt, *A Man for All Seasons* (New York: Vintage, 1990), 65-66.

40. St. Paul, *Letter of the Ephesians*, 6:12.

41. See note 9, *supra*.

42. As Tugwell rightly puts it, "the court remained, when it recovered from Taney, the final arbiter . . . The Justices had relieved the people of responsibility for their Constitution." Tugwell, 100.

43. Abraham Lincoln, "The Perpetuation of Our Political Institutions," speech at Springfield, Illinois, January 27, 1838 in Roy P. Basler, ed., *Abraham Lincoln: His Speeches and Writing* (New York: Grosset & Dunlap, 1962), 82-83.

44. "Leader" or "leaders" occurs fourteen times in *The Federalist*, twelve times in a negative context: "avarice" (33), "artful" (479), "ambitiously" (59), "factious" (64, 418), "surreptitious invasions" (103), "intrigues and bribes" (113), "mercenary instruments for inveigline their countrymen" (116), "the ambition of enterprising leaders" (292), "conspiracy to prevent an election" (402), "tools of the most cunning or the most numerous faction" (440), and "from leaders and favorites to become despots" (588). Twice it is used in a positive context, each time with respect to revolution: "leaders of the revolution" (88) and "patriotic leaders" (341).

45. Let me end by stressing that the judicial usurpation of politics usually occurs when the Court fails to respect the people's right to resolve the meaning of ambiguous constitutional language. This truth was stated long ago by a progressive who followed Charles Beard in regarding "judicial review" as a creation of conservatives to protect property against majority rule: "[F]ew of these laws apparently striking at freedom of speech or the press or at minority rights are clear violations of specific constitutional provisions. . . . They involve interpretation of clauses of the Constitution inevitably ambiguous—clauses like 'due

process of law' or 'deprivation of liberty' or even 'abridging' freedom of speech or of the press." Henry Steele Commager, *Majority Rule and Minority Rights* (New York: Oxford University Press, 1943), 68. Given this ambiguity, these clauses' meaning "is not to be determined by legal research but by 'considerations of policy'" (43) and this constitutionally belongs to the people, the Congress, and the president, but not the Court.

6 DEMOCRACY IN AMERICA

1. EOD, 154, 147.
2. Alexis de Tocqueville, *Democracy in America*, trans. George Lawrence, ed. J.P. Mayer (New York: Harper & Row, 1969), 418; hereafter DIA.
3. DIA, 704.
4. EOD, 4.
5. EOD, 5.
6. EOD, 4.
7. EOD, 3.
8. EOD, 4.
9. EOD, 41.
10. EOD, 10.
11. EOD, 12.
12. EOD, 24.
13. EOD, 26-27.
14. EOD, 81.
15. DIA, 541.
16. DIA, 19.
17. DIA, 541.
18. EOD, 17.
19. EOD, 31.
20. EOD, 68.
21. DIA, 530.
22. DIA, 530.
23. DIA, 531.
24. DIA, 530.
25. DIA, 530-31.
26. DIA, 531.
27. DIA, 531.
28. DIA, 540.
29. DIA, 540.
30. DIA, 542.
31. DIA, 542.

32. DIA, 444.
33. DIA, 546.
34. EOD, 6.
35. EOD, 144.
36. EOD, 154.
37. EOD, 75.
38. EOD, 77.
39. EOD, 74.
40. DIA, 544.
41. DIA, 429-30.
42. DIA, 544.
43. DIA, 430.
44. EOD, 160.
45. EOD, 77-78.
46. EOD, 3.
47. EOD, 7-8.
48. EOD, 41.
49. EOD, 82-83.
50. DIA, 533-34.
51. DIA, 12, 19.
52. DIA, 705.
53. DIA, 296.

7 THE QUEST FOR EQUITY

1. The most comprehensive study of equity and the U.S. Constitution is Gary L. McDowell, *Equity and the Constitution* (Chicago: University of Chicago Press, 1982).

2. See Edward McWhinney, *Judicial Review* (Toronto: University of Toronto Press, 1965) for an account of how judicial review has spread throughout the world since the end of World War II.

3. Aristotle, *The Poetics*, trans. Theodore Buckley (London: George Bell and Sons, 1920), book 1, chapter 13.

4. Ibid.

5. Aristotle, *Nicomachean Ethics*, trans. and ed. John Warrington (London: Dent, Everyman's Library, 1954), 113.

6. Ibid, 114.

7. Thomas Hobbes, *A Dialogue between a Philosopher and a Student of the Common Laws of England*, ed. Joseph Cropsey (Chicago: University of Chicago Press, 1971), 26.

8. Thomas Hobbes, *Leviathan*, ed. Michael Oakeshott (Oxford: Basil Blackwell, 1960), 117.

9. Ibid, 174.

10. Ibid, 101.

11. Ibid, 174.

12. Ibid, 176.

13. Ibid.

14. Ibid.

15. Francis Bacon, *The Essays or Counsels, Civil and Moral of Francis Ld. Verulam* (New York: The Peter Pauper Press, 1963), 210.

16. Ibid., 211.

17. Ibid., 215.

18. R. J. Walker and M. G. Walker, *The English Legal System* (London: Butterworths, 1970), 40.

19. *Re National Funds Insurance Co.* (1878) 10 Ch.D. 118, 128.

20. George Burton Adams, *Council and Courts in Anglo-Norman England* (New York: Russell and Russell, 1965), 205.

21. Baron Montesquieu, *The Spirit of the Laws* (New York: Hasner Library, 1956), 153.

22. Ibid.

23. Ibid.

24. William Blackstone, *Commentaries on the Laws of England*, 4 vols. (Chicago: University of Chicago Press, 1979), 1:10.

25. Ibid., 61-62.

26. Ibid.

27. John Austin, *The Province of Jurisprudence Determined*, intro. H.L.A. Hart (London: Weidenfeld and Nicolson, 1965), 1:191.

28. McDowell, 110.

29. Ibid., 98.

30. See Edwin W. Patterson, "The Case Method in American Legal Education: Its Origins and Objectives," *Journal of Legal Education* 4 (1951).

31. See Lon L. Fuller, "American Legal Philosophy at Mid-Century," *Journal of Legal Education* 6 (1953-54): 457.

32. See Lon L. Fuller, "The Place and Uses of Jurisprudence in the Law School Curriculum," *Journal of Legal Education* 1 (1948-49): 495. See also Lon L. Fuller, "Pure Theory of Law and Analytical Jurisprudence," *Harvard Law Review* 55 (1941): 44.

33. Erwin N. Griswold, "Report on the National Law Student Conference on Legal Education," *Journal of Legal Education* 1 (1948-49): 64.

34. Paul Eidelberg, *The Philosophy of the American Constitution* (New York: The Free Press, 1968), 202.

35. McWhinney, 236.

36. At the time of writing, this case has not yet been reported in

the official printed form. All quotations from the judgment are taken from the reasons for judgment that appeared in the *Globe and Mail*, Toronto, 3 April 1998.

37. Ibid. This decision was, of course, applauded by Canadian social activists. It is one of the great ironies of Canadian public life that the very people in Canada who opposed the free trade agreement with the United States, on the grounds that it would mean American control of the Canadian economy, welcome this American judicial intrusion into the democratic process.

38. Madam Justic Claire L'Heureux-Dubé, "Making a Difference: The Pursuit of a Compassionate Justice," *University of British Columbia Law Review* 31 (1997): 1. She makes it clear that she is following in the footsteps of her predecessor, Madam Justice Bertha Wilson, who was the first woman appointed to the Supreme Court of Canada and applauded the use of the Brandeis brief. See her comments in *Regina v. Lavellee* (1990) 1 SCR 852.

39. Ibid.

40. McDowell, 122.

8 THE INAUGURATION OF EXTRAORDINARY POLITICS

1. EOD, 3-62.

2. "The Ninth Circuit's Fatal Overreach," *First Things* 63 (May 1996): 13.

3. EOD, 122-23.

4. EOD 95-97.

5. EOD, 129-33.

6. EOD, 143-55.

7. "Neocon v. Theocon: An Exchange," *New Republic* (February 3, 1997): 28-29.

8. "On the Future of Conservatism," *Commentary* 103:2 (February 1997): 14-43. Contributors to the *Commentary* symposium include: Robert L. Bartley, Peter Berger, Walter Berns, William F. Buckley, Jr., Midge Decter, David Frum, Francis Fukuyama, Mark Helprin, Gertrude Himmelfarb, William Kristol, Michael Novak, Norman Podhoretz, Irwin M. Stelzer, George Wiegel, and Ruth R. Wisse.

9. Joseph Blenkinsopp, "The Summer of our Discontent," *Common Sense* 11:1 (October 1996), 1.

10. Senate Proceedings Minutes, September 11, 1996.

11. Notre Dame Faculty Senate Resolution, December 3, 1996.

12. Pamela Schaeffer, "Irish Fighting: Faculty denounces ND President," *National Catholic Reporter*, December 13, 1996.

13. Only three signatures (Solomon, Lentricchia, and Wuthnow) appeared in the *Chronicle* (February 7, 1997) because of its policy of printing no more than three for any given letter. All of the signatures appeared in the *Observer* (February 6, 1997).

14. David Burrell to NCR, excerpted by Pamela Schaeffer, January 31, 1997.

15. Cited in Blakey, "Dissenting Views," p. 10.

16. "Student Finds God at Notre Dame," "Is Dorothy Day's Laetare Medal in Jeopardy?" and "ND Professor defends Baxter," *Houston Catholic Worker* XVII:1 (Jan-Feb, 1997).

17. Pamela Schaeffer, "Notre Dame Dispute May Signal a Shift: Countercultural Catholic Voice Stirs a Storm," *National Catholic Reporter*, January 31, 1997.

18. "On the Future of Conservatism," 27.

19. David Glenn, "The Schism," *Lingua Franca* (February 1997), 26.

20. EOD, 43.

21. Richard McBrien, Ed., *HarperCollins Encylopedia of Catholicism* (New York: Harper Collins, 1995), 1180.

22. Ibid. Schaeffer, NCR, January 31, 1997.

23. Alasdair MacIntyre, *Three Rival Versions of Moral Enquiry* (Notre Dame, Ind.: University of Notre Dame, 1990).

24. McBrien, 1180.

25. EOD, 154.

26. EOD, 129-33.

27. Schaeffer, NCR, January 31, 1997.

28. Ibid.

29. Richard Rorty, "Wild Orchids and Trotsky," in *Wild Orchids and Trotsky*, edited by Mark Edmundson (New York: Penguin, 1994).

30. Schaeffer, NCR, January 31, 1997.

31. Stanley Fish, "Boutique Multiculturalism, or Why Liberals are Incapable of Thinking about Hate Speech," *Critical Inquiry* 23 (Winter 1997): 378.

32. EOD, 8.

33. Thomas Kuhn, *The Structure of Scientific Revolutions* (Chicago: University of Chicago Press, 1962). In many respects, I am reluctant to use Kuhn here because the notion of "paradigm shifts" has become so over-used as to be trite. Rhetorically, however, the analogy does lend itself well to the more important idea of "extraordinary politics."

34. George Parkin Grant, *English-Speaking Justice* (Notre Dame: University of Notre Dame Press, 1985).

35. Wendy Kaminer, "The Last Taboo: Why America Needs

Atheism," *New Republic* (October 14, 1996): 24-32.

36. Richard Cohen, "When Morality Begets Violence," *Washington Post* (January 23, 1997): A17.

37. Jean Bethke Elsthain, "The Hard Questions: Civil Rites," *New Republic* (February 24, 1997): 23.

38. Stanley Fish, "Liberalism Doesn't Exist," *There's No Such Thing as Free Speech, and It's a Good Thing, too* (New York: Oxford, 1994), 134-38.

39. Stanley Fish, "What Makes an Interpretation Acceptable?" *Is There a Text in This Class?* (Cambridge: Harvard University Press, 1980), 338.

40. Baxter and Hauerwas affirm similar versions of pacifism. For their differences with Neuhaus on the Gulf War see Hauerwas and Neuhaus, "Pacifism, Just War, and the Gulf," *First Things* 13 (May 1991): 39-45.

41. Richard John Neuhaus, "Religion within the Limits of Morality Alone," *First Things* (April 1997): 61.

42. Richard John Neuhaus, "The Liberalism of John Paul II," *First Things* 73 (May 1997): 16-21.

43. Stanley Hauerwas, "The Church's One Foundation is Jesus Christ our Lord," *Theology Without Foundations: Religious Practice and the Future of Theological Truth*, eds. Stanley Hauerwas, Nancey Murphy, and Mark Nation (Nashville: Abingdon, 1994), 144.

44. I personally believe this distinction to be a very important one.

45. James Wm. McClendon, Jr., "The Baptist Idea of a University," Unpublished presentation, Baylor University, September 15, 1995.

46. Ibid, p. 3.

47. Gertrude Himmelfarb, "The Christian University: A Call to Counterrevolution," *First Things* 59 (January 1996): 16-19.

48. Richard John Neuhaus, "The Christian University: Eleven Theses," *First Things* 59 (January 1996): 20-22.

49. Christopher Shea, "'Natural Law' Theory is at the Crux of a Nasty Intellectual Debate," *Chronicle of Higher Education* (February 7, 1997): A14.

50. EOD, 113.

51. EOD, 90.

52. EOD, 90.

53. Stanley Hauerwas, "In Praise of *Centesimus Annus*," *In Good Company: The Church as Polis* (Notre Dame, Ind.: University of Notre Dame Press, 1996), 128.

54. *Centesimus Annus*, 32.

55. Ibid., 39.

56. Ibid., 31.
57. Ibid., 34.
58. *Evangelium Vitae*, 70.
59. Ibid.

9   THE PHILADELPHIA CONSTITUTION: DEAD OR ALIVE?

1. Whether there are really any "in-between" theories is debatable. But those that have attempted to find some middle ground between originalism and activism would include: John Hart Ely, *Democracy and Distrust* (Cambridge: Harvard University Press, 1980); Jesse Choper, *Judicial Review and the National Political Process* (Chicago: University of Chicago Press); Michael Perry, *The Constitution, the Court and Human Rights* (New Haven: Yale University Press, 1982). For a devastating critique of Choper and Ely see Christopher Wolfe, *The Rise of Modern Judicial Review: From Constitutional Interpretation to Judge-made Law* (New York: Basic Books, 1985).

2. I am borrowing this formulation from Justice William Brennan's speech, "The Constitution of the United States: Contemporary Ratification," delivered at Georgetown University (October 12, 1985). This speech is generally regarded as one of the most lucid arguments for an activist Court.

3. In *The Federalist*, Number 47, Madison writes: "The Accumulation of all powers legislative, executive and judiciary in the same hands, whether of one, a few or many, and whether hereditary, self appointed, or elective, may justly be pronounced the very definition of tyranny." Hamilton, Madison, and Jay, *The Federalist*, eds. George W. Carey and James McClellan (Dubuque, Iowa: Kendall/Hunt, 1990), 249. All subsequent references to *The Federalist* are to this edition.

Article XXX of the Massachusetts Constitution of 1780 provided that "the legislative department shall never exercise the executive and judicial powers, or either of them: The executive shall never exercise the legislative and judicial powers, or either of them: The judicial shall never exercise the legislative and executive powers, or either of them: to the end it may be a government of laws and not of men." *The Popular Sources of Political Authority: Documents on the Massachusetts Constitution of 1780*, eds. Oscar and Mary Handlin (Cambridge: Harvard University Press, 1966), 327.

4. Lino A. Graglia, "How the Constitution Disappeared," *Human Life Review* (Spring, 1986): 71.

5. For an interesting account of this episode and other acts of judicial activism, see Paul Craig Roberts and Larry M. Stratton, *The New Color Line: How Quotas and Privilege Destroy Democracy* (Wash-

ington, D.C.: Regnery Publishing, 1995).

6. *The Federalist*, 103-04.

7. James B. Thayer, "The Origin and Scope of the American Doctrine of Constitutional Law," in *Taking the Constitution Seriously*, ed. Gary L. McDowell (Dubuque, Iowa: Kendall/Hunt, 1981), 57.

8. Ibid.

9. *The Federalist*, 403-04.

10. This stands in sharp contrast to the Populist and Progressive critics of the Constitution who looked upon the Court as a final and authoritative check on the leveling excesses of rampant majorities. See, for instance, James Allen Smith, *The Spirit of American Government* (New York: The Macmillan Co., 1907).

11. EOD, 10.

12. EOD, 27.

13. The desegregation decisions are *Brown v. Board of Education*, 347 U.S. 438 (1954) and *Bolling v. Sharpe*, 347 U.S. 497 (1954).

14. Charles S. Hyneman, *The Supreme Court on Trial* (New York: Atherton Press, 1963), 199.

15. *Roe v. Wade*, 410 U.S. 113 (1973).

16. There are difficulties which each of these observations. First, some activists argue that limiting the appellate jurisdiction of the Court would be unconstitutional. In any event, the Court would be able to rule on the constitutionality of any effort to limit its authority. Second, the appointment process does not seem to work very well in changing the direction of the Supreme Court. All sorts of arguments come into play here. Some argue that individuals should not be subject to "litmus" tests that would reveal their outlook because this would tend to politicize the Court (not that it isn't already). The arguments that are marshaled against using the appointment process as a means to change are based on the traditionalist model which holds that the Court's mission requires those learned in the law. Finally, whenever amendments are suggested supporters of judicial activism are among the loudest in proclaiming that the Constitution should not be trivialized with such amendments.

17. EOD, 19.

CONTRIBUTORS

HADLEY ARKES is Ney Professor of Jurisprudence at Amherst College.

J. BUDZISZEWSKI is associate professor of politics and government at the University of Texas at Austin.

GEORGE W. CAREY is professor of government at Georgetown University.

ROBERT P. GEORGE is associate professor of politics at Princeton University.

GARY D. GLENN is professor of political science at Northern Illinois University.

RUSSELL HITTINGER is Warren Professor of Catholic Studies and Research Professor of Law at the University of Tulsa.

CARSON HOLLOWAY is assistant professor of political science at Concord State College in Athens, West Virginia.

SCOTT H. MOORE is assistant professor of philosophy at Baylor University.

MITCHELL S. MUNCY is editor in chief of Spence Publishing Company.

RICHARD JOHN NEUHAUS is editor in chief of *First Things*.

FREDERICK VAUGHAN is emeritus professor of political science at the University of Guelph in Canada.

Index

280

This book was designed and set into type
by Mitchell S. Muncy,
with cover art by Stephen J. Ott,
and printed and bound
by Edwards Brothers, Inc.,
Ann Arbor, Michigan.

The text face is Caslon,
designed by Carol Twombly
and issued in digital form by Adobe Systems,
Mountain View, California, in 1989.

The paper is acid-free and is of archival quality.